A PRACTICAL SPIRITUALITY

A Spirituality for the Third Millennium

Father J.J. Edward and Paul J. Buisson

iUniverse, Inc.
New York Bloomington

A Practical Spirituality
A Spirituality for the Third Millennium

Copyright © 2009 J.J.Edwards

All rights reserved. No part of this book may be used or reproduced by any means, graphic, electronic, or mechanical, including photocopying, recording, taping or by any information storage retrieval system without the written permission of the publisher except in the case of brief quotations embodied in critical articles and reviews.

iUniverse books may be ordered through booksellers or by contacting:

iUniverse
1663 Liberty Drive
Bloomington, IN 47403
www.iuniverse.com
1-800-Authors (1-800-288-4677)

Because of the dynamic nature of the Internet, any Web addresses or links contained in this book may have changed since publication and may no longer be valid. The views expressed in this work are solely those of the author and do not necessarily reflect the views of the publisher, and the publisher hereby disclaims any responsibility for them.

ISBN: 978-0-595-53401-2 (pbk)
ISBN: 978-0-595-63459-0 (ebk)

Printed in the United States of America

iUniverse rev. date: 3/11/09

Contents

Foreword vii

Part 1   Spirituality

1. Spirituality and its Challenges 3
2. Basic Elements of Spirituality 8
3. A Spirituality of Ownership 11
4. A Spirituality of Praise 16
5. Realistic Spirituality 23
6. A Spirituality of Aging 36
7. A Spirituality of Awareness 41
8. A Spirituality of Mission 52
9. Spirituality as a Journey 63
10. A Spirituality of Success 71
11. A Spirituality of Work 82
12. Compulsions in Spirituality 88
13. A Spirituality of Devotion 92
14. A Spirituality of Intimacy And Undivided Heart 96
15. Vigilance and Discernment in Spirituality 105
16. Planetary Spirituality and Globalization 110
17. An Ecological Spirituality 119

Part 2   Service

18. Burn with Fire Without Burning out 129
19. The Cheerful Giver 134
20. Devils of the Apostolate 141
21. It's a Matter of Love 147
22. Reconciliation: Celebrating Forgiveness 156
23. The Eagle in You 164

Part 3   Prayer

24. Mystic Journey 173
25. Demons of Prayer 175
26. The Essentials of Prayer 181

27. How to Pray 190
28. Meditation 201
29. Zen Meditation 207
30. God Hunger 211
31. The Art of Creating Affluence and Resourcefulness 220

Part 4   Religious Life

32. Obedience in Religious Life 229
33. Holy Indifference and Obedience 233
34. Inner Freedom 239
35. Dialogue: The Path to Community 246

Appendix I.   Twelve Steps for Christian Living 251
Appendix II.   An Approach to Life 253
Appendix III. General Guidance to Souls 255
Appendix IV. The Examination of Consciousness 257
Appendix V.   Contemplation 259
Appendix VI. Sixteen Steps for Discovery and Empowerment 261

Bibliography **263**

Foreword

What we need in the third millennium is a spirituality to be able to handle life in all its forms. A human being has to develop himself into a man of hope, faith and love. A human has to develop himself spiritually to handle life with all its complications in society.

We have entered the era of information, mind and psyche development. Todays society with its potential for greater leisure and less mechanical work is better suited for mental, psychic and spiritual development. A human being is not a finished product and will experience an infinite number of changes and developments. A new human being is being born and the consciousness is rising and will continue to rise.

We propose to use the age old perennial accepted values and apply them to todays issues. We have to work on ourselves in order to adapt and respond proactively.

Fr. J. J. Edward PhD & Paul J. Buisson

Part 1

Spirituality

Spirituality and its Challenges

The third Millennium will be meant for the spiritually fit. The agricultural and industrial era is over and the post industrial society with its emphasis on the service element has become the main characteristic of the present age. Information and information related industries are dominating the field of business and commerce. We have reached the saturation point perhaps in science and technology, but we are in an infantile stage in spirituality, mysticism and psychic power. There will be more and more leisure and the spiritual and psychic area will find suitable environment for their development.

St. Paul used the word spiritual (1 Cor.2: 14-15) to distinguish the "spiritual person" from the "natural person." Paul was not contrasting the spiritual with the material, the good with the evil, but the person under the influence of the spirit of God with the merely natural human being. The term "spirituality" is being used today to denote some experiential reality, which characterizes all the religions.

We need a spirituality that can question our preoccupations, in order to arrive at an ever richer and more authentic human life. Spirituality is an activity of human life, which is open to engagement with the Absolute. Raymundo Panikkar, for example, defines spirituality, as "one typical way of handling the human condition.[1] Spirituality is "the experience of consciously striving to integrate one's life in terms not of isolation and self-absorption but of self transcendence within and toward the horizon of ultimate concern. If the ultimate concern is God revealed in Jesus Christ and experienced through the gift of the Holy Spirit within the life of the Church, one is dealing with Christian Spirituality.

Nature of Spirituality
Spirituality can be defined as the field of study that attempts to investigate in an interdisciplinary way spiritual experience as such i.e. in the technical sense of ultimate meaning and value, which have transcendent, and life-integrating power over individuals and

groups. Van Harvey calls spirituality a field-encompassing field[2]. In that sense, spirituality is a reality that must touch all of ones life or it touches none of one's life.

There is now a profound and authentic desire for synergy, symbiosis, interdependence and wholeness and for community. Human beings are spirits in the world, and spirituality is the effort to understand and realize the potential of that extraordinary and paradoxical condition. This is the very point which cultural anthropologist, Ernest Becker makes in his study of the human condition, "the denial of Death", at the end of the book: "The distinctive human problem from time immemorial has been the need to spiritualize human life"[3].

New Concerns and Challenges
1. Authenticity
If one of the challenges of the first centuries of the Christian era was the development of orthodoxy, certainly the challenge of the next centuries will be that of authenticity and credibility. It will not be enough to believe, the Gospel will have to be lived. Evangelization will not mean more Christians, but rather being more Christian. The traditional Christian faith will continue to be challenged, and doctrine will continue to develop, but the greater challenge will be whether we live what we say we believe.

2. Solidarity with the Poor, the Women and Children
One of the major contributions of the theology and spirituality that emerged within Latin America in the past thirty years is its emphasis on liberation, praxis, and solidarity with the poor. The poor keep us grounded and focused on basic realities of life. There is greater awareness of the need for the gender equality and balance. The child has acquired greater concern and respect and any violation against the child is met with severe punishment.

3. Liberation of Cultures
Africa has taught us that there is no liberation apart from inculturation and respect for cultures and there is no inculturation or true evangelization of cultures without socio-economic liberation. (the challenges of 'the other') The goal of dialogue is not to evaluate

the various religious traditions, not even to compare them, although that may happen along the way, but the goal is simply that we might learn from one another and get healed and ennobled by another. True religion brings about unity while respecting diversity. If the diversity is divisive, it is no longer true religion. That God is a poor God, if he is worshipped only in one way. The dialogue between the West and East, and among religions and the interreligious denominations has begun. There can be no liberation or inculturation without dialogue and a genuine commitment to the values of other religious traditions. We respect peoples, their traditions, their cultures, values and God's work in cultural pluralism.

5. Challenge of Contemplation

Early in the twentieth century, Teilhard de Chardin had already spoken about matter as having two sides: a 'within' and a 'without.' There is no 'within' without a 'without,' and no 'without' without a 'within.' The outer world and the inner world must move together in harmony. The modern West has an overdeveloped 'without' and an underdeveloped 'within'. The earth has no future separated from the contemplative quest. Each of us is called to that contemplative venture, the journey to truth, the uprooting of egoism from which all true compassion emanates. This interior journey or the genuinely mystical journey will only blossom as the dialogue among all the religions of the world deepens.

6. The Challenge of 'the Other' and Solidarity

Is there space in our world for more than one culture? We have become one, and yet remain many, and the ever present challenge is how to be one without destroying the many. One of Latin America's great and lasting contributions to theology and spirituality is the emphasis it places on the option for the poor. God's reign is inclusive. That which separates us from God is self-righteousness, according to the Gospels; God's love extends to all, but particularly to those who are outsiders from the social and economic points of view. God reaches out especially to those most in need, those most abandoned by their societies. Those whom the structures of the world have cast out, God includes in a very special manner.

The challenging question raised centuries ago by the first Domnican preachers, the question that touched the conscience of Bartolome de las Casas, is perennial: Are they not human too? The challenges will be whether we will live the Gospel or only proclaim it. Will we be able to move beyond the barriers that divide, the barriers of gender, of race, of class? God's dream is not that there be no diversity in creation. Nations, states and ideologies may crumble but even humanity is the only value God envisions in future for all of creation.........

7. The Challenge of Cosmic Vision
There are also the voiceless, the marginalized, the ostracized, the outcasts and untouchables of our world, the poor. Here we are actually concerned with a dialogue with the majority of the world. The challenge of Jesus is that we love our neighbor and ourselves, to make solidarity with 'others' as important as solidarity with God, which is the basis for a human society.

There is more to God's creation, God's dream, than human solidarity alone. There is a cosmic solidarity as well (Romans 8:18-25). Teilhard de Chardin, Sri Aurobindo, and Ken Wilber are among some of the prophets of the past century who have offered us the keys to the next millennium. We together with all of creation form one eco-system. Humans are that part of creation that is aware. As St. Paul writes, 'All of creation is groaning and in travail. There is an order in the universe. Molecules are more advanced than atoms, cells more advanced than mega molecular substances, multi-cellular organisms more advanced than single cells, the human nervous system and brain more complex than those of the pre-hominids, reflective intelligence and advance beyond sensation. Creation is not there for humankind. The fact that God has given us dominion over the earth doesn't mean that we are entitled to domination of the earth. The Spirit is asking of us "to act justly to love tenderly, to walk humbly with God"(Micah 6:8).

End notes
1. Raymundo Pannikkar, the Trinity and the Religious Experience of Man: Icon – Person – Mystery (Maryknoll, N.Y. Orbis, 1973).

2. Van A. Harvey, The Historian and the Believer: The Morality of Historical Knowledge and Christian Belief (Philadelphia: Westminster, 1966) 139-140.

3. Ernest Becker, the Denial of Death, (New York: Macmillan, 1993.

Basic Elements of Spirituality

Spirituality refers to situating God at the center of one's heart. A spiritual person is led by the Spirit. A spiritual person refuses to derive total satisfaction from the things of the world. Holiness is the capacity to pass God's life to others. Spirituality is openness and response-ability vis-à-vis reality[1]. Openness means letting oneself be affected by these realities, to see one's relatedness to all reality. It is to allow reality to "come and invade, enter, disturb, challenge, mould and move us to joy, to tears, to anger, to action".

A devotee passes through several stages
1. Awakening to the divine reality, often abruptly
2. Realization of one's finiteness; need for discipline and mortification; detachment from the senses, the stage of purgation, a stage of effort and pain, active dark nights of the senses and spirit.
3. Detachment from sense has been accomplished; virtues acquired; joy and pleasure in prayer and life; contemplative prayer; illumination of the intellect.
4. Passive dark nights of the senses and spirit; purification at the very center of "I"hood; spiritual crucifixion; seeming abandonment by the absolute; journey to total surrender and receptivity to the Divine;
5. Oneness with the Divine; peaceful joy, enhancement of powers; intensity of certitude. Virtues especially compassion and apostolic activities.

Every Spirituality has seven elements in common

1. **A capacity to live morally.** Every religion and spirituality emphasize the moral aspect. All the spiritual practices will lead to nothing, if one does not respect the laws of life and love. A person, who meditates and performs spiritual practices without leading a moral life, only amuses himself or herself. Spiritual life is not possible without a moral character, but morality is only the beginning.

2. **Non-violence.** This kind of non-harming extends to all sentient beings and to the planet itself. Love shows itself in tenderness, attunement with all the things around. This culture of peace demands compassion and love and informs every action.

3. **Solidarity with all life and the Earth itself.** A deeply spiritual, person is in communion with nature and the whole universe. Like an expectant mother, God prepares the "oikos" (home) for her offspring to be born. At every point of creating something "God as Mother exclaims with joy: God saw that it was good" (Gen 1:4,10,12,18). Whenever the equilibrium in nature tilts, there is a danger of nature losing its goodness.

The human being is part of this one system. Any imbalance in the ecosphere affects humans. (Cosmo-theandric vision). Nature is a sacrament of God, a sign of God's enduring presence. "The whole earth is full of His Glory"(Is 6:3) whither shall I flee from thy presence? If I ascend to heaven thou art there: If I make my bed in Sheol, thou art there" (Ps 139:8)

> *The God who is in the fire*
> *The God who is in the water*
> *The God who has entered into the world.*
> *The God who is in the plants and trees,*
> *adoration to that God, adoration to him*
> *(Bhagavad Gita 18:61*

Father Bede Griffiths painfully observes

> *The modern age has banished God from the world and therefore it has banished beauty. Everything has become "profane" exiled from the sphere of the 'holy' and therefore everything has lost its meaning.[2]*
> *Having banished God, the humans are fearless. They freely commit the threefold sins of the ecological crisis: genocide, ecocide and biocide"[3]*

4. **A Spiritual Practice and self-knowledge.** No spirituality is effective without spiritual discipline. By this means, one grows in depth and awareness. Transformation happens as we gain self-knowledge and uncover hidden motives that lie deep within us.

5. **Simplicity of life.** We have to simplify our lives if the ecological age has really to take root. "Live simply so that others may simply live". One avoids a profligate life-style. We have to take only what is ours and the rest is to be shared.

6. **Selfless Service.** True spirituality is always open to service and never evades service, especially as the need arises. Service is the rent we pay for being on this earth.

7. **Prophetic Action.** It is the ability to speak out when injustice, oppression or the violation of human rights, or the rights of other species occur. The prophetic gift springs from one's deep passion for God and His people.

End Notes

1. An Indian Search for a Spirituality of Liberation" in Asian Christian Spirituality: Reclaiming Traditions V. Fabella and others(eds). New York: Orbis Books, 1992, p.76.

2. Bede Griffiths. *Return to the Center* p.22

3. Mathew Fox, Original Blessings p.12 New Mexico, Bear & Company, 1983.

A Spirituality of Ownership

A Spirituality of ownership defines the right attitude to the material environment. The basic truth is that nothing is mine. Everything passes through my hands. As long as we live in this world, we have the right to our due share. It is through work that we earn the right to consume and enjoy the goods of this world.

Poverty is a lifetime experiment in truth. We feel inspired to trust God a little and release our hold on something. This leads us to more trust and the release of something else, and so on. It's lifetime, because we will never run out of things to let go of. In our experience, we see that these peacemakers who stand out in any century were people of great poverty, e.g. Francis, the poor man of Assisi; Mahatma Gandhi, the Indian leader, Thomas Merton, the Trappist and Dorothy Day. They are not remembered because they were deprived, they are remembered because they gave up much and had much to give.

Bible Perspective
The earth is the Lords' and all who dwell in it. It is communal, undivided and the source of life and nature is given to and for all.

> *Take heed lest you forget the Lord, your God. When you have eaten your fill and built fine houses and your silver and gold is multiplied, take heed lest your heart by puffed up and you forget what the Lord God brought you. Do not say to yourself, "My power and the might of my hand have gathered me this wealth". (Deuteronomy)*

Once the land loses the context of earth, they become ever more divisive, dispossessing many kings. Lack of desire to defend one's possessions would make war improbable and unnecessary. Wars are usually started for economic reasons. During the reign of Solomon there were definite warnings against wealthy producer-consumer economy. (1 kings 4)

The social order became center-periphery, in which a powerful and wealthy regime at the center saw itself as normative, while the periphery including foreign slaves existed as a support system for the center. Their sons were enlisted in the king's armies, their daughters taken as servants, paying taxes to keep the prosperous in place (1 Samuel 8).

Prophets

God will not be mocked forever, and in his own time he raised up prophets, from Amos onwards to challenge the dominant regime. What were during Solomon's reign listed as God's blessings are now listed as blasphemy by prophets before God. Wealth and power are not evil in themselves, but they become evil when they are enjoyed while God's poor go hungry. The essence of God's covenant, which is the solidarity of God's people as a people, has been forgotten. The prophets warn that however competent and smooth the dominant regime may appear, the producer-consumer military ethic contains within itself the seeds of its own destruction.

Temptation to Play God

In all our involvement with God's created gifts we are tempted to play God ourselves, to use those gifts for our own programs, to redefine reality to our own liking. The serpent in the garden and Satan in the desert with Jesus play on this possibility. We can handle them as gifts with reverence, patience and solidarity. All God's gifts, material, intellectual, affective and cultural are of God, but none of them are God. Only God is good and other gifts are always ambivalent, mixed blessings. Fire can purify or devour; water can cleanse or drown. This ambivalence is especially true of gifts of wealth, power and learning.

> *Not from your own do you bestow upon the poor man. You return what is his, what has been given as common for the use of all? You appropriate to yourself alone. The earth belongs to all. Not to the rich…you are therefore paying a debt, not bestowing a bounty. (Ambrose 333-307 A.D).*

> ***Because the rich were the first to occupy common goods, they*** *take these goods as their own. If each would take what is sufficient for one's needs, leaving what is in excess to those in distress, no one would be rich, no one poor. (St. Basil 333-379 A.D.)*

Idols are those good things in life, which instead of being handled as gifts and servants of life, we treat them as absolutes. They are good substitutes, look-alikes. We are living in the false security of the right car, the right house, and the right bank balance.

Simple Life Style
Adopt a simple life style through dependent and limited use of material things. The individuals and the institutions should embrace this life style. Apostolic poverty is at the service of the apostolate. Simplicity in material things has evangelical value. Our simple life style enables us to deeply share till it hurts. Our communities can practice poverty and deep hospitality, welcoming the stranger and offering them the spaces of our heart. We are called to frugality as opposed to profligacy. "He who possesses God wants nothing. God alone suffices", says St. Therese of Avila.

Attitude of Celebration and Compassion
We have to celebrate God's gifts and gifts that flow from God's love. We have to enjoy them without being addicted to any one of them. We are called to think abundance and celebrate the whole of creation, together with compassion. We are called to enjoy life but not to get intoxicated through surfeit. Wealth is filthy lucre but a good fertilizer. It helps us to share our wealth and enlarge the capacities of the heart. We have to take personal and institutional stand against unbridled consumerism in our own lives. Pedro Arrupe, the former Superior General of the Jesuits speaks of 'homo consumens' and the homo serviens. The homo consumes' stands for the egocentric, egotistical individual who is obsessed with having rather than being a slave of created needs, whose moral principle is to pile up wealth. Every human being should strive to be homo serviens, (a serving human being) one who has no desire, for more possessions, but for

more being, who seeks to develop a capacity for service to others in solidarity with a modest sense of what is sufficient.[1]

Non-Possessive Love of things

As Thomas Aquinas puts it "The first foundation for attaining fullness of love is voluntary poverty." We are called upon to have a non-possessive love of things. Jesus the itinerant preacher expected his followers to rely on the providence of God and to transcend everything else for the sake of the kingdom.

The Object of the Religious Vow

1. The object of the vow is to lead a life that is poor in spirit and in fact.
   a. A slum dweller whose heart is not set on riches is poor in spirit and in fact.
   b. A slum dweller whose heart is set on riches is not poor in fact, but not in spirit.
   c. A rich person whose heart is set on riches is neither poor in spirit or in fact.
   d. A rich man whose heart is not set on riches is poor in spirit but not in fact.

2. To make us moderate and industrious
   a. Not destitution but tangible moderation, frugality and simplicity.
   b. Live on the income of our labor.
   c. Renounce luxuries

3. Dependent and limited in the use and disposal of goods.

Concrete Ways of Witnessing

1. Reducing personal and community possessions
2. Living a simple and hardworking way of life
3. Simplifying the standard of living, in building, furnishing, equipment, travel, food and clothing
4. Taking a clear stand against the consumerism of our day.

5. Contributing to the support of one's self and of one's community.
6. Living with a modest, but realistic ceiling of income
7. Taking responsibility for the care of things kept in common
8. Being satisfied with what the community provides.

"There is one thing more you must do. Go and sell what you have and give it to the poor" (Math 10:21). It is an effort of love to accept as a cross and to rejoice in the poverty of the indigent. We make our home with them and never leave them.

End Notes

1. Religious. life–Donum Dei,24, RCP.114

A Spirituality of Praise

The secret of spiritual living is the power to praise. Praise is the harvest of love. Praise precedes faith. First we sing, and then we believe. The fundamental issue is not faith but sensitivity and praise, being ready for faith.

To praise God is to express our acceptance of something that God permits to happen. So to praise God in difficult situations, as sickness and disaster, means literally that we accept what is happening, as part of God's plan to reveal his perfect love for me. We cannot really praise God without being thankful for the thing we are praising Him for. And we cannot really be thankful unless we believe that an omnipotent, loving Father is working for our good. Praising, then, involves both gratitude and joy. (Rom. 8:28). The fact that we praise God and not some unknown fate also means that we are accepting the fact that the God is responsible for what is happening and will always make it work for our good. Otherwise, it would make little sense thanking Him for it.

Always be Joyful
Always be joyful. Always keep on praying. No matter what happens, always be thankful, for this is God's will for you who belong to Christ Jesus. (1 Thess.5.16, 18). But God has a perfect plan for our understanding, and when we use it His way, it isn't a stumbling block, but a wonderful aid to our faith. For God is King of all the earth. (Ps 47.7). Our understanding gets us into trouble when we try to figure out why and how God brings certain circumstances into our lives. This is the basis of our praise. God wants us to understand that he loves us and that He has a plan for us. And we know that all that happens to us is working for our good, if we love God and are fitting into His plans. (Rom. 8.28) Are you surrounded by difficult circumstances right now? Try to accept with your understanding that God loves you. Accept that God has allowed those circumstances because He knows that He can bring good out of this for you. Praise him for what he has brought into your life, do it deliberately and with your understanding.

A Spirituality of Praise

Accept the Situation as it is
Chinese spirituality will use the word 'Yielding'. We praise God, not for the expected results, but for the situation just as it is. Praise is based on an acceptance of the present as part of God's loving and perfect will for us. We praise God not for what we expect will happen in or around us, but we praise him for who he is and where and how we are right now. It is of course a fact that if we honestly praise God, something does happen as a result. His power obviously flows into the situation and we will soon notice a change in us or around us. Praise is not a bargaining position, we don't say, "I'll praise you so that you can bless me, Lord. To praise God is to delight ourselves in Him. Be delightful with the Lord. Then he will give you all your heart's desires (Ps. 37.4).

First delight and then Express Your Heart's desires
We don't mention our heart's desires and then delight ourselves in the Lord in order to get them. We're first to be delighted. Once we have experienced being really delighted with God, we'll discover that everything else becomes secondary. Still, it is true that God does want to give us all our heart's desires. Nothing short of this is his wish and plan for us. God does have a perfect plan for your life and for mine. God has a perfect plan for our lives, but he cannot move us to the next step of His plan until we joyfully accept our present situation as part of that plan. What happens next is God's move, not ours.

Power and Praise
There is power in our words of praise; there is power in our attitude of thankfulness and joy. But God is omnipotent and retains absolute control. We need to remind ourselves of that fact frequently. It is easy to fall into the trap of thinking that we have the power to manipulate or change a situation simply by reciting a certain form of prayer. We must sincerely accept and thank God for our situation, believing that he has allowed it to come about. Then there is, released into that situation, a supernaturally divine force that causes change. This is God's power at work in human lives. Any form of sincere prayer opens the door for God's power to move into our lives. But

the prayer of praise releases more of God's power than any other form of petition.

Acceptance Before Understanding
Even if we realize our own powerlessness to cope with the enemy, we are afraid to let go and trust ourselves to God's power. God's word makes it clear that the only way out of that dilemma is a step of faith on our part. Believing that God's promises are true, accepting them, and daring to trust in them leads to understanding. Acceptance comes before understanding. The reason for it is simple. Our human understanding is so limited that we can't possibly grasp the magnitude of God's plan and purpose for us. If our understanding had to come before our acceptance, we'd never be able to accept very much.

Jesus Praised and Gave Thanks
Before multiplying the loaves Jesus looked up to heaven and praising God gave thanks and broke the bread (Mark 6.41-3). Before raising Lazarus: He said Father, I thank you for hearing (John 11.41.) Praise is an active response to what we know God has done and is doing for us-in our lives and in this world, through his son Jesus Christ and the Holy Spirit. If we doubt in our hearts what God has done and is doing, we cannot wholeheartedly praise him. If we want to be able to praise God for everything, we need to have our foundation solid and without cracks of doubt and uncertainty.

Praise in Scripture
With enthusiasm and confidence the Psalmist proclaims resolutely: "I will bless the Lord at all times; his praise shall be ever in my mouth" (Ps 34:2). God himself praises His gentle servant: "Here is my servant whom I uphold, my chosen one in whom my soul delights" (Is 42:1) in reference to Jesus: "This is my beloved Son, on whom my favor rests". Listen to him (Mt. 17:5; see Lk 9:35; Mk 9:7). Throughout Scripture, the central meaning of praise seems to indicate the human person as receptive and responsive: receptive to the discernible presence of God, responsive in the expression of wonder and awe. Praise is the key element in the life of the spirit.

Praise: It's Nature
Praise is an expression of approval, a positive affirmation. To praise God is to acclaim, magnify, honor, and glorify him. Praise is a co-mingling of wonder, awe, adoration and thanksgiving. To praise is to acknowledge lovingly and accept gratefully not only what God is in himself, but also what he is for the human person. Authentic praise involves sensitivity to the sacred, and awareness of indebtedness to God. It seems to be born when the mystery of God and the mystery of the human person meet.

Praise, Lewis maintains, is the dynamic response of a creature who knows himself or herself to be the object of God's infinite love. Lewis personally gave "praise" for coming to this discovery after a slow and hesitant faith-struggle of more than thirty years.

Praise is the "correct, adequate, and appropriate response" to someone or something that deserves it. Therefore, the Psalmist can state, "Praise is rightfully yours, O God" (Ps 65:2). "Praise the Lord, for he is good; sing praise to our God, for he is gracious; it is fitting to praise Him" (Ps 147:1; Ps 33:1). Thus, the issue of praise is not primarily our feelings and our words; the issue of praise is God. Essentially then, to praise is to discover a value, appreciate it, and in some way express this appreciation. The word appreciation for him means to love and delight in. The beginning of praise is appreciation and the beginning of appreciation is a sense of humble awe in the face of the mystery of the enduring love and goodness of God. In the light of this we could perhaps say that praise is a form of the truth to be grasped by the spirit. To praise is to forget the self and break down the walls of self-absorption and resistance of God. Praise is fueled by love; therefore, selfishness smothers praise. The humblest, and at the same time the most balanced and capacious minds praise most, while the malcontents praise the least.

Praise and Creation: Matter Really Matters
There is no good trying to be more spiritual than God. God never meant man to be a purely spiritual creature. He likes matter. He invented it. "God saw that it was good" is a refrain repeated seven times with the first thirty-one verses of Genesis (Gen.1: 4, 10, 12,

and 18). The Biblical words about the Genesis of heaven and earth are not words of information but of appreciation. The story of creation is not a description of how the world came into being but a song about the glory of the world's having come into being; "And God saw that it was good" (Gen. 1:25)

Not to praise what God has created is not to see. Elizabeth Barrette Browning's pertinent observation in the poem "Aurora Leigh".

> *Earth's crammed with heaven,*
> *And every common bush afire with God;*
> *And only he who sees takes off his shoes*
> *The rest sit around and pluck blackberries.*

The world is "crammed" with the marvelous. Yet our perception is fragile and lacks intensity. We can be blind and deaf and dumb. Even Screwtape, the senior devil in Lewis' **Screwtape Letters** attests to the truth that God is a hedonist at heart.

> *Out at sea, there is pleasure and more pleasure. He makes no secret of it; at his right hand are pleasures forevermore.*

Praise and the Present Moment: Time Touches Eternity
Without doubt, Lewis roots praise in an appreciation of what is "extraordinary" in the ordinariness of the present moment. The "present is the point at which time touches Eternity". God's loving and caring presence is presumed through the present moment. This notion is crucial in the great theological vision of Julian of Norwich's statement "All shall be well" is rooted in the reality of the "All is well." A splendid text in Romans also embraces the vision: "We know that God makes all things work together for the good of those who love Him" (Rom. 8:28). Thus, a realization that the present moment is enlivened with an incarnation and vision is crucial to spiritual growth.

Praise and Joy: The Serious Business of Heaven
Praise is an act of buoyancy and spontaneity. Praise transmutes

feeling into delight. Praise is the "mode of love which always has some element of joy in it." In human experience praise is intimately intertwined with joy. Profound joy can generate praise and praise is the springboard for joy. All enjoyment spontaneously overflows into praise. We delight to praise what we enjoy because the praise not merely expresses but it is never complete until it is expressed.

Praise and Suffering: A Sacrifice of Praise

If a primal and central quality of praise is joy, what are we to understand in Scripture's invitation to offer the Lord a "Sacrifice of Praise"? We have already noted that a reverently surrendered heart is the wellspring of praise. Nothing so hampers the capacity to praise as the desire to control and the temptation to manipulate. The focus of praise is not the self; therefore, praise is part of asceticism. The proper good for a creature is to surrender itself to its Creator to enact intellectually, volitionally and emotionally that relationship which is given in the mere fact of being a creature. In the world as we now know it, the problem is how to recover this self-surrender.

"Self-surrender" demands courageous fidelity to the demands of discipleship. It urges that we cut through all the indulgence of the ego, that we become the instrument of hollowing and hallowing, a means of rooting our security in God. We shall draw nearer to God, not by trying to avoid the sufferings inherent in all loves, but by accepting them and offering a "Sacrifice of Praise" Thus, "Obedience" is at the heart of offering a sacrifice of praise. God's design is to keep us on tiptoe, to nourish our thirst for Him with little "glimpses" into what will some day be forever. "The patches of goodnight" in the woods of our experience summons us to move beyond. To offer a "sacrifice of praise" is to allow our innate appetite for the Infinite, our thirst for God himself, to dislodge us, whenever we are inclined to settle down.

Praise and Adoration: Fused Moments of Felicity

Authentic praise sometime goes beyond the scope of emotion; it is the threshold to the transcendent. Praise is intimately linked with appreciative love. "We give thanks to you for the great glory." God can awaken in man, toward Himself a supernatural appreciative love.

We often discover a level where we are stunned by the ineffable. At such moments the human person deeply experiences the disparity between desire for expressions and the means of expression. Even though a loving heart has no words, it cannot contain itself. St. Augustine gifts us with a memorable image: "Love grown cold is the heart's silence."

Fully to enjoy is to glorify. In commanding us to glorify him, God is inviting us to enjoy him. The contemporary milieu, with its unhealthy emphasis in utilitarianism and materialism continues to strangle and corrode our sense of wonder. St. Augustine invites us to glory in the splendor of the truth and goodness of praise with our whole being:

> *Sing praises with your whole being: that is, praise God not only with your tongue and your voice, but with your conscience, with your life, with your deeds.*

Realistic Spirituality

To deny our errors is to deny ourselves, for to be human is to be imperfect, somehow error-prone. To be human is to embody a paradox. For according to that ancient vision, we are "less than the gods, more than the beast, yet somehow also both Spirituality accepts that "if a thing is worth doing, it is worth doing badly. It is more interested in questions than in answers, more a journey toward humility than a struggle for perfection. "First of all, we have to quit playing God"

Story Telling
In the midst of sorrow and in the presence of joy, both mourners and celebrants tell stories. But especially in times of trouble, when "a miracle" was needed and the limits of human ability were reached, people turned to storytelling as a way of exploring the fundamental mysteries:" Without imperfections namely the "gap between intentions and results," there would be no story.

Through Others
Our salvation comes through other human beings, God speaks through events and through human beings who play significant roles in our lives.

The great master Mat-su, as a youth, was a fanatic about sitting in meditation for many hours at a time. One day, his patriarch's disciple Huai-jang asked him what on earth he hoped to attain by this compulsive cross-legged sitting. "Buddha hood," said Mat-su. Thereupon Huai-jang sat down, took a brick, and started to polish it assiduously. Mat-su looked at him, perplexed, and asked what he was doing. "Oh," said Huai-jang, "I am making a mirror out of my brick". "You can polish it till doomsday," scoffed Mat-su, "you'll never make a mirror out of a brick!" "Aha!" smiled Huai-jang. "Maybe you are beginning to understand that you can sit until doomsday, it won't make you into a Buddha."[1] This story suggests the hope and, ultimately, the promise of our shared journey:

When Humans Meet in Love it is Holy Ground

When the world was young, two brothers shared a field and a mill. Each night they divided evenly the grain they had ground together during the day. Now as it happened, one of the brothers lived alone; the other had a wife and a large family. One day, the single brother thought to himself: "It isn't really fair that we divide the grain evenly. I have only myself to care for, but my brother has children to feed." So each night he secretly took some of his grain to his brother's granary to see that he was never in want. But the married brother said to himself one day, "It isn't really fair that we divide the grain evenly, because I have children to provide for me in my old age, but my brother has no one. What will he do when he is old?" So every night he secretly took some of his grain to his brother's granary. As a result, both of them always found their supply of grain mysteriously replenished each morning. Then one night, the brothers met each other halfway between their two houses, suddenly realized what had happened, and embraced each other in love. The story is that God witnessed their meeting and proclaimed, "This is a holy place-a place of love-and here it is that my temple shall be built."

The holy place, where God is made known, is the place where human beings discover each other in love.

Earthly Things

We are not spirits but human beings with material and visible existence. Let us not pretend to be angels.

Abba Poemen was visited one day by a dignitary, who was most anxious to discuss his troubled soul and receive the monk's advice, But as soon as the visitor started talking, the Abba averted his gaze and refused to speak to him. Confused and straight, the visitor left the room and asked one of the holy man's followers what was going on-why did the Abba ignore him? The disciple spoke to Abba Poemen, who explained, "He is from above and speaks of heavenly things, but I am of the earth and speak about earthly things. If he had spoken to me about the passions of his soul, then I should have answered him. But if he speaks about spiritual things, I know nothing of them." Fortified with this knowledge, the dignitary tried again, beginning with the question, "What shall I do, abba, I am dominated by the passions of my soul?" and abba Poemen replied; "Now you are speaking rightly."[2]

Acceptance of Truth
Whether we are weak or not, the most important thing in spirituality is that we are absolutely honest with ourselves. Rabbi Elimelech Lizensker said: "I am sure of my share in the World-to-come. When I stand to plead before the bar of the Heavenly Tribunal, I will be asked: 'Did you learn, as in duty bound?' To this I will answer: 'No.' Again, I will be asked: 'Did you pray, as in duty bound'? Again my answer will be 'No.' The third question will be 'Did you do good, as in duty bound'? And for the third time, I will answer: 'No.' Then judgment will be awarded in my favor, for I will have spoken the truth."

Its all right that it's not all right
Therapy offers explanations; spirituality offers forgiveness. Therapy may release one from addiction; spirituality releases for life. Spirituality prefers the language of weakness and flaw and favors the ancient image of the archer's arrow falling short of its mark. I'm not all right, and you're not all right, but that's okay- that's all-right. Man is the creature who wants to be God," Jean-Paul Sartre observed. The realistic spirituality wrestles directly with that quest, assuring that "first of all, we have to quit playing God".

God Comes to Us through Our Wounds
Jungian analyst Marion Woodman identifies addiction as one of the "wounds" that let "God" in: At the very point of the vulnerability where the surrender takes place-that is where God enters. God comes through the wound.[4] The "problem" is not material realities but our attachment to material possessions. Possessions can lead to obsessions. Obsession with possessions crowds out the spiritual.

Opening and Closing Doors
An everyday event is to be mastered and that is the key to higher and spiritual things. Merton once met a Zen novice who had just finished his first year of living in a monastery. He asked the novice what he had learned during the course of his novitiate, half expecting to hear of encounters with enlightenment, discoveries of the spirit,

perhaps even altered states of consciousness. But the novice replied that during his first year in the contemplative life, he had simply learned to open and close doors. The quiet discipline of not acting impetuously, of not running around slamming doors, of not hurrying from one place to another was where this novice had to begin (and perhaps end) in the process of spiritual growth. Merton loved the answer and often retold the story, for it exemplified for him the need to do the ordinary; while being absorbed in it intensely and utterly.[5] Only by embracing the "dark side" of our ambiguous natures, can we ever come to know "the light." We find ourselves only by giving up ourselves; we gain freedom by submitting to the will of others, we attain autonomy by not insisting on our own rights.

You are Right

Everyone thinks that he is right when he does even a wrong thing. The insight of sages and saints is that we are either ignorant or weak consequently we are. We operate at our own level of consciousness.

> *A rabbi was asked to adjudicate a case. The first man presented his argument, and the rabbi, after hearing his evidence, said to him, "You are right!" Then the second man presented his argument and the rabbi, after hearing his evidence, said, "You are right!" At this point, the rabbi's wife turned to her husband and asked, "How can both of these men be right?" The rabbi thought for a moment and said, "Darling, you are right!"*[6]

The Reality of Limitation

There is a crack in everything God has made says Ralph Waldo Emerson.[7] One devotee complained, "Look at me; I've been here for thirty-eight years, and I have not yet attained pure prayer. Another man present said, "It's a sad story all right, but the sadness consists in the fact that after thirty-eight years in a monastery he's still interested in pure prayer."[8] In the verse "Therefore be perfect as your heavenly father is perfect,"

Mt 5: 48: the term perfect is translated from the Greek 'teleios', which means more accurately "fully complete." It means to be compassionate in a way that treats all others fairly or equally.

Fundamental to the life of the desert fathers was the insight not to judge but to love.[9] "When Jacob's sons said to Joseph: 'We are upright men', he answered: 'that is why I spoke to you saying: Ye are spies.' But later, when they confessed the truth with their lips and with their hearts, and said to one another, 'We are verily guilty concerning our brother,' the first gleam of their redemption dawned. Overcome with compassion, Joseph turned aside and wept."[10]

"The chiefs sanctity of a temple is that it is a place, to which men can go to weep in common," wrote the Spanish philosopher Miguel de Unamuno. When Riziner was imprisoned, he wept. He was asked: 'Why do you not accept this affliction as intended in love?' He answered: 'when God sends bitterness, we ought to feel it.'"[11] The Russians have a proverb: "You cannot kiss your own ear." We cannot directly know our own being.

Spirituality is Nurtured in Community
While spirituality can be discovered in solitude-by retreating to a cell of some kind, by reading, thinking, meditating, praying-it can be fulfilled only in community. Abba Poemen offered a telling observation: "It's possible to spend a hundred years in your cell without ever learning anything."

Not Magic, But Miracle
Magic refers to quick fix tactics and strategy. If you wear a medal you will be protected from harm. Real spirituality consists in daily work with prayer. The volume of work and the result of our sustained efforts appear to be a miracle.

> *In the remote mountains of northern Greece, there once lived a monk who had desired all of his life to make a pilgrimage to the Holy Sepulchre-to walk three times around it, to kneel, and to return home a new person. Gradually through the years he had saved what money he could, begging in the villages nearby, and finally, near the end of his life, had enough set aside to begin his trip. He opened the gates of the monastery and, staff in hand, set out with great anticipation on his way to Jerusalem.*

> But no sooner had he left the cloister than he encountered a man in rags, sad and bent to the ground, picking herbs. "Where are you going, Father?" the man asked. "To the Holy Sepulchre, brother. By God's grace I shall walk three times around it, kneel, and return home a different man from what I am." "How much money to do that do you have, Father?" inquired the man. "Thirty pounds," the monk answered. "Give me the thirty pounds," said the beggar. "I have a wife and hungry children. Give me the money, walk three times around me, then kneel and go back into your monastery." The monk thought for a moment, scratching the ground with his staff, then took the thirty pounds from his sack, gave the whole of it to the poor man, walked three times around him, knelt, and went back through the gates of his monastery. He returned home a new person, of course, having recognized that the beggar was Christ himself–not in some magical place far away, but right outside his monastery door close.

It is no wonder, then, that "locating divinity in drugs" becomes a kind of spiritual death. Drunkenness can be a kind of shortcut to the higher life, the attempt to achieve a higher state without an emotional and intellectual effort. Midas, King of Phrygia and friend of Dionysus was granted his magical wish that everything he touched might turn to gold. The result, of course, was that Midas then found it impossible both to eat and to embrace his child.[14]

> Once upon a time, but not very long ago, in a kingdom both near and far away, a canny scientist longed for the love of a beautiful woman. Wise women were wary of the man, and so he lived a very lonely life. One day, the man decided to use his science to win love, and he set about to concoct a chemical that would cause the object of his affections to fall madly in love with him. Soon his research succeeded, he produced the chemical, and as luck would have it, at just that time he met a beautiful, talented and good woman–the ultimate woman of his dreams. The scientist arranged for friends to introduce them, and at

their first meeting, he poured it into her beverage. Lo and behold, his fantasy came true! The exquisite creature fell instantly and completely in love with him, and they soon married. But was our hero happy? Alas, no. In a short time, he became gaunt from not eating, his work fell by the wayside, and eventually he could not even bring himself to touch his beloved, as he spent every waking moment torturing himself, trying to devise some kind of test to answer his agonized question: "Would she love me if it were not for the chemical?" Our scientist did crave love, and love cannot be commanded.

We have to accept the inevitable and the true test of maturity is that we are reconciled to the fact that we cannot change many things. Another sign is the awareness that we may be wrong.

I was anxious and depressed and selfish. Everyone kept telling me to change. I resented them, and I agreed with them, and I wanted to change, but simply couldn't, no matter how hard I tried. My best friend kept insisting that I change. So I felt powerless and trapped. Then, one day, another friend said to me, "Don't change. I love you just as you are." Those words were music to my ears: "Don't change. Don't change. I love you as you are." I relaxed. I came alive. And suddenly I changed. Now I know that I couldn't really change until I found someone who would love me whether I changed or not[13]

You may directly will	**but not**
Knowledge	Wisdom
Pleasure	Happiness
Congratulations	Admiration
Reading/Listening	Understanding
Going to bed	Sleeping
Meekness	Humility
Dryness	Sobriety

"Story," the novelist John Gardner observed, "details the gap between intentions and results." To live with an awareness of story is to recognize that "We are never more than the co-authors of our own stories."[15] Every story details a mixture of what Niccolo Machiavelli named necessity, virtue, and fortune: cause, choice, and chance. The very combination of the three reveals that we are neither completely controlled nor completely in control. We can will, in other words, but we must also be willing. We are all looking for, but we find what we are looking for only by being looked for. We find miracle only when we stop looking for magic.

The Real End is the Journey

The realistic spirituality offers an alternative image for the spiritual life: that of journey. The word journey originally meant, "the distance traveled in one day". A journey becomes a pilgrimage as we discover, day by day, that the distance traveled is less important that the experience gained. "When you're on a journey, and the end keeps getting further and further away, then you realize that the real end is the journey," quoted Joseph Campbell.[16] As the fourth-century monk Macarius emphasized, all improvement in spirituality is "a matter of falling and getting up again, building something up and then being knocked down again."

> *We shall not cease from exploration*
> *And the end of all our exploring*
> *Will be to arrive where we started*
> *And know the place for the first time.*[17]

A Pervasive Spirituality

Our spirituality should pervade all the aspects of our life. Nothing is left out. There is no value-free action. Everything is value- laden.

> *In a faraway place and a long-ago time, there was once a rich man who gave all his money to the poor, joined a band of hermits, and went to live with them in the desert and worship God. One day the man was sent to town with another hermit to sell two donkeys that had grown old and could no longer carry their burdens. He went and stood in the marketplace, where shoppers looking for donkeys came to ask if his were*

worth buying. "If they were worth buying, do you think we'd be selling them?" he replied. "And why do they have such ragged backs and tails?" he was asked." Because they're old and stubborn," he said. "We have to pull their tails and thrash them to make them move". Since there were no buyers for the donkeys, the man returned with them to the desert, where his companion told the other hermits what had happened. All of them demanded to know why he had frightened the buyers away. "Do you imagine for a moment," he answered, "that I left home and gave everything away, all my camels and cattle and sheep and goats, in order to make a liar of myself for the sake of two old donkeys?"[18]

"Experience is not what happens to a man. It is what a man does with what happens to him" remarks Aldous Huxley [19]. Wisdom is the certainty and joy of having done something.

The young salesman approached the farmer and began to talk excitedly about the book he was carrying. "This book will tell you everything you need to know about farming," the young man said enthusiastically. "It tells you when to sow and when to reap. It tells you about weather, what to expect and when to expect it. This book tells you all you need to know." "Young man," the farmer said, "that's not the problem. I know everything that is in that book. My problem is doing it."[20]

Letting Go

Blaise Pascal offered another perspective on the theme of "attachment" and "detachment." We suffer from various libidinal enslavements that bloat our egotistical self: (1) the libido dominandi or lust for power over others and over nature; (2) the libido sentiendi, or lust for intense sensation; and (3) the libido sciendi, or lust for manipulative knowledge, knowledge that is primarily used to increase our own power, profit, and pleasure.[21] Spirituality involves the "letting go" of three needs: the need to be in control, the need to be effective, and the need to be right.

Humility

St. Bernard, asked to list the four cardinal virtues, answered:

"Humility, humility, humility and humility." For humility signifies, simply, the acceptance of being human, the acceptance of one's human being. It is the embrace of both the saint and the sinner, both the beast and angel that constitute our very being as human. Humility involves learning how to live and take joy in the reality. As a Sufi saying suggests: "A saint is a saint unless he knows that he is one."[22] One day a rabbi, in a frenzy of religious passion, rushed in before the ark, fell to his knees, and started beating his breast, caring, "I'm nobody! I'm nobody!" "To be humble is not to make comparisons." The alcoholic's problem is not when he thinks, 'I am a worm.' The alcoholic's problem is that he is convinced: "I am a very special worm." For the words human, humor, and humility all have the same root-the ancient Indo-European ghom, best translated by the English humus. Humus is "a brown or black substance resulting from the partial decay of plant and animal matter.

Tolerance

A man who took great pride in his lawn found himself with large and recurring crops of dandelions. Although he tried every method he knew to get rid of them, they continued to plague him. Finally, in desperation, he wrote to the Agriculture Department of the State University, enumerating all the things he had tried and concluding with the question: "What shall I do now?" After a somewhat prolonged time even for such correspondence, the reply finally came: "We suggest you learn to love them."[23]

We need to reclaim anger for its proper purpose. It is always a waste of good anger to get annoyed with other human beings. What the ascetic needs to do is to focus his attention on the fact that he is annoyed. Instead of seeing some other being angrily, he tries to see his own anger. He can then begin to fight against it.[24] Anger and sadness butt against each other, steel against stone. The danger of anger lies not in anger itself, but in resentment, the clinging to and prolonged attachment to anger. For the opposite of "resentment" is forgiveness, recognized by centuries of spiritual thinkers as "the endpoint of human life."

We are a Community of Sinners

A man was looking for a good church to attend and he happened to enter one in which the congregation and the preacher were reading from their prayer book. They were saying, "We have left undone those things which we ought to have done, and we have done those things which we ought not to have done." The man dropped into a seat and sighed with relief as he said to himself, "Thank goodness, I've found my crowd at last."[25]

I Need Lots of Clapping

A young priest stopped to talk to a parishioner and her five year-old daughters, Carmine. The little girl had a new jump rope, and the priest began to demonstrate the intricacies of jumping rope to her. After a while Carmine began to jump, first once, then twice. Mother and priest clapped loudly for her skill. Eventually, the little girl was able to jump quite well on her own and wandered off with her newfound skill. Priest and mother chatted a few moments until Carmine, with the saddest, wisest eyes imaginable, returned dragging her rope. "Mommy," She lamented, "I can do it, but I need lots of clapping."[26]

A realistic spirituality is characterized by a series of farewells: To youth, beauty strength, influence and usefulness. It is a journey towards humility and tenderness. It is spirituality of acceptance and forgiveness. We compare ourselves to God and not to others. We adopt the attitude that we are ordinary and ignorant and stand in need of God and that we are not ourselves gods.

End Notes

1. Versions of the story also appear in William Bausch, Storytelling: Imagination and Faith (Mystic, CT: Twenty-Third Publications, 1984), pp. 68-69,

2. See Simon Tugwell, Ways of Imperfection (Springfield, IL: Templegate, 1985), p.20. The full story may be found in *The Sayings of the Desert Fathers*: The Alphabetical Collection, trans. Dom Lucien Renault (Solesmes: Bellefontaine, 1985);

34   *A Practical Spirituality*

3. The Worlds of Existentialism: A Critical reader (Chicago: University of Chicago Press, 1964), p. 33,

4. Marion Woodman, "Worshipping Illusions," Parabola 12:2 (May 1987), p. 64.

5. Belden C. Lane, "Merton as Zen Clown." Theology Today 46:3 (October 1989), 259-60.

6. Gregory M. Corrigan, Disciple Story: Every Christian's Journey (Notre Dame, IN: Ave Maria Press, 1989), p. 93

7. The Great Quotations (New York: Lyle Stuart, 1960), p. 238, citing The Works of Ralph Waldo Emerson, 1913.

8. Thomas Hopko, "Living in Communion: An Interview with Father Thomas Hopko," Parabola 12:3 (August 1987), 50-59.

9. Benedicta Ward, Harlots of the Desert: A Study of Repentance in Early Monastic Sources (Kalamazoo, MI: Cistercian Publications, 1987), p. 87

10. Martin Buber, Tales of the Hasidim: The Later Masters (New York: Schocken Books, 1948) pp. 187-88; Polsky and Wozner retell the story, citing this source in Everyday Miracles, p. 259.

11. The Unamuno quotation is from Miguel de Unamuno, The Tragic Sense of Life, trans. J.E. Crawford Flitch (New York: Dover, 1954 [1921], p. 17; the Passover story is from Newman, Hasidic Anthony, p. 485.

12. The story of the lost little girl is form Polsky and Wozner, Everyday Miracles, p. 3.

13. De Mello, Song of the Bird, pp. 67-68.

14. A concise summary of the Midas story may be found in Herbert Spencer Robinson and Knox Wilson, Myths and Legends of All Nations (Savage, MD: Rowman and Littlefield, 1976 [1950]), p. 92,

15. The John Gardner's quotation is form *The Art of Fiction* (New York: Vintage, 1985).

16. This story draws on information from Bill's widow, Lois, 1977 interviews, and conversations with his secretary, Nell Wing.

17. Andre Lacocque and Pierre-Emmanuel Lacocque, The Jonah Complex (Atlanta: John Knox Press, 1981), p. 54.

18. Sadeh, Jewish Folktales, p. 179.

19. Huxley is quoted without citation by Laurence J. Peter, Peter's Quotations (New York: Wm. Morrow & Co., 1977), p. 185.
20. Retold by Joseph Gosse, "Inexhaustible Springs," Spiritual Life 36:1 (Spring 1990), 39.
21. See Mark D. Hart, "Reconciliation of Body and Soul: Gregory of Nyssa's Deeper Theology of Marriage,2 Theological Studies 51: (1990), 450-78
22. Although this insight appears in many forms in many traditions, this most succinct statement of it is borrowed from Shah, Learning How to Learn, p. 121.
23. Retold by de Mello, Song of the bird, p. 65. It can also be found in Fuller, Thesaurus of Anecdotes, and pp. 408-9.
24. As presented and interpreted by Tugwell, ways of Imperfection, p. 29; see also Ernest A. Wallis Budge, ed. And trans., Stories of the Holy Fathers (London: Oxford University Press, 1934), pp. 294ff.
25. Told by L. Patrick Carroll and Katherine M. Dyckamn, "Lend Each Other a Hand," Praying 29, p. 5.
26. This story is constructed from Joseph T. Shipley, The Origins of English Words (Baltimore: The Johns Hopkins University Press, 1984), p. 163, and Thomas Bullfinch, The Age of Fable (London:

J.M. Dent & Sons, 1973, pp. 266-67

A Spirituality of Aging

We cannot avoid sickness, old age and death. Human life is constantly changing and we are challenged to move with those changes. We move through the stages of childhood and maturity into old age, which demand that we leave behind one way of living to face life in a new and different way. The adjustments are difficult and may take many years to accomplish.

John the Baptist, said: "He must increase and I must decrease." John saw that his disciples were leaving him and following Jesus. He sensed that his basic work was completed and his role in God's plan had been fulfilled. He did not try to hold on to his disciples nor did he need to continue his previous work of preparing for the Messiah. He stepped back and let Jesus proclaim his message, trusting that God was working through and through others. In a sprit of trust he lived his statement: "He must increase and I must decrease." This would be a suitable model for the aging.

As we grow older many things are taken from us. As they diminish in body, mind, and spirit their influence in the world around them is lessened, and they are called upon to find God in these losses. Instead of emphasizing generosity as they did as a young religious, they are called to accept these diminishments and even to rejoice in them. Instead of giving themselves more fully to apostolic involvement, they are called to withdraw from such assignments. Above all they are called to trust, to believe that as they decrease, Jesus increases. They are called to trust that their diminishment is part of God's way of furthering the kingdom.

1. Preparation for Death.
The spirituality of an old person should include a serious preparation for death. Death is not simply something that happens to us. It is one of the most important actions of our lives, for in death, we go back to the womb of God. The period of aging has been given to us by God as a time of intense preparation for death. It would be a mistake to be so busy with our work and other affairs that we give

no time, thought, or effort to this approaching event in our lives. We may want to die with our boots on, but such an attitude may possibly manifest a lack of faith. We are, of course, called by God to do our share of the work of building the kingdom. But our faith affirms that we are called by God to pass beyond this world to live with him in an eternal kingdom. It would be wrong in our present lives to be so occupied with the "God of this world" that we ignore the "God of the future"

1.1. Putting Things Aside
One way of preparing for death is to begin to *put things aside*. Since in death we will be forced to leave our engagements in this world, a preparation would be to step back from these, to become less absorbed in our concern for the achievement of goals and the attainment of success. Nature aids such stepping back, since for an aging person, the world often becomes rather "tasteless." The process of aging may not only reduce the sensitivity of our taste, but also diminish our hunger for the activities and concerns of the world around us. We can find ourselves not caring which songs are the most popular, or who is the most popular movie star. When we were young, such things made a difference, but as we grow older, we find ourselves losing touch with these "popular" concerns.

1.2 Focus on Important and Leaving Unimportant Things
The tendency to lose touch need not be conceived as a sad thing, or a loss. As we move towards death we are challenged to free ourselves from all that is unimportant in life. How wonderful it would be, if the contemplation of death could make us truly "free" of all these petty things so that we might live for what is truly important.

1.3. Meeting God
The preparation for death demands a positive focus on that meeting with God, which is found in death. Preparing for death thus invites us to turn toward God and give ourselves directly to God. We have more time for prayer and more time for God.

2. A challenge to Accept.
2.1 Physical deterioration.
One major characteristic of the spirituality of aging is that it places emphasis on a person's acceptance of diminishment. As we grow older various things are taken from us. There is a basic lessening of energies as we grow older. Vision and hearing begin to deteriorate. Health fails as we encounter various illnesses and pains. Control over one's body can be lost; hands become clumsy and our feet unsteady. There may be a lessening of mental powers as memory goes; concentration becomes difficult and the mind tend to wander. In our daily lives we are no longer able to control situations the way we did, when we were young.

Spiritual Losses
There may even be spiritual losses, as we grow older. The apostolic zeal we had as young religious may have vanished. The patience that was once part of our character becomes more difficult as physical pain makes us more irritable. Sometimes the spiritual devotions that were once so vital and moving no longer move us.

God takes my health and my prayer says 'yes'.
God takes my energies and my prayer says 'yes'.
God takes away my meaningful work and my prayer says 'yes'.
The Lord gives, and the Lord takes away; Blessed be the Name of the Lord."

3. A challenge not to Live in the Past
One problem that all aging people face is the natural tendency to become absorbed in the past, to relish past joys, and to fight the battles we had when we were children. We may even tend to assume the attitudes we had when we were children. When new situations with their new demands disturb us and cause us pain, we tend to run away from this pain, and hold on to our old ways of doing things. This tendency may seem to be rather harmless, but the danger is that in our absorption in the past and in the old ways of doing things, we may miss the wonderful challenges of the present.

4. Invitation to Find New Values in One's life
One's aging years offer an invitation to find new values in one's life. We live in a milieu that tends to value persons basically in terms of

their work. Influenced by this attitude, when we come to the point of our lives when we do less work-or do no work at all, we tend to find our life less valuable and less meaningful. In such a situation we are invited to set aside this false way of seeing others and ourselves and to adopt Jesus' way of seeing human life. For Jesus, the work of Martha was important, but Mary sitting before him and listening to him had the "better part." In her prayerful absorption in Jesus, Mary found a most worthwhile way of living.

As we age, we are challenged to believe first of all in the value of just being alive-to believe that there is something precious and holy in waking up each morning to a new day. We can rejoice in the simple actions of eating, washing, and walking. Furthermore we are challenged to believe in the value of the praise and gratitude we offer God. Like the prayer of Mary, the prayer of the elderly is a precious treasure. In the book of Revelation, we are given a vision of twenty-four elders who surround the throne of God in heaven and worship. They throw their crowns down in front of God's throne and shout, "Our Lord and God! You are worthy to receive gory, and honor, and power." We, too, are given the wonderful opportunity to pray, to be elders before the throne of God, to cast our crowns before God, and to offer our praise. We are able to anticipate what we will be doing for all eternity.

5. Challenge to learn to receive
For those who are aging there is **challenge to learn to receive.** Learning to receive may be a difficult lesson for us to learn. Our mature existence has emphasized giving. The meaning in our lives has usually been found in the contribution that we make to others and to society. But as we become older, our capacity to give is lessened and we increasingly need others to give us. We need others to be kind to us, to be patient with us and to help us. We need to resist the conviction that it is always better to give than to receive. When we are open to receive, we give other people the opportunity to be kind, to be patient, to be generous. Other people are able to grow and to become more mature and holy through our need for their help. Aging also gives us the opportunity to receive not just from other people but also from God. During our mature lives we have placed

our emphasis on our giving to God. This situation guides us to be more passive and to receive from God.

Such a change of attitude was dramatically accomplished by Pedro Arrupe, the Superior General of the Jesuits, after he suffered a stroke. In his mature years, Father Arrupe had been constantly active. After his stroke he was led to be more passive. He wrote: "More than ever, I now find myself in the hands of God. This is what I have wanted all of my life, from my youth. But now there is a difference: the initiative is entirely with God. It is indeed a profound spiritual experience to know and feel myself so totally in his hands, in the hands of this God who has taken hold of me".

6. Aging offers us an invitation to faith

Christians believe that apostolic fruitfulness is the greatest when they are most united with Jesus the poor and crucified. Aging people experience the poverty of their own physical and spiritual weaknesses. So much of what they did when they were younger is no longer possible. The wisdom of the world sees such poverty and weakness as a loss, a state of deprivation. But Christians who believe in the Cross affirm the opposite, that God's grace is most present in such poverty. God builds his kingdom in a non-worldly way. The Cross-is salvific. Thus aging Christians are invited to lead lives of faith, to believe in the power of the Cross present in the poverty and weakness of their living. We are indeed invited to believe that in dying the grain of wheat brings forth much fruit.

A Spirituality of Awareness

Do you have eyes but fail to see, and ears but fail to hear?
(Mk 8:18)

1.1 Awareness is Essential for Spirituality

The story is told of one master, who even on the day of silence obliged a pilgrim's request for a word of guidance. He silently wrote on a piece of paper just a single word: awareness. But the inquirer did not make out what the master meant to say. So the master took back the paper and wrote again simply, "awareness, awareness." The confused seeker asked the master, "but what does it mean?" So the master wrote again: "Awareness means just that: awareness." Self-awareness according to Eckhart, is an essential aspect of spirituality

> *A man has many skins in himself, covering the depth of his heart. Man knows so many things; he does not know himself. Why, thirty or forty skins or hides, just like an ox or a bear's, so thick and hard, cover the soul. Go into your own ground and learn to know yourself there* [1]

The one practice which they harp on over and over again is "paying attention to yourself," and by this we are able to diagnose exactly what is going on at any given moment.

1.2 Awareness is a Result of Shock

A few years ago, a man was shocked to read his own obituary in the morning paper. His death was mistakenly reported. But what shocked him most was how the obituary described him: as someone who had devoted his whole life to making weapons of war. That morning he resolved to turn his energies in a new direction: working for world peace and human betterment. That man was Alfred Nobel, founder of the Nobel Peace Prize.

1.3 Awareness is Emotional Knowledge

Awareness is intellectual knowledge charged with emotion. It is as if we begin to smell, taste and touch the foolishness and wickedness of our unloving behavior. The goal of prayer is this kind of awareness. St Ignatius of Loyola wrote in his Spiritual Exercises "It is not much knowledge that fills and satisfies the soul, but the interior understanding and relish of truth." With awareness we acquire a new heart to see, as the prophet Ezekiel puts it:

> *I will give you a new heart and put a new spirit in you: I will remove from you your heart of stone and give you a heart of flesh. And I will put my spirit in you and move you to follow my decrees and be careful to keep my laws. Ezekiel, 36:2-27*

Awareness, then, helps us to understand the petty games we play to feel complacent by duping others and ourselves. We begin to see things almost as God sees them.

> *The disciple asked the Master where God was.*
> *"He is right in front of you", replied the Master.*
> *"Why is it that I cannot see Him?"*
> *"Why is it that the drunkard cannot see his house?" said the Master:*

1.4 Awareness is Inner Freedom
People who grow in awareness are not the victims of outdated and meaningless customs. They would be like Christ who condemned the meaningless rituals like cleaning cups and hands. These gestures were to symbolize cleanliness and purity of heart. William Barclay tells how a jailed Rabbi nearly died of thirst, because he used his small daily ration of water for ritual washing.

1.5 Awareness is Accepting Both Wheat and Cockle
With awareness we are not surprised or disappointed unduly by the cruelty, treachery or wickedness of people. They have an experiential knowledge that the world and the people in it are like a field with wheat and cockle, a mixture of good and bad (Mt. 13:24-30). Tony De Mello used to say, "Do not see people as good or bad; see them as good, kind, loving, just and wicked, cruel and selfish." "Behold, I send you out as sheep in the midst of wolves" (Mt. 10:16).

2. Obstacles to Awareness
2.1 Pride. Selfishness or pride is the primary block to awareness in our lives. Love is the greatest virtue: Love your neighbor as yourself. If love is the sum of all virtues, pride is the root of all evil, because it destroys love and true brotherhood. The trouble with the Pharisee who went up to pray in the temple along with the tax collector was not that he was fasting and observing all the laws, but he looked down on and judged his neighbor, the tax collector. In putting him down, the Pharisee felt he was 'somebody'. (Lk 18:11.). We are proud when we feel that we are better than others. Humility is refusing to compare ourselves with others. Euripides wrote two thousand five hundred years ago: 'When God wishes to destroy someone he first drives him mad with pride."

2.2 Desire. Buddha would ask one to get rid of 'desire'; while Gita would require one to cultivate desireless action) ('niskama karma)'; and St. Ignatius would ask the retreatant to rid himself of all inordinate attachments. A.S. Neill, the author of 'Summer Hill' says the sign of a sick child is that he is always hovering around his parents. The healthy child has no interest in persons. He is interested in things. When a child is sure of his mother's love he forgets his mother; he goes out to explore the world; he is curious. So we were given a taste of various drug addictions: approval, attention, success, making it to the top, prestige, getting your name in the paper, power, being the boss. To live with people in this state involves a never-ending tension.

3. Means to Grow in Awareness
There are basically four ways by which we grow in wisdom:

    1. Experience   2. Reflection
    3. Feedback   4. Prayer

3.1 Experience
The Prodigal son went through an experience, which taught him what it was to live outside his father's house. This helped the young man to grow in wisdom, and to return to his father. St Vincent de Paul wanted to become a priest not so much to witness to God's love,

mself and his family. Thus he got himself
...eteen, five yeas before the canonical age.
...from 1600 to 1611, his aim in life was to
...benefice, even a bishopric. For this purpose
...influential people. Even as late as 1610 he
...m obliged to stay on in Paris looking for an
...tion which my disasters have so far robbed me."
...ers that slowly opened the eyes of Vincent to the
vanity of worldly riches and prestige.

An alcoholic priest was so drunk one night that he tumbled into a gutter and slept there the whole night. What he saw when he woke up, well after sunrise, was a small crowd watching him lying in the gutter. He never drank again. Experiences, especially painful ones, like an illness, financial failure, death of a dear one, betrayal by a friend are often an eye-opener to most of us.

3.2 Reflection
Sudden illness confines us to bed and compels us to think and reflect. Reflection will help us to understand our hidden motives and the silly games we play, in a dispassionate way.

3.3 Feedback or Corrections
Feedback or corrections, remarks and suggestions given to us by friends or even foes can open our eyes to reality. All of us have blind spots, areas of our behavior of which we are not aware. St Teresa once wrote to her friend St John of the Cross about the Novice Master of his congregation: "If Fr. Espinol were a little less holy, at least others could have told him the harm he is doing." St Teresa had little appreciation for 'holiness' that refused feedback and thus was devoid of awareness and maturity. A sign that we are getting mature and holy is that others are not afraid to tell us what annoys them in our behavior. Feedback is the voice of God. So the way we give feedback or corrections should resemble as much as possible the way God would give it. It has to be given in great love. Secondly, it has to be done gently, choosing the appropriate time and place so that it will be accepted. Thirdly it has to be done in such a way that one leaves the other the freedom to accept or reject the feedback. Fourthly

feedback is to be given only as far as the other has the strength to receive it. The professional counselors often give feedback in this manner and that is why they usually are so effective.

3.4 Prayer

Prayer is one of the most effective ways to grow in awareness. In fact the goal of prayer is growth in awareness. Advance in prayer is advance in love. St Paul tells this in the following words.

> *The Spirit helps us in our weakness. We do not know what we ought to pray for, but the Spirit himself intercedes for us with groans that words cannot express (Rom 8:2-27)*

The example and teaching of Christ and of all spiritual masters are clear on that.

Jesus prayed at his baptism	(Lk. 3:21);
Before preaching and healing	(Mk 1:35);
After preaching and healing	(Lk. 5:16);
Before picking his apostles	(Lk. 6:12);
Before teaching his disciples how to pray	(Lk. 11:1);
At the last supper	(Jn 17:1-26);
On the Mount of Olives	(Lk. 22:41);
On the Cross	(Lk. 23:3);

4. Realization of Some Basic Realities
4.1 Transitoriness and Creatureliness

In the last analysis we have to accept our transitoriness, creatureliness, imperfection and the limitation. Our journey is towards humility. At the same time we have to celebrate the life that we have received from God and cultivate remembrance of the Lord, become ever thankful of the divine energy that flows through us.

4.2 We Belong to the Sky

A man found an eagle's egg and put it in a nest of a barnyard hen. The eaglet hatched with the brood of chicks and grew up with them. All his life the eagle did what the barnyard chicks did. He scratched the earth for worms and insects. He clucked and cackled. One day he saw a magnificent bird above him in the cloudless sky. It glided in graceful majesty among the powerful wind currents, with scarcely a beat of its strong golden wings. The old eagle looked up in awe. "Who's that?" he asked. "That's the eagle, the king of the birds, " said his neighbor. "He belongs to the sky. We belong to the earth – we're chickens." So the eagle lived and died a chicken, for that's what he thought he was.

We are programmed to tend to God. We are primarily spirits with a human existence not humans with spiritual existence.

4.3 Don't Renounce, See Through
When you renounce something, you're stuck to it forever. What you resist insists. When you fight something, you're tied to it forever. The only way to get out of this is to see through it. Don't renounce it; see through it.

4.4 Spirituality Means Waking Up
Spirituality means waking up. Most people, even though they don't know it, are asleep.

The father shouts, "Get up, you have to go to school." The son says, "I don't want to go to school." "Why not?" asks the father. "Three reasons," says the son. "First, because it's so dull; second, the kids tease me; and third, I hate school." And the father says, "Well, I am going to give you three reasons why you must go to school. First, because it is your duty; second, because you are forty-five years old, and third, because you are the headmaster."

There's a story about Ramirez. He is old and living up there in his castle on a hill. Old as he is, leaning on a cane, his enemy is climbing up the hill slowly and painfully. His enemy opens the door, comes straight to the bedroom, puts his hand inside his cloak, and pulls out a gun. He says, "At last, Ramirez, we're going to settle scores!" Ramirez tries his level best to talk him out of it. He says, "Come on, Borgia, I'm no longer the man who ill-treated you as that youngster years ago, and you're no longer that youngster. Come off it!" "Oh no," says his enemy, "Your sweet words aren't going to deter me from this divine mission of mine. It's revenge I want and there's nothing you can do about it." And Ramirez says, "But there is something that I can do!" "What?" asks his enemy? "I can wake up," says Ramirez. And he did; he woke up!

4.5 Observe Experience as if it were Happening to Others

Self-observation means to watch everything in you, as if it were happening to someone else. The reason you suffer from your depression and your anxieties is that you identify yourself with them. You say, "I'm experiencing a depression right now." When there is something happening to you, you must see it as if it were happening to someone else, with no comment, no judgment, no attitude, no interference, no attempt to change, only to understand. As you do this, you'll begin to realize that increasingly you are disidentifying from "me"

4.6 Fear – The Root of Violence

Some say love and fear are the only two things in the world. There's only one evil in the world, fear. There's only one good in the world, love. The person who is truly nonviolent, who is incapable of violence, is the person who is fearless. It's only when you're afraid that you become angry. Think of an angry person, maybe someone you're afraid of. Can you see how frightened he or she is? We always hate what we fear. When you fear somebody, you dislike that person. You dislike that person insofar as you fear that person.

4.7 Drop Your Illusions

As the Japanese Zen masters say, "Don't seek the truth; just drop your opinions." Drop your theories; don't seek the truth. Truth isn't something you search for. Suffering is a sign that you're out of touch with the truth. Suffering is given to you that you might open your eyes to the truth. True happiness is uncaused. You cannot make me happy. Happiness is our natural state. You've got to drop illusions. You don't have to add anything in order to be happy. You've to drop something: your illusions, your ambitions and your greed your craving comes from having identified with all kinds of labels

4.8 All's Right With The World

According to one view everything happens according to law of cause and effect. "If you do this, this will happen."

There's a powerful story about a little boy walking along the bank of a river. He sees a crocodile who is trapped in a net. The crocodile says, "Would you have pity on me and release me. I have a mother's heart. I came this morning in search of food for my young ones and got caught in this trap!" So the boy says, "Ah, if I were to help you out of that tap, you'd grab me and kill me." The crocodile asks, "Do you think I would do that to my benefactor and liberator?" So the boy is persuaded to take the net off and the crocodile grabs him. As he is being forced between the jaws of that crocodile, he says, "So this is what I get for my good actions." And the crocodile says, "Well, don't take it personally, son, this is the way the world is, this is the law of life." The boy sees a bird sitting on a branch and says, "Bird, is what the crocodile says right?" The bird says, "The crocodile is right. Look at me. I was coming home one day with food for my fledglings. Imagine my horror to see a snake crawling up the tree, making straight for my nest. I was totally helpless. It kept devouring my young ones, one after the other. I kept screaming and shouting, but it was useless. The crocodile is right, this is the law of life and this is the way the world is." But the boy says, "Let me ask someone else."

There was an old donkey passing by on the bank of the river. "Donkey," says the boy, "this is what the crocodile says. Is the crocodile right?" The donkey says, "The crocodile is quite right. I've worked and slaved for my master all my life and he barely gave me enough to eat. Now that I'm old and useless, he has turned me loose, and here I am wandering in the jungle, waiting for some wild beast to pounce on me and put an end to my life. The crocodile is right, this is the law of life, and this is the way the world is," says the crocodile.

The boy sees a rabbit passing by, and he says, "Rabbit, is the crocodile right?" The rabbit sits on his haunches and says to the crocodile. "We've got to discuss this." But the rabbit says, "How can we discuss it when you've got that boy in your mouth? Release him; he's got to take part in the discussion, too." The crocodile says, "You're a clever one. The moment I release him, He'll run away." The rabbit says, "If he attempted to run away, one slash of your tail would kill him." "Fair enough," says the crocodile, and he released the boy. The moment the body is released, the rabbit says, "Run!" And the boy runs and escapes. Then the rabbit says to the boy, "Don't you enjoy crocodile flesh? You didn't really release that crocodile; most of his body is still caught in that net. Why don't you go to the village and bring everybody and have a banquet." He goes to the village and calls all the men folk. They come with their axes and spears and kill the crocodile. The boy's dog comes, too, and when the dog sees the rabbit, he gives chase, catches hold of the rabbit, and throttles, him. The boy comes to the scene too late, and as he watches the rabbit die, he says, "The crocodile was right, this is the way the world is, this is the law of life."

5. Four Steps To Wisdom

The first thing you need to do is get in touch with negative feelings that you're not even aware of. Lots of people have negative feelings they're not aware of. Lots of people are depressed and they're not aware they are depressed.

The second step is to understand that the feeling is in you, not in reality. Negative feelings are in you, not in reality. Stop trying to change the other persons. We spend all our time and energy trying to change external circumstances, tying to change our spouses, our bosses, our friends, our enemies, and everybody else. Negative feelings are in you.

The third step: Never identify with that feeling. It has nothing to do with the "I". Don't define your essential self in terms of that feeling. Don't say, "I am depressed. If you want to say, "It is depressed, "that's all right. There's an African tribe where capital punishment consists of being ostracized. If you were kicked out of New York, or wherever you're residing, you wouldn't die. How is it that the African tribesman dies? He thinks he will not be able to live if he does not belong. You want to be desired. You want to be applauded, to be attractive, to have all the little moneys running after you.

The fourth step: How do you change things? You are the one who needs to change, who needs to take medicine. You keep insisting, "I feel good because the world is right." Wrong! The world is right because I feel good. That's what all the mystics are saying.

6. Attitudes to be Adopted
What Does It Matter
Excessive preoccupation and intensity kill interest and thrill. Ultimately one realizes the futility of everything and inevitability of things.

There's a story of a disciple who told his guru that he was going to a far place to meditate and hopefully attain enlightenment. So he sent the guru a note, every six months, to report the progress he was making. The first report said, "Now I understand what it means to lose the self." The guru tore up the note and threw it into the wastepaper basket. After six months he got another report, which said, "Now I have attained sensitivity to all beings." He tore it up. Then a third report said, "Now I understand the secret of the one and the many." It too was torn up. Finally no reports came in. After a time, the guru became curious and one day there was a traveler going to that far place. The guru said, "Why don't you find out what happened to that fellow." Finally, he got a note from his disciple. It said, "What does it matter?" And when the guru read that, he said, "He made it! He finally got it!"

Not Clinging To Illusion
The nature of the rain is the same and yet it produces thorns in the marsh and flowers in the garden." A woman, for example, is absorbed in a movie. It's a comedy and she's roaring with laughter and in that blessed moment she's forgotten to remind herself that nobody loved her. She's happy! Then she comes out of the theater and finds her friend going with a boyfriend, leaving the woman all alone. So she starts thinking, "All my friends have boyfriends and I have no one.

I'm so unhappy. Nobody loves me!" You become happy by contact with reality. That's where you'll find happiness.

Freedom from Obstruction

When a sailboat has a mighty wind in its sail, it glides along so effortlessly that the boatman has nothing to do but steer. He makes no effort; he doesn't push the boat. "If the eye is unobstructed, it results in sight; if the ear is unobstructed, the result is hearing; if the nose is unobstructed, the result is a sense of smell; if the mouth is unobstructed, the result is a sense of taste; if the mind is unobstructed, the result is wisdom." "If the heart is unobstructed, the result is love."

A Spirituality of Mission

As Monika Hellwig describes, mission refers to the sending of someone to do something on behalf of another. Mission is first of all "missio Dei"[1], God's self-communication and saving act which stretches from creation to new creation. The mission of the Church is a participation in this saving act of the Triune God, namely in the love of the Father made known in Christ Jesus through the power of the Holy Spirit.[2] People of different faith communities work together in our common struggle for justice, peace, solidarity, reconciliation and love in order to build a greater communion of the scattered children of God (Jn. 11:52).

1. Dialogue as the Way of Mission

Mission consists in being in dialogue. On the subjective level it presupposes that I respect the other person as a subject with autonomy and freedom as myself. From this perspective dialogue is the basic attitude of respectful listening to others and of openness to communicate oneself to others. On the objective level, it presupposes that every person and every human community has some valuable experience of the ultimate meaning of life, which they can share with others. The ultimate Truth is always greater than my own experience and knowledge, and no one; no institution can claim to possess the whole truth.

Dialogue is the only viable way of mission. If dialogue is the basic attitude of being open to others, then dialogue does not contradict the proclamation of the Gospel at all. What is necessary is that we proclaim the Good News in a dialogical way, not primarily by words but by our life. St. Francis of Assisi once said: "Always preach, if necessary use words". We ought to dialogue even with the oppressors in order to break the circle of violence. In politics we have some shining examples of people like Mahatma Gandhi, Martin Luther King and Nelson Mandela. Their lives have become a prophetic affirmation that only dialogue can transform the vicious circle of violence into a virtuous circle of justice, forgiveness, reconciliation and peace. Dialogue is another name for the Gospel message, an appeal to love even your enemy.

1.2 Prophetic Dialogue
The Christian attitude of dialogue in mission is more appropriately expressed in terms of "prophetic dialogue".[3] A prophet listens and proclaims the Word of God. The prophet also criticizes injustice and evil elements in society, which are contrary to the will of God, with the consequence that the prophet might undergo persecution and suffering. The same is true with dialogue in mission. What we are supposed to do is to listen, follow, witness and proclaim the Word of God. However, since we believe that God has spoken also to other peoples of others cultures and religions, mission means first of all listening to the Word of God coming to me, through others.

1.3 Both the Church and the Community are Missionary
If the Church is missionary by its nature, then every Christian community is the addresser of mission. However, within the Christian communities there are people who in a very special way dedicate themselves to mission and therefore are called missionaries. The people are sent in the name of the Lord by the Christian communities and they in turn remind Christian communities of their missionary call. The missionaries are the addressers of mission par excellence. We have the threefold dialogue, namely dialogue with people of other cultures, with people of different religions and with the poor. We can add another category of faith seekers and so speak of a "fourfold prophetic dialogue".[4]

a). The first aspect is dialogue with faith seekers and people who have no faith community. In our contemporary world there are more and more people who do not belong to any faith community. In France, for instance, 47 % of the population describe themselves as a-religious or atheists; in Germany 38 % profess no religion.

b). Dialogue with the poor and marginalized.
In many parts of Asia, Christians live among a great mass of very poor people. Mission, among the poor means being in solidarity with them, participating in their life and their struggle. As Pieris

puts it: "The poor (the destitute, the dispossessed, the displaced and the discriminated) who form the bulk of Asian peoples, plus their specific brand of cosmic religiosity constitute a school where many Christian activities re-educate themselves in the art of speaking the language of God's reign, which is the language of liberation which God speaks though Jesus. Neither the academic nor the pastoral Magisterium is conversant with this evangelical idiom".[5]

c). Dialogue with people of different cultures.

The main issue in the dialogue with people of different cultures is the inculturation of the Gospel and the evangelization of culture, which are two aspects of the same missionary dialogue. For many centuries in the Catholic Church, the Universality (catholicity) of the Church tended to be identified with the uniformity of doctrines (formulated in dogmas), of rites and laws. What we call "universal Church" is the ecclesia ecclesiarum, the communion of Christian communities in the Lord. In the case of art, if somebody simply copies the work of another artist, he or she is not a real artist but an epigon. It is a paradoxical truth of art that the more unique and original a work of art is, the more universal value it has. The more authentic the art is the more universal can it become. If, however the local Church simply imitates what is done in Rome then it is an imitation Church, not yet an authentic Church rooted in the local soil.

d). Dialogue with people of other religions.

Inter-religious dialogue can take various forms. The first form is the <u>dialogue of life</u> where people of various religions live together in the same society with tolerance and respect for each other. Secondly, through <u>dialogue of action,</u> they collaborate on some concrete projects such as helping the victims of natural disaster, promoting human rights, improving education for poor children and so on. Thirdly, people of different religions can also pray together and share their faith. After the big riot in Jakarta, May 13-15, 1998, when 1190 people were killed, women activists of different religions (Islam, Christian, Hinduism, Buddhism) organized several prayer meetings where they openly denounced the act of violence and prayed together for justice, reconciliation and peace in a wounded nation. Finally there can be dialogue on the theological or doctrinal level. Dialogue of life and action paves the way for theological dialogue. In its turn theological dialogue should enlighten and promote dialogue of life and action. Through creative inter-religious dialogue we may hope that people of various religious traditions can work together for a new spirituality, which can inspire human beings in a post-modern world.

2. New Approaches to Mission
2.1 Mission from the Position of Weakness

a) **First, political superiority:** At the beginning they came from a colonizing country to a colonized country. It was the sending Church that planted new local churches namely the target Church. They also enjoyed protection and certain privileges granted to them by colonial government.

b) **Secondly, cultural superiority**. They came from a developed country to the so-called underdeveloped country. They built schools, centers of training and education using the standard and curriculum of Europe. They were also financially supported by Christian communities in their home counties for many social projects.

c) **Thirdly, religious superiority**. The missionary pioneers from Europe knew very well that they were commissioned by the hierarchy in the name of the Lord in order to preach the Gospel. In comparison to the former missionaries from Europe, the Asian missionaries today seem to be sent empty handed. We know that former missionaries preached Gospel, taught catechism, and baptized people; but they were also actively involved in education, heath care, and in promoting social and economic development.

Today many of these jobs have been taken over by the state or secular institutions. This kind of weakness can and should be the strength of the new missionaries. If you have nothing in your hand, and if you do not have any kind of superiority, then you have to rely on the people to whom you are sent. Missionaries are expected to work not simply for the people from a position of superiority, but to work with the people. Above all, this approach presupposes that missionaries believe in the One who calls and sends them. "I am with you always to the end of time" (Mt. 28:20).

2.2 Mission from a Contemplative Presence
Contemplation means living in intimate union with God. Every authentic mission flows from contemplation, just as every poetic word is born out of silence. Mission without contemplation would be empty; contemplation without mission would be lame and mute. Mission and contemplation are two fundamental aspects of Christian life. Hence those who live in the contemplative orders are called to be missionaries in silence like Theresa of Lisieux. Missionaries who are actively working with people have to practice a "contemplation in via" like Theresa of Calcutta. Mission is passing over to people of other cultures, other social classes, other religions and convictions in order to gather the scattered children of God into a greater and deeper communion.

2.3 Mission needs a Narrative Theology
All doctrines are to be understood in relation to the narrative. But every narrative is open to multiple interpretations. It is in the process of interpretation that a story is decontextualized and decontextualized. The living Word of God is reincarnated every time a believing community reads the Bible, appropriates its meaning for itself and puts it into practice in everyday life. Narrative is all the more important because, as Ricoeur and others have shown, the identity of a person and that of a human community is a narrative identity.[6] Narrative tends to hold the creative tension between unity and plurality. The unity of the same story remains, but a different people in a different context understands it in a different way.

2.4 Liberation and Communion in the Reign of God
After the Second World War, many colonized counties in Asia and Africa declared their independence and became free nations. But political independence is only one step in the struggle for greater liberation. Our contemporary world is marked by globalization, a great process transforming our world into a global village. Through the ecological movement we have come to realize that we are all living in a very small planet called "Earth" where water, land, air, and

all natural resources are limited. For this reason there has been more international collaboration for the preservation of the ecological system.

Through both processes of liberation and communion, we discern the saving acts of God within our contemporary world. Liberation without communion tends to divide and scatter; communion without liberation tends to dominate and oppress. In concrete situations, however, these great signs should be deciphered and actualized more concretely in acts of solidarity, of defending the rights of the marginalized, of helping the victims, of resolving the conflicts, of healing the wounds, of reconciliation and so on.

It is important that we avoid domineering and dividing attitudes in our missionary approach. The following passage from the Chinese mandate of Heaven will be helpful.

Blunt your sharpness, untangle the knots, soften your glare, and become one with the dusty world. By lowering oneself and becoming one of the people, the sage is able to gradually purify the dirty waters of the world. Water flows down and loves to stay in the lower place. The empty vessel, which can hold various foods, the empty space of the building, which gives us room to dwell and the empty area of musical instruments, which makes it possible for air to go through-all these natural signs of the Tao, point us toward getting rid of our selfish concerns and opening our vision for the bigger picture. The mission of the Taoist sage is not aggressive, but only helps a spontaneous flowering to happen.

The Tao Te Ching, chapter 57 describes the sage thus:

I take no action and the people are transformed of themselves;
I prefer stillness and the people are rectified of themselves;
I am not meddlesome and the people prosper of themselves;
I am free from desire and the people of themselves become simple like the uncarved block.

2.5 The Religions are Allies

Another helpful attitude is that religions are allies, in our pursuit of the kingdom of God. The church is not the kingdom; it is its symbol and servant. The yin and the yang of the Chinese tradition seek harmony in dynamic movement. The images of the peaceful sitting 'Buddha' and the dancing 'Nadaraja'(the god of dance) are Indian expressions of harmony that manifest an Absolute that is inclusive and integrating. The Tibetan 'mandalas' are meditative instruments conducive to inner harmony. Harmony with the cosmos is also promoted in terms of symbols and rituals, particularly music. Other religions enrich our vision and provide us with tools that are lacking in our religion.

2.6 Accompaniment

Mission apostolate can be viewed as an effort to accompany the other in his life. The image of Jesus on the road to Emmaus with the disciples in Luke 24, and the charge in the scroll of Isaiah, which Jesus reads in the synagogue in Nazareth in Luke 4, provide powerful images for this sense of missionary spirituality.[7] Solidarity is the consequence of accompaniment, of living a life of dialogue, of inserting oneself into another's reality. Reconciliation is first and foremost the work of God in our lives.

3. Major Breakthroughs
3.1. Universal Availability of Salvation

As recently as in 1949, the Vatican had to step in to correct Fr. Leonard Feeney's insistence that the availability of salvation applied exclusively to members of the Catholic Church. Prior to the Middle Ages, the common perception was that the inhabited world and the Mediterranean world were one and the same. Then came the geographic discoveries of the late Middle Ages, revealing vast populations on the other side of the world where the Gospel was not yet known and the embrace of Christianity was impossible.

3.2 Mission not only a function but of the very nature and essence of the church

Prior to Vatican II, it was commonplace to think of mission as one among many other activities, the church was called to engage in, by its Founder. With the practicing of the corporal and spiritual works of mercy, and undertaking various educational and cultural ministries, there was the call to proclaim the Gospel to the world. This arrangement made sense until the term "mission" began to be applied not only to the church, but also to God.

3.3. Local church too is Missionary
Prior to seeds planted by Vatican II, and their germination in the postconciliar church, it was taken for granted that local churches were basically pastoral rather than missionary communities. While there was openness to and interest in bringing unbelievers into the Christian fold, the main responsibility of these communities did not extend to full-scale missionary activity. Local church is also considered missionary now.

3.4. No Distinction between mission-sending and mission-receiving churches: shift to mutuality in mission.
The age-old distinction between churches that send missionaries and those that receive them began to whither away in the Protestant world when the International Missionary Council was integrated into the World Council of Churches in the latter's Third Assembly in New Delhi in 1961. Based on the principle that mission is the very essence of the church, this integration received full articulation in the meeting of the Commission on World Mission and Evangelism of the World Council of Churches in Mexico City in 1963. The distinction between the sending Church and the target church is beginning to blur and mutuality in being accepted.

3.5. From Minimal to Full Participation of the Laity
Until the developments set in motion by the Second Vatican Council, the experience of laypeople in the church might have told them that the vocation to carry the Gospel to the world as missionaries is reserved for Christians who have been called either to priesthood or to religious life. The lay people were seldom if ever targeted in campaigns to swell the ranks of field missionaries in the church.

3.6. From one to five components of evangelization
Paul VI in Evangelii Nuntiandi, echoing the conclusions of the

Third Synod of Bishops made it clear that the witness of living the Gospel is already a silent proclamation of the Good News and a very powerful and effective one. Without compromising the special importance of formally proclaiming the Gospel, new forms of evangelizations were formally identified: 1. Presence and witness; 2. Human development and liberation; 3. Liturgical life, prayer and contemplation; 4. Interreligious dialogue; and 5. Proclamation and catechesis.

3.7. Culture-Intensive Evangelization.

In this new world, missionaries are sent to those who are other than us, who are distant from us because of their culture, faith or history. They are far away but not necessarily physically distant they are strangers though they may be our neighbors. The expression "the global village" sounds cozy and intimate, as if we all belong to one big happy human family.

4. Presence, Epiphany and Proclamation

Presence: Being a missionary is not what I do; it is who I am. Jesus is the one who is sent (Heb 3:1). Nicholas Boyle wrote that "the only morally defensibly and conceptually consistent answer to the question 'who are we now?' is 'future citizens of the world. The Missionary is not a tourist. Perhaps the challenge for the young missionary is learning that stamina, that enduring fidelity to the other, faced with our own fragility and anxiety. Presence is not merely being there. It is staying there and making our home with the people to whom we are committed.

Epiphany: The celebration of Christ's birth used to begin with Epiphany, the disclosure of the glory of God among us. When Simeon receives the child Jesus in the Temple, he rejoices, "For my eyes have seen thy salvation which you have prepared, in the presence of all peoples" (Lk 2:30, 31f). To be someone important today is to achieve "icon status"! The experience of God is the "genetic moment". The genetic moment is trans-formation, newness, creativity in which God irrupts into our lives. Every genetic moment is a mystery. It is dawn, discovery; spring, new birth, awakening, transcendence, liberation, ecstasy, forgiveness, reconciliation, revolutions, faith, hope, love. So the challenge for our mission is how to make God visible through gestures of freedom, liberation, transformation, little "happenings" that are signs of the end.

Proclamation At the end of Matthew's Gospel, the disciples are sent out to all the nations to make disciples, and to teach all that Jesus has commanded. The Word becomes flesh, but the flesh also becomes word. Here we encounter what is perhaps the deepest crisis in our mission today. There is a profound suspicion of anyone who claims to teach, unless they come from the East or have some strange New Age doctrine. Missionaries who teach are suspected of indoctrination, of cultural imperialism, of arrogance. In 'Christianity Rediscovered' Vincent Donovan describes how he worked for many years as a missionary with the Maasai, building schools and hospitals, but never proclaiming his faith. He was not encouraged to do so by his superiors. Finally he could restrain himself no longer and he gathered together the people and told them about his belief in Jesus. And then the elders said, "We always wondered why you were here, and now at last we know. Why did you not tell us before?" We do not always have the freedom to speak, and we must choose well the moment, but it would ultimately be patronizing and condescending not to proclaim what we believe to be true. Indeed it is part of the Good News that human beings are made for the truth and can attain it. As *Fides et* Ratio puts it, "One may define the human as the one who seeks the truth" (n. 28), We have, "a *propensio ad veritatem*", *(LCO* 77.2), an inclination to the truth. Any spirituality of mission has to include a passion for the truth.

St Thomas says that the object of faith is not the words we speak; but God whom we cannot see and know. The object of our faith is beyond the grasp and dominion of our words. We will only be confident and humble preachers if we become contemplative. Mission begins in humility and ends in mystery. Rowan Williams wrote that "what we must rediscover is the discipline of silence not an absolute, unbroken inarticulacy, but the discipline of letting go of our own easy chattering about the Gospel so that our words may come again from a new and different depth or force from something beyond our fantasies. This love is very risky. In this dangerous world careering away towards an unknown future, the only solution is to take risk.

Risk is the characteristic of a society that looks to the future. Risk is the mobilizing dynamic of a society bent on change, that wants to determine its own future rather than leaving it to religion, tradition or the vagaries of nature. Our mission invites us to a risk beyond imagining. This is the risk of love. It is the risk of living for the other who might not want me; the risk of living for a fullness of truth, that I cannot capture, the risk of letting myself be hollowed out by yearning for the God whose Kingdom will come. This is most risky and yet most sure.

End Notes

1. Redemptoris Missio (RM) no. 12-20
2. Ad Gentes
3. In Dialogue with the Word, p.31.
4. Ibid. pp. 30-36.
5. Aloysius Pieris, "An Asian Paradigm: Inter-religious Dialogue and Theology of Religions", Month, April 1993, p. 130.
6. Paul Ricoeur, Time and Narrative Vol.3 (Chicago: University of Chicago Press, 1988), pp. 244-249
7. John Paul II, Ecclesia in Asia, November 6, 1999, art. 44 p. 41. He recommends to religious in Asia: "the search for God, a life of fraternal communion, and service to others are the three chief characteristics of the consecrated life which can offer an appealing Christian testimony to the peoples of Asia today."

Spirituality as a Journey

God All along the Way
The metaphor of journey is useful to describe spiritual life. As in other human journeys, we reach the destination of our spiritual pilgrimage only gradually. While alive, we will never fully reach our goal of union with God and others. God is to be enjoyed not only at the end of the search, but all along the way. The Christmas story of the Magi illustrates this truth. God was present to them not only when they joyfully arrived at the cave in Bethlehem, but also in the original stirrings that sent them off in search of the promised Messiah. God's presence was also experienced in a guiding star that directed them through dark nights and in a dream that warned them of Herod's threat. God is more present to us than we think.

I will be with you
Our search for union with God is life-long, often a strenuous trek punctuated by dark passages. If we are to persevere, we must take courage in God's abiding presence all along the way. Even as we are travelling towards God as destiny, Emmanuel is already with us in manifold ways. The disciples of Jesus were once given a dramatic lesson about how Christ is ever present. One day they were crossing the Lake of Galilee when a fierce storm enveloped their little boat. Frightened by violent winds, the apostles were stricken with panic. Suddenly, Jesus appeared to them walking on the water. He told them, "It is I. Do not be afraid" (Jn 6:21). Jesus then calmed the storm and the boat quickly came to shore.

Shedding of Illusions
The journey metaphor most accurately reflects reality when it is seen as a zigzag pattern rather than as an uninterrupted straight line. Our life is punctuated by numerous disillusionments. As we commit ourselves to life's stagnations, we shed the old images we have had of life. We usually stick to ideas we have acquired during the mature period of our lives. Human growth consists in giving up unrealistic views of life. The journey is one of humility.

Forgiveness: The End Point of Life

The contemporary tendency is to think that the goal of our existence is perfection and absolute fulfillment. Forgiveness is the endpoint of human life. In the end, we will fully enjoy the unconditional acceptance of God, not because we are flawless, but in spite of our imperfections. Our merciful God's gift of forgiveness means that we cannot and need not measure up to the conditions of worth of others . When forgiveness, and not fulfillment, is seen as the endpoint of our lives, we can live with greater acceptance of our weaknesses and with greater hope in God's power to complete what grace started. The promise of ultimate forgiveness "allows us to be incomplete and yet complete, estranged and yet related, distorted and yet fulfilled. When our journey reaches its termination, we will be wrapped in God's merciful arms, like the prodigal son. "You are forgiven" will be the final words we will hear at the death bed. "Success and failure are accidental", writes Adrian Van Kamm "The joy of the Christian is never based on success but on the knowledge that (one's) Redeemer lives".[1]

Accept the Mystery of Iniquity

The Lord will never ask how successful we were in overcoming a particular vice, sin, or imperfection. He will ask us, "Did you humbly and patiently accept this mystery of iniquity in your life? How did you deal with it? Did it teach you to trust not your own ability but my love? Did it enable you to understand better the mystery of iniquity in the lives of others?"[2] Our lack of perfection will never separate us from God, because the Lord's forgiveness is always perfect and total.

The Problem of Ideals

Ideals like stars may never be reached; but they are useful to steer our lives by. Ideals can hinder us, however, and discourage us from trying, when the fear of performing poorly paralyses us. Furthermore, ideals are injurious when they lure us into thinking that we can earn God's approval by doing everything perfectly. Paul refers to this as seeking a perfection that comes from the law rather than from faith in Jesus (Ph. 3:9). No matter how grand our ideals, they can only be achieved through small but steady steps. As the Chinese sage Lao Tze stated centuries ago, "The journey of a thousand miles begins with one step." We must dispose ourselves to be receptive to the sanctifying action of God's touch.

God's Work

Jesus is the vine and we are the branches. The Father prunes us so that we might bear fruit (Jn 15:1-2). Spiritual growth is passive in the sense that purification and progress are the direct results of God's action upon us. The evangelist Mark reinforces the centrality of God's action in his parable about the seed growing by itself.

> *This is what the kingdom of God is like. A man throws seed on the land. Night and day, while he sleeps, when he is awake, the seed is sprouting and growing; how, he does not know. Of its own accord the land produces first the shoot, then the ear, then the full grain in the ear. And when the crop is ready, he loses no time; he starts to reap because the harvest has come (Mk 4:26-29).*

Notice that the farmer's work is described with a minimum of words. The emphasis falls on the mysterious process of growth. Just as the earth produces fruit spontaneously, so God's reign comes by divine power alone. A classical biblical text used to illustrate the need for docility to God's formative action in our lives is Jeremiah's description of the potter. Watching the artisan working at his wheel, the prophet noticed that he continued to shape and reshape the clay until he created what he was envisioning. Then the word of Yahweh came to Jeremiah as follows: "Houses of Israel, can I not do to you what this potter does? Yes, like in the potter's hand, so you are in mine, House of Israel" (Jr. 18:1-6).

Spiritual Growth through Trial and Error

The ideals of Christian spirituality cannot be achieved without immersing ourselves in the messiness of nitty-gritty experience. Learning how to love God and others in an integrated way comes only through daily practice. As theologian John Dunne states, "Only one who has tried the extremes can find this personal mean. On the other hand, trying the extremes will not necessarily lead to finding the mean. Only the person, who perceives the shortcomings of the extremes will find it. Even at the end of a lifetime of effort, we will still need to be completed by the finishing touch of the divine Artist. God will then bring to completion in us the eternal design of persons destined to love wholeheartedly.

Experience as Manure in the Spiritual Field

In the spiritual project of transformation into Christ, effort is what counts, not unremitting success. Acclaiming the value of practice in spiritual growth, the Eastern guru Chogyam Trungpa speaks of the "manure of experience" Our experiences, our mistakes, and even our failures function like fertilizer. According to Trungpa, what appears to be useless trash contains potential nutrients for life. But, to convert our deficiencies into positive value, we need to pile them on a compost heap, not sweep them behind a bush.

Harvesting Silence: Desert Spirituality

A desert is a most carefully constructed work of art. Nature, and God, has taken great effort and artistry to create an empty backdrop, a single sandy sheet. A desert is not only beautiful, but functional as well. In the desert's emptiness there is nothing to hide behind, nothing to conceal; there is nothing to distract. By the very fact of its emptiness, the desert is a perfect place for evaluation, a perfect place for confrontation. A desert is not geographical; it is an attitude, a condition and a state of the soul. Nor are deserts fixed areas of terrain. Deserts can appear overnight or sometimes in a single, often climatic moment. God creates deserts in our lives whenever God's patience turns dry. God creates deserts out of the lushness of our lives to force an issue we have otherwise avoided. Duties, tasks, responsibilities, projects are the trees, plants and shrubbery that have been planted within our lives but which have grown out of control.

Only What We Must Do

The passage from Ursal Le Gun's *A Wizard of Earth Sea* is a story about a young man struggling to become a wizard. At one point in his training a sage gives him this bit of advice.

You thought, as a boy, that a mage is one who can do anything. So I thought once. So did we all. And the truth is that as a man's real power grows and his knowledge widens, the way he can follow grows narrower: until at least he chooses nothing, but does only and wholly what he must do. The trick, it would seem, is to find what he must do. The key to the finding seems to revolve around getting in touch with limitations, the paucity of resources and talents wherein lies our realistic avenue of growth. The desert seems a fitting place for recognizing one's limits, the truth about oneself. Sit in the desert and watch a parade go by. There are clowns and bands, important people smiling and waving. Each one wants those on the sidelines to join them, to take up ranks behind them. It is the parade of the unnecessary. Clowns, bands, and crowds make almost as much noise as winds, earthquakes and fires. To hear it, one must wait and listen attentively.

Intense Silence Cleanses

A desert is anything but empty; despite all appearances to the contrary, it is filled with an intense silence. It is so silent and calm and still that every breath, every heartbeat booms. It is incredibly difficult, if not impossible, to be unaware in a desert. The scarcity of scenery seems somehow to cleanse the senses. The silence that is both vocal and visual washes over the eyes and ears and all the other senses. In the desert, where there is nothing to hear but the howling of the wind, we learn how to listen to the spirit. Self-consciousness is not necessarily knowledge and recognition of the truth.

Old Routine no Longer works

There is another quality to deserts. They are excellent places to get lost. There are very few landmarks in a desert. Even the sand dunes shift. That is why people who traverse the desert often do so at night, when they can at least use the stars as navigational guides. All of this is quite distressing, especially to those inexperienced with desert life. Most of us have lived with paths well worn from daily routines, habits, and regular patterns of behavior. One way of knowing that we have been spiritually teleported into a desert is when the old routine no longer works. The stability has become instead sterility. Our first response to this is frequently anger, then panic. The anger is a response to the realization of how illusory is the illusion that we are in control of our lives, that we indeed are not the masters of our destiny.

A Journey towards Tenderness

What we desire most is to do away with suffering by fleeing from it or finding a quick cure for it. As busy, active, relevant ministers, we want to earn our bread by making a real contribution. Solitude leads to the awareness of the dead person in our own house and keeps us from making judgments about other people's sins. In this way real forgiveness becomes possible. The following desert story offers a good illustration;

> *"A brother committed a fault. A council was called to which Abba Moses was invited, but he refused to go to it. Then the prior sent someone to him, 'Come, for everyone is waiting for you' He took a leaking jug, filled it with water, and carried it with him. He said," My sins run out behind me and I don't see them, and today I am coming to judge the error of another".*

Journey in Silence

Abba Tithoes once said, "Pilgrimage means that a man should control his tongue." The expression "To be on pilgrimage is to be silent" (*Peregrinare est tacere*), expresses the conviction of the Desert Fathers that silence is the best anticipation of the future world. Silence protects the inner fire. Silence guards the inner heat of religious emotions. This inner heat is the life of the Holy Spirit within us. Thus, silence is the discipline by which the inner fire of God is nourished and kept alive. Diabochus of Photiki offers us a very concrete image: "When the door of the steam bath is continually left open, the heat inside rapidly escapes through it; likewise the soul, in its desire to say many things, dissipates its remembrance of God through the door of speech, even though everything it says may be good. Let us at least raise the question of whether our lavish ways of sharing are not more compulsive than virtuous. Vincent van Gogh knew about the temptation to open all the doors so that passersby could see the fire and not just the smoke coming through the chimney. His own life is a powerful example of faithfulness to the inner fire.

Word Emerges From Silence

A word with power is a word that comes out of silence. A word that bears fruit is a word that emerges from the silence and returns to it. The literal translation of the words "pray always" is "come to rest." The Greek word for rest is *hesychia*; hesychism is the term which refers to the spirituality of the desert. A hesychist is a man or a woman who seeks solitude and silence which is the way to unceasing prayer. "To pray is to descend with the mind into the heart, and there to stand before the face of the Lord, ever-present, all-seeing, within you." Prayer is standing in the presence of God with the mind in the heart; that is, at that point of our being where there are no divisions or distinctions and where we are totally one.

Finishing touch of the Artist

Even at the end of a lifetime of effort, we will still need to be completed by the finishing touch of the divine Artist. God will then bring to completion in us the eternal design of persons destined to love wholeheartedly. While awaiting that unifying touch of divine grace, we pilgrims are called to follow the way of Jesus. A rabbi was asked, "What is a blessing?" He gave a riddle.

> *After finishing his work on each of the first five days, the Bible states, "God saw that it was good." But God is not reported to have commented on the goodness of what was created on the sixth day when the human person was fashioned. "What conclusion can you draw from that?" asked the rabbi. Someone volunteered. "We can conclude that the human person is not good." "Possibly," the rabbi nodded, "but that's not a likely explanation." He then went on to explain that the Hebrew word translated as "good" in Genesis is the word "tov," which is better translated as "complete."*

God did not declare the human person to be "tov." Human beings are created incomplete. It is our life's vocation to collaborate with our Creator in fulfilling the Christ-potential in each of us.

End Notes

1. Henri J.M.Nouwen. The Way of the Heart, Darton, Longman, Todd, London 1981.
2. Ibid, p. 15.
3. Bendicta Ward, trans., *The Sayings of the Desert Fathers* (London & Oxford: Mowbrays, 1975), p.8
4. Ibid., P.117

A Spirituality of Success

Success in life could be defined as the continued expansion of happiness and the progressive realization of worthy goals. Success is the ability to fulfill your desires with effortless ease. We need a more spiritual approach to success and to affluence, which is the abundant flow of all good things to you. We should nurture the seeds of divinity inside us. In reality, we are divinity in disguise, and the gods and goddesses in embryo that are contained within us seeking to be fully materialized.

The source of all creation is pure consciousness, pure potentiality seeking expression from the unmanifest to the manifest. And when we realize that our true self is one of pure potentiality, we align with the power that manifests everything in the universe.

You are what your deep, driving desire is.
As your desire is, so is your will.
As your will is, so is your deed.
As your deed is, so is your destiny. (Brihadaranyaka Upanisad IV. 4.5)

True success is therefore the experience of the miraculous. It is the unfolding of the divinity within us. Law is the process by which the unmanifest becomes the manifest. It's the process by which the observer becomes the observed; it's the process by which the seer becomes the scenery; it's the process through which the dreamer manifests the dream. All of creation, everything that exists in the physical world, is the result of the unmanifest transforming itself into the manifest. Consciousness in motion expresses itself as the objects of the universe in the eternal dance of life.

We should guard against our desire to attain material reputation. It is misleading with its attractive vision like an oasis of green trees, but it is simply a mirage in the desert of this world of repeated birth and death. It will cause your utter spiritual destruction.

1. Law of Pure Potentiality and Consciousness

This law is based on the fact that we are, in our essential state, pure consciousness. Pure consciousness is pure potentiality; it is the field of all possibilities and infinite creativity. Pure consciousness is our spiritual essence. The Law of Pure Potentiality could also be called the Law of Unity, because underlying the infinite diversity of life is the unity of one all pervasive spirit. There is no separation between you and this field of energy. The field of pure potentiality is your own Self.

The need for approval, the need to control things, and the need for external power are needs that are based on fear. When we experience the power of the Self, there is an absence of fear; there is no compulsion to control, and no struggle for approval or external power. It is immune to criticism, it is unfearful of any challenge, and it feels beneath no one. When one is well attuned one feels neither superior or inferior to anyone.

Ego based power will only last as long as those things last. As soon as the title, the job, the money go away, so does the power. Self-power, on the other hand, is permanent, because it is based on the knowledge of the Self. It draws people to you, and it also draws things that you want to you. It magnetizes people, situations, and circumstance to support your desires. This is also called support from the laws of nature. It is the support of divinity; it is the support that comes from being in the state of grace.

One way to access the field is through the daily practice of silence, meditation, and non-judgment. Spending time in nature will also give you access to the qualities inherent in the field: infinite creativity, freedom, and bliss. Practice of silence means making a commitment to take a certain amount of time to simply be. Experiencing silence means periodically withdrawing from the activity of speech. It also means periodically withdrawing from such activities as watching television, listening to the radio, or reading a book. If you never give yourself the opportunity to experience silence, this creates turbulence in your internal dialogue. Set aside a little time every once in a while to experience silence. Or simply make a commitment to maintain silence for a certain period each day. Practicing silence periodically as it is convenient to you is one way to experience this law. Spending time each day in meditation is another. Ideally, you should meditate at least thirty minutes in the morning, and thirty minutes in the evening. Through meditation you will learn to experience the field of pure silence and pure awareness. Stillness is the first requirement for manifesting your desires, because in stillness lies your connection to the field of pure potentiality that can orchestrate an infinity of details for you.

"Be still, and know that I am God." When you are constantly evaluating, classifying, labeling, analyzing, you create a lot of turbulence in your internal dialogue. This turbulence constricts the flow of energy between you and the field of pure potentiality. There is a prayer that states, "Today I shall judge nothing that occurs." Non-judgment creates silence in your mind.

This world of energy is fluid, dynamic, resilient, changing, forever in motion. And yet it is also non-changing, still, quiet, eternal, and silent. Stillness alone is the potentiality for creativity; movement alone is creativity restricted to a certain aspect of its expression. But the combination of movement and stillness enables you to unleash your creativity in all directions- wherever the power of your attention takes you. Wherever you go in the midst of movement and activity, carry your stillness within you.

2. The Law of Giving

> *The universe operates through dynamic exchange. Giving and receiving are different aspects of the flow of energy in the universe. And in our willingness to give that which we seek, we keep the abundance of the universe circulating in our lives. This frail vessel thou empty again and again, and fill it ever with fresh life. Thy infinite gifts come to me only on those very small hands of mine. Ages pass, and still thou pour, and still there is room to fill.*
> *Rabindranath Tagore, Gitanjali.*

Every relationship is one of give and take. Giving engenders receiving, and receiving engenders giving. In reality, receiving is the same thing as giving, because giving and receiving are different aspects of the flow of energy in the universe. The more you give, the more you will receive, because you will keep the abundance of the universe circulating in your life. In fact, anything that is of value in life only multiplies when it is given. That which doesn't multiply through giving is neither worth giving nor worth receiving. If you give grudgingly, there is no energy behind that giving. Don't give because it is your duty to give or because you have to give. Give in a spirit of thanksgiving. Give because you have more than enough to give. That which you have not given is lost.

The act of giving has to be joyful – the frame of mind has to be one in which you feel joy in the very act of giving. Then the energy behind the giving increases many times over. Practicing the Law of Giving is actually very simple; if you want joy, give joy to others, if you want love, learn to give love, if you want attention and appreciation, learn to give attention and appreciation, if you want material affluence, help others to become materially affluent. In fact, the easiest way to get what you want is to help others get what they want. This principle works equally well for individuals, corporations, societies, and nations.

We are localized bundles of consciousness in a conscious universe. It doesn't have to be in the form of material things; it could be a flower, a compliment, a payer. You can bring a compliment. The more you give, the more confidence you will gain in the miraculous effects of this law. And as you receive more, your ability to give more will also increase. Our true nature is one of affluence and abundance; we are naturally affluent because nature supports every need and desire. We lack nothing, because our essential nature is one of pure potentiality and infinite possibilities.

3. The Law of Cause And Effect

> *Every action generates a force of energy that returns to us in like kind. What we sow is what we reap. We*

> *choose actions that bring happiness and success to others. Our thoughts, our words, and deeds are the threads of the net, which we throw around ourselves. Swami Vivekananda*

The third spiritual law of success is the law of action and the consequence of that action, it is cause and effect simultaneously, because every action generates a force of energy that returns to us in like kind. "What you sow is what you reap." Obviously, if we want to create happiness in our lives, we must learn to sow the seeds of happiness. Unfortunately, a lot of us make choices unconsciously, and therefore we don't think they are choices – and yet, they are. If I were to insult you, you would most likely make the choice of being offended. If I were to pay you a compliment, you would most likely make the choice of being pleased or flattered. But it's still a choice.

Ask yourself two things: first of all, "What are the consequence of this choice that I'm making?" In your heart you will immediately know what these are. Secondly, "Will this choice that I'm making now bring happiness to me and to those around me?" If the answer is yes, then go ahead with that choice. If the answer is no, if that choice brings distress either to you or to those around you, then don't make that choice. When you make that one choice, it will result in a form of behavior that is called spontaneous right action. Spontaneous right action is the right action at the right moment. It's the right response to every situation as it happens.

4. The Law of Least Effort

> *Nature's intelligence functions with effortless ease, harmony, and love. And when we harness the forces of harmony, joy, and love, we create success and good fortune with effortless ease.*
>
> *An integral being knows without going, sees without looking, and accomplishes without doing. Lao Tzu*

The fourth spiritual law of success is the Law of Least Effort. This law is based on the fact that nature's intelligence functions with effortless ease. This is the principle of least action, of no resistance. This is therefore, the principle of harmony and love. When we learn this lesson from nature, we easily fulfill our desires. If you observe nature at work, you will see that least effort is expended.

Grass doesn't try to grow, it just grows. Fish don't try to swim, they just swim. Flowers don't try to bloom, they bloom. Birds don't try to fly, they fly. This is their intrinsic nature. The earth doesn't try to spin on its own axis; it is the nature of the earth to spin with dizzying speed and to hurtle through space. This principle is known as the principle of economy of effort, or "do less and accomplish more." What is commonly called a "miracle" is actually an expression of the Law of Least Effort. Least effort is expended when your action is motivated by love, because nature is held together by the energy of love. When you seek power and control over other people, you waste energy. When you seek money for personal gain only, you cut off the flow of energy to yourself, and interfere with the expression of nature's intelligence. But when you actions are motivated by love, there is no waste of energy. When your actions are motivated by love, your energy multiplies and accumulates – and the surplus energy you gather and enjoy can be channeled to create anything that you want, including unlimited wealth.

The first component is acceptance. Acceptance simply means that you make a commitment: "Today I will accept people, situations, circumstances and events as they occur." This means I will know that this moment is as it should be because the whole universe is as it should be. This moment – the one you're experiencing right now – is the culmination of all the moments you have experienced in the past. You accept things as they are, not as you wish they were at this moment. You can wish for things in the future to be different, but at this moment you have to accept things as they are. When you feel frustrated or upset by a person or a situation, remember that you are not reacting to the person or the situation, but to your feelings about the person or the situation.

This leads us to the second component of the Law of Least Effort: responsibility. Responsibility means not blaming anyone or anything for your situation, including yourself. Having accepted this circumstance, this event, this problem, responsibility then means the ability to have a creative response to the situation as it is now. Whatever relationships you have attached in your life at this moment are precisely the ones you need in your life at this moment. There is a hidden meaning behind all events, and this hidden meaning is serving your own evolution.

The third component of the Law of Least Effort is defenselessness, which means, that you have relinquished the need to convince or persuade others of your point of view. If you observe people around you, you'll see that they spend ninety-nine percent of their time defending their points of view. If you just relinquish the need to defend your point of view, you will in that relinquishment, gain access to enormous amounts of energy that have been previously wasted. When you become defensive, blame others, and do not accept and surrender to the moment, your life meets resistance. Any time you encounter resistance, recognize that if you force the situation, the resistance will only increase. You don't want to stand rigid like a tall oak that cracks and collapses in the storm. Instead, you want to be flexible like a palm tree that bends with the storm and survives. "The past is history, the future is a mystery, and this moment is a gift. That is why this moment is called 'the present'." When you remain open to all points of view – not rigidly attached to only one – your dreams and desires will flow with nature's desires. Then you can release your intentions, without attachment, and just wait for the appropriate season for your desires to blossom into reality. You can be sure that when the season is right, our desires will manifest. This is the Law of Least Effort.

5. The Law of Intention and Desire

> *Inherent in every intention and desire is the mechanics for its fulfillment. Intention and desire in the field of pure potentiality have infinite or organizing power. And when we introduce an intention in the fertile ground of pure potentiality, we put*

> *this infinite organizing power to work for us. In the beginning there was desire, which was the first seed of the mind; sages, having mediated in their hearts, have discovered by their wisdom the connection of the existent with the non-existent.*
>
> *(The Hymn of Creation, The Rig Veda)*

The fifth spiritual law of success is the Law of Intention and Desire. This law is based on the fact that energy and information exist everywhere in nature. In fact, at the level of the quantum field, there is nothing other than energy and information. The quantum field is just another label for the field of pure consciousness or pure potentiality. And this quantum field is influenced by intention and desire. Let's examine this process in detail. A flower, a rainbow, a tree, a blade of grass, a human body, when broken down to their essential components, are energy and information. The whole universe, in this essential nature, is the movement of energy and information. The only difference between you and a tree is the informational and energy content of your respective bodies. On the material level, both you and the tree are made up of the same recycled elements: mostly carbon, hydrogen oxygen, nitrogen, and other elements in minute amounts. The real difference between the two of you is in the energy and in the information. We experience this field subjectively as your own thoughts, feelings, emotions, desires, memories, instincts, drives, and beliefs.

The conscious change is brought about by the two qualities inherent in consciousness: attention and intention. Attention energizes, and intention transforms. Whatever you put your attention on will grow stronger in your life. Whatever you take your attention away from will wither, disintegrate, and disappear. Intention, on the other hand, triggers transformation of energy and information. Intention organizes its own fulfillment.

Nature is a symphony. The human body is another good example of this symphony. Any single cell in the human body is doing about six trillion things per second, and it has to know what every other cell is doing at the same time. What is remarkable about the nervous system of the human species is that it can command this infinite organizing power through conscious intent. Intent in the human species is not fixed or locked into a rigid network of energy and information. It has infinite flexibility. In other words, as long as you do not violate the other laws of nature, through your intent you can literally command the laws of nature to fulfill your dreams and desires. Intention lays the groundwork for the effortless, spontaneous, frictionless flow of pure potentiality seeking expression from the Unmanifest to the manifest. The only caution is that you use your intent for the benefit of mankind. Intention is the real power behind desire. Intent alone is very powerful, because intent is desire without attachment to the outcome. Desire alone is weak, because desire in most people is attention with attachment. And when action is performed in present-moment awareness, it is most effective. Your intent is for the future, but your attention is in the present. As long as your attention is in the present, then your intent of the future will manifest, because the future is created in the present. You must accept the present as it is. Accept the present and intend the future. The future is something you can always create though detached intention, but you should never struggle against the present.

The past, present, and future are all properties of consciousness. The past is recollection, memory; the future is anticipation, the present is awareness. Only present, which is awareness, is real and eternal. It is an eternal field of possibilities experiencing itself as abstract forces, whether they be light, heat, electricity, magnetism, or gravity. These forces are neither in the past nor in the future. They just are. Intention, grounded in this detached freedom of the present, serves as the catalyst of the right mix of matter, energy, and space-time and events to create whatever is that you desire. Learn to harness the power of intention, and you can create anything you desire.

6. The Law of Detachment

> *Attachment is the great fabricator of illusion; reality can be attained only by someone who is detached*   Simone Weil

The sixth spiritual law of success is the Law of Detachment. The Law of Detachment says that in order to acquire anything in the physical universe you have to relinquish your attachment to it. This doesn't mean you give up the intention to create your desire. You don't give up the intention, and you don't give up the desire. You give up your attachment to the result. The Law of Detachment does not interfere with the Law of Intention and Desire–with goal setting. You still have the intention of going in a certain direction, you still have a goal. However, between point A and point B, there are infinite possibilities. When you understand this law, you don't feel compelled to force solutions. When you force solutions on problems, you only create new problems. Good luck is nothing but preparedness and opportunity coming together. This is the perfect recipe for success, and it is based on the Law of Detachment.

7. Purpose In Life
The seventh spiritual law of success is the Law of Purpose. Each of us is here to discover our true Self, to find out on our own that our true Self is spiritual, that essentially we are spiritual beings that have taken manifestation in physical form. We're not human beings that have occasional spiritual experiences – it's the other way round: we're spiritual beings that have occasional human experiences. The other as pect of this law is service to humanity – to serve your fellow human beings and to ask yourself the questions, "How can I help? How can I best be suited to serve humanity? Answer that question, and put it into practice. Discover your divinity, find your unique talent, serve humanity with it, and you can generate all the wealth that you want. When your creative expressions match the needs of your fellow humans, then everything will spontaneously flow from the Unmanifest into the manifest, from the realm of the spirit to the world of form.

Today the average life span is 25,550 days. A life devoted to things is a dead life, a stump; A god –shaped life is a flourishing tree (Prov. 11:28). You were made by God and for God and until we understand that, life will make no sense. God was thinking of you long before you ever thought about him. His purpose for your life predates your conception. He planned it before you existed, without your input.

A Spirituality of Work

There is a God within us and we grow when he stirs us. (Ovid)
God gives the birds their food, but he doest not throw it into their nests.
Greek Proverb.

Heaven is blessed with perfect rest but the blessing of earth is toil. Nothing happens until people go to work. The right attitude toward work multiplies achievement. Everything depends on what you think about your work, how you feel about your work, and what you do about your work. It is seeing it as freedom to create and build and help. It is striving to find work you can love, a job to which you can harness your heart. It is doing your present work so well that it will open doors to new opportunities. Tasks done at a high standard pave the way to bigger things.

Co-Creative Species
As creation-centered spiritual writers like Teilhard de Chardin, Gibson, Matthew Fox, Brian Swimme and Thomas Berry have reminded us, the starting point for spirituality is the affirmation of creation. We humans are co-creative species. We are discovering that creation is a developmental process, a continuing journey and an unfolding flower. This process begins its creativity with the primal explosion of matter, spread outward in the formation of the galaxies and deepens still more with the developmental emergence of life, from the simplest forms up to the mammals. Finally it achieves reflective consciousness in the human species. Human consciousness, as Pierre Teilhard de Chardin has expressed, is the evolutionary point at which planet earth, and perhaps the whole universe, begins its conscious phase. Human beings are that part of the universe which is aware. When humans make tools, cities and nations, they by their work, act as co-creators.

The Power beyond Measure
Nelson Mandela speaks of the hidden potentialities that must be awakened and brought to the fore.

Our deepest fear is not that we are inadequate. Our deepest fear is that we are powerful beyond measure. It is our light, not our darkness that most frightens us. We ask ourselves who am I to be brilliant, gorgeous, talented and fabulous? Actually who are you not to be? You are a child of God; your playing small doesn't serve the world. There is nothing enlightened about shrinking so that other people will not feel secure around you. We are born to make the glory of God that is within us .It is not in just some of us; it is in everyone. And as we let our own light shine, we unconsciously make people do the same. As we are liberated from our own fear; our presence automatically liberates others.[1]

Work for a Purpose

It is in work that we find our spiritual expression. Do your work as perfectly as you can. Any act of work can be made a symbol of the inner life. Joy comes not merely when our work is what we want it to be, but when we make it expressive of our aspirations, even though it is to dig the soil, or to saw wood, or add up a list of figures. Use the work deliberately for a spiritual purpose, even though it is merely knocking nails into packing cases. The value is not in the work, but in your attitude to it. The soul gives significance to the simplest and humblest acts.

Enthusiasm

It is working with enthusiasm that pays rich dividends. It is putting the stamp of our unique personality on the work you do. It is pouring your spirit into your task. It is making your work a reflection of your faith, your integrity, and your ideals. It is only through work that you can express yourself and make a contribution to human progress. We have some work to do. God has given this life a segment of eternity to contribute our share to this life.

Sing at Your Work

We should not work hard. We should play hard. Now it has become clear that the work for justice, peace and joy in humanity is considered nobler than any other pursuit. Give us, therefore, the man who sings at his work, says Carlyle, he will do more—he will do it better—he will persevere longer. One is scarcely sensible of fatigue whilst he marches to music. The very stars are said to make harmony as they revolve in their spheres. Wondrous is the strength of cheerfulness. In the matter of choice it is best to follow the principle "Follow thy bliss". We work in a spirit of playfulness like children building sand castles on a beach and skipping along the shore.

Work and Leisure

The rower reaches the shore partly by pulling, partly by letting go.
(Egyptian proverb)

The book of Genesis tells us that God works. The creation story shows God is busy creating the sun and the moon and the living creatures. In ancient civilization most people of the time envisioned their gods as not working, but rather romping about on mountaintops or lazily lying around snacking and snoozing. God enjoys and delights in working. Rest or leisure is an integral part of the work process. During a jubilee year there was no planting or harvesting of crops. The land was allowed to lie fallow during that year thus giving it a needed rest. He who cannot relax cannot work.

Benefits
The following are the benefits from our faithful work.
More knowledge by learning more and more.
More power and influence and more responsibility.
Immense faith, confidence and thoroughness.
Truthfulness, boldness and courage.
Contentment and peace of mind.
Real happiness.
Better health.
Better opportunities for advancement.
Better methods and improved ways and means.
Good character and good capacity.
Name, fame and respect.
More privileges and more freedom.
Originality, resourcefulness and initiative.
Success in life generally.

Conducive to Health

There is only one medicine, better and more reliable than all the drugs in the world: work. Work is the anodyne to worry. It is not work that kills man; it is worry. It is not the revolution that destroys machinery; it is the friction. Thank God every morning when you get up that you have something to do which must be done, whether you like it or not. Being forced to work, and forced to do your best, will breed in you temperance and self-control, diligence and strength of will, cheerfulness and content, and a hundred virtues, which the idle never know. The man who rolls up his shirt sleeves is rarely in danger of losing his shirt. Nothing is so fatiguing as the eternal hanging on of an uncompleted task.

Work as an Artist

"No matter how humble your work may seem," said Marden, "do it in the spirit of an artist, of a master. In this way you lift it out of commonness and rob it of what would otherwise be drudgery." Even if it's a little thing, do something for those who have need of help, something for which you get no pay but the privilege of doing it. The man who not only does his work superbly well, but also adds to it a touch of personality through great zeal, patience, and persistence, making it peculiar, unique, individual, distinct, and unforgettable, is an artist. And this applies to each and every field of human endeavor—managing a hotel, a bank, or a factory, writing, speaking, modeling, or painting. It is that last indefinable touch that counts; the last three seconds he knocks off the record that proves the man a genius.

Concentration and Devotion

No one has the right to be careless in his work, to demoralize his character by failing to put into the task at hand one's best efforts. Every thing that passes through our hands, everything we do, everything we touch, bears our trademark. When you are in any contest you should work as if there were to the very last minute a chance to lose it. The more intelligent rich men work nearly as hard as if they were poor. When the chief aim of your daily life is to produce intrinsically the best, and not merely the outwardly attractive, you can then attend to disregard the approval and praise of men. Let your thought be of quality, not quantity. To do good work you must be interested in it. And to be interested in it you must like it. All the master builders have been earnest, intense, conscientious workers.

The Will to Labor

The infinite capacity for taking pains is Carlyle's definition of genius. Ever since the morning of time, humans have made a name for themselves, a name for greatness. The road to distinction is paved with years of self-denial and hard work, heartaches, headaches, nerve-aches, disheartening trials, discouraged hours, fears and despair. Successful achievement was attained when humans learned to overcome these trials of life. The grit, determination, the capacity for keeping on, for conquering, for attaining perfection, lifted our heroes of history out of the mass of humanity and rewarded them with a place in the hearts of mankind. Most of these men and women became superior to other men and women because they took more pains than other men and women. The hands of a clock make sourly approaches to the point and yet proceed so slowly to escape observation.

Perseverance

No matter if it does cost you the pleasure, the thousand early gratification of life, stick to the thing and carry it through. The work an unknown good man has done is like a vein of water flowing hidden underground, secretly making the ground green. Nature does not thrust powers and accomplishments upon us, if we are half hearted. We must plod on even if the results are not in sight. Remember that it is only through your work that you can grow to your full height. Execute your resolutions immediately. Thoughts are but dreams; still their effects are to be tried. As regards intellectual work, it remains fact, indeed, that great decisions in the realms of thought and momentous discoveries and solutions of problems are only possible to an individual, working in solitude. To work with a view to serve your brothers is the only motive that can justify any work and it will pay dividends during our life. Those who work hard will succeed. If not today, tomorrow or another day, the forces of nature, impatient, will help and start their work in a way unknown to the worker.

Nature Loves to See Human Work

Nature loves to see humans work. She loves sweat, weariness, and self-sacrifice. She crowns the unconscious head of the busy man. You obtain an accurate measurement of your capacity of performance. Go to your task with love in your heart, and you will go to it lighthearted and cheerful. To begin is half the work. Let the half still remain; again begin thus, and you will have finished. The three great essentials to achieve anything worthwhile are according to Einstein, first, hard work; second, stick-to-activeness; third, common sense.

The ingredients of successful work are training and experience in the subject being addressed; good general intelligence and ability; a capability of high affinity; a tolerance of pain; and the ability to communicate and receive ideas. The things you are doing today are the things about which the world will know in the future. All the hard labor and toil you are putting into your work will be of service to you later. You will wake up some morning after years of labor to find that the world wants your time. Work each day a few hours longer. Always do more than is expected of you. The workers are the saviors of society, the redeemers of the race.

End Note

1. Nelson Mandela. Inaugural Speech, 1994.

Compulsions in Spirituality

Spirituality enables us to face life with confidence. It is meant to liberate us for action. The following are the hang-ups or obstacles. The faithful man is free and the free man is faithful.

Perfectionism
The virtue of doing things 'perfectly', or the 'be perfect' behavior is a typical example of the compulsion of perfectionism. It is good to aim at doing things neatly. But if doing things perfectly becomes a sort of compulsion, then the person is likely to take a disproportionate amount of time to do what he or she does, just to make sure that it is done perfectly. For fear of not being able to do a perfect job, these people often hesitate or refuse to accept to do things which those who do not suffer from perfectionism will not be afraid to take up. Chesterton remarks: "What is worth doing is worth doing badly." In short, these perfectionists are not free to do what they can and be at peace with what they have done; nor are they free to tolerate imperfection in others. A perfectionist takes infinite pains and gives half of it to others.

There are particularly five behavior patterns with their sub modalities which, though good in themselves, become vices beyond a point. They are please me, be perfect, be strong, try hard and hurry up. We are not saying that these behavior patterns are not good. They are. We should try to cultivate these. What is wrong is that, beyond a point, they become counterproductive as explained above.

Please Me
Please me driver urges one to go out of one's way to please others. It is of course good to behave in a pleasing way. Socialization means just that. But 'Please me' driver is such a compulsion to please others that one is afraid to say 'no' even to requests that have to be refused, for fear that the others might be displeased. People who suffer from this urge fear that others do not or will not appreciate them. These people are afraid to take up responsibilities for they know that they

will have to displease others now and then in the execution of their jobs. Being liked by other is too important for them.

Be Strong
This driver makes one insensitive to finer feelings of life, compassion, sadness, grief, etc. There will be situations in life in which it is helpful to be insensitive, as when one tries to manipulate us. But if one is insensitive to feelings all the time, one misses a lot from life such as warm and intimate friendships, capacity to be compassionate, the supreme joy of forgiving and being forgiven and the ability to understand the sufferings of others.

Try Hard
A person with this driver tries hard, but not productively. He concentrates so hard on what he does that he gets tense, does not, for example, grasp what he reads and develops a headache. He may repeat a question or an answer to get right. A person needs concentration to study, to work or to do anything serious. But if he is not reasonably relaxed, concentration becomes counterproductive. If you meet, say, at the ticket reservation counter one who, after going through your application picks up one book, to put it back to take another and then put it aside to open a third, asking you in between, a clarification that is already in the application form, you have met one who is driven by the "Try Hard" driver. We should play hard and not work hard. A bird does not fly hard, but enjoys flying with great facility.

Hurry Up
One may be in a tremendous hurry. He would start brushing his teeth, meanwhile go to the cupboard to take out the clothes for the day, then go back to brushing, and while doing it, make sure that he had the correct papers in the file. He was too much in a hurry to get things done; this friend is driven by the 'hurry up' driver.

What has been said of these five drivers can be said of many other behavior patterns like being gentle, being angry, working hard, being sensitive, being respectful of superiors, etc. If we cannot behave also in the opposite manner when needed, we have become compulsive.

Drivers and Physical health

These drivers can cause even physical harm, because they create tension within. Any tension, especially if it lasts for a long time, has unhealthy repercussions on the body. Secretions resulting from tension are introduced into the blood stream and slowly begin to affect the weaker parts of the body. If we blow up a balloon beyond a limit, it develops a bulge and bursts. In much the same way these tensions resulting from drivers can affect the weaker parts of the body causing diseases like arthritis, ulcers, backache, asthma, etc. It is not implied that drivers are the sole cause of these diseases. Research has, however, shown that about seventy per cent of serious diseases have psychological stress as one of their major causes. Yes, sound spirituality is good for health.

It is Never Too Late

The first step in restoring mental peace is to recognize the drivers in us. Is there an unhealthy behavior pattern in you, like taking extra care in doing things well or keeping things clean or being punctual, that causes in you or others negative emotion like irritation, anger, etc? Do certain situations like someone being late or slow, make you unduly tense? These situations point towards a driver.

The second step is to accept the fact that we have a particular driver or drivers and that we are not going to get rid of them easily. Serene acceptance of the reality relaxes us and that creates the atmosphere for healing, though slowly.

The third step is to realize that drivers are learned behavior patterns and therefore can be unlearned. We will accept the responsibility for our present behavior. We will not excuse our driver behavior by blaming others, for example, we may tell others, "look, I'm annoyed because you are too slow." He may be slower than normal people. But those of us with 'hurry up' drivers are a little too fast than most people.

A fourth step is to realize that we acquired these drivers, in our attempt to please our parents or those who were in authority. Consequently as children we had often to give up our spontaneity and childlike behavior and thus suffer or get emotionally wounded. Hours of prayerful silence and reflection over our lost childhood and re-experiencing the pain of the child and then surrendering it all to the Lord, helps healing.

The fifth step is to gently and consciously go counter to our driver behaviors. The awareness that we gain by reflection and prayer should lead to action. "Not every one who says to me, 'Lord, Lord, shall enter the kingdom of heaven, but he who does the will of my father in heaven" (Mt. 7:21). So the one with 'Hurry Up Driver' will walk slowly, speak slowly, work slowly. The perfectionist will not go back to his work to take a second or third look at what he has done in order to give the 'final' touch. While the lazy one has to strive to overcome his laziness, the perfectionist would have to do just the opposite. It is hard to get rid of them. All that we can and need to do is to be aware of them, accept them serenely, take responsibility for our present driver behavior and gently and perseveringly go counter to them.

Jesus
There was something special about the character of Jesus, a union of many opposites. He knew what intimacy was. He experienced it in the company of Lazarus and his sisters. At the same time he could be totally detached even from his mother if that was the will of God. He could be simple like a dove and behave so towards children and honest seekers of truth. Yet he could be wise like a serpent towards people who played games with him. He enjoyed the company of people and could spend hours on end teaching and healing people. Yet he equally relished the long hours he spent in silent communion with his Father at night or in lonely places. He was at home with nature. Lilies of the field and birds of the air could speak to him of God and his ways. He could weep unashamedly at he death of a friend. Yet he could stand like a rock, when he had to face his enemies. He could experience extreme fear, as in the garden of Gethsemane. Yet he could experience courage enough to drive out the money-changers and other traders who were converting the temple into a market place.

A Spirituality of Devotion

To give one's love and attachment to a highly qualified person or to the Deity is called devotion. It is the unceasing attention and love coming from the heart of a person for a spiritually advanced and noble soul. Devotion is a spontaneous current of attraction, which draws one towards the Beloved. Repetition, austerity, pleasures, comforts, honor, fame, power are all worth sacrificing for one infinitesimal bit of love. That eye is very fortunate through which pearls of tears are shed in remembrance of the beloved. That heart is blessed, which is being burned in the fire of separation for the beloved because the teardrops falling on the ground of the heart are responsible for bringing forth the blossoms of the mysteries of God. Just as the merciful rain produces multicolored flowers on the earth similarly the eyes that are drenched with tears of remembrance of the Lord bring forth flowers of spirituality.

God is love and therefore the best method of meeting him is love. One has developed love when one is filled with it all the time. In order to tread this path one has to sacrifice himself without a murmur. Love rules out arrogance and self-conceit.

Love demands great detachment. A truly detached person lives in this world but does not become entangled in it. He does not consider it necessary to leave the world in order to rise above it. He sees the presence of God in everything. Those who try to become detached without fully realizing its implications cannot be truly happy or peaceful. Such people are restless in this world.

A devotee must have faith. Firm faith turns into devotion, and eventually it culminates in love. Knowledge and discipline are practice for attaining communion with God, but devotion is both a practice and the reward for such a practice.

A Spirituality of Devotion

The Principles of Devotion

1. There should be the firm belief and awareness that God is the creator of all and is omniscient.
2. One should be happy in the will of God and should remain contented and grateful for whatever happens to him. Trouble is meant to elevate the condition of our mind. One should never complain.
3. One should consider it to be the greatest sin to hurt the feelings of others. To provide comfort and happiness to others should be considered the highest obligation because it is the highest form of religious duty. The lover should not be in a state of enmity or hatred with anyone.
4. No other idea should creep into the mind except that of the beloved. A woman who has one husband is "sohagan" happily married. Intimate contact with more than one is impure and leads to disputes and other troubles. In devotion, it is considered sinful to give place in one's mind to thoughts of love for more than one object because that brings no results.
5. All types of fear should be removed.

"Satsang" True Association

We should stay in the company of persons who have devotion fully established in their minds. One should become a devotee by taking support from his Guru or Master, so that by being in contact with such a higher being one may also eventually attain the same stage. One should talk only of Him, so that in due course there will be nothing but him. A greedy person cannot because of the greed freely use the secret fires of his soul. It is difficult to understand true devotion because it is achieved without any selfish motive and by freeing one's self from all ambition.

We get warmth by sitting near a master, if we sit near a highly evolved soul, his spiritual rays will certainly bestow his influences on us. To tap electricity you need a finite switch. The currents of love emanating from the heart of a devotee strikes against the heart of the master, draw power from it and return to the heart of the disciple with a double force. A Disciple should merge completely in his

Guru like a dead body going into a grave. Just as water cannot enter a stone even if the stone is immersed in it for a long time similarly those who are without devotion are as impregnable as the stone (Adi Granth) A Master has a unique magnetic power by which we are attracted to him. True and intense love can be experienced only through another human being. A human being needs a master in the physical form, who will enable him to rise out of the physical body (die daily) make him finer (pure spirit) and thus make him capable of loving the Lord.

Devotion in Bhagavat Gita

The Bhagavat says that devotion is of nine different kinds.

1. Listening to the Guru's words with rapt attention and fixing those in one's mind.
2. Singing hymns and engaging in spiritual talk
3. "Sunvan" Repetitions and remembrance. Go on repeating the name of the Lord. All the trouble and anxiety will by obliterated. (Adi granth)
4. Physical service
5. Worship
6. Prayer
7. Humility
8. Feeling, love and reverence for the Master
9. Complete surrender.

Basis of all Evil

1. Action which is done underhandedly. Concentration of the will in this case is lost.
2. Action which compels the doer to talk in defense to substantiate his arguments. He goes on thinking of arguments to support it.
3. To think evil of others. If we think ill of somebody we forget the connection of our soul with the other.
4. Lust, Wealth, lack of Faith and talking about enemies create obstacles in the Path of Devotion. The worst is pride in one's

own wealth, power, offspring, knowledge, intellect, caste, creed family status, good character, beauty and so forth.

A head that does not bow down in reverence to the Lord should be cut into pieces. The body that has not entertained a desire to meet the Lord should be burned. (Guru Angad) Intense longing has a very deep influence because of its powerful current of energy. Even the ill furnished and dilapidated hut is beautiful if it is brightened with the spark of love. The physical love is like a bridge and a bridge is meant only to cross the river and not to live on. Those who stay on the bridge do not achieve any progress in their endeavor to meet the Lord. As soon as it is steeped in love, a crow becomes a swan and troubles no one. If you wish to know about love you should ask a worshipper of love or you may ask a nightingale that has fallen in love with a rose, or you may ask a moth that sacrifices its life, without hesitation in the flames. Do not ask about love from any other person except the lover himself, because he alone can tell you anything about it. Love is a constant magnet. A lover prefers to be wounded by the arrows of love than to wound another person with them. Ordinarily a sword cuts one into two but the sword of love unites two into one. As the mind becomes free from desires, to that extent is it filled with love. A human heart is far better than a thousand places of worship. A man made temple may be a place to worship a deity, but the heart is the place of pilgrimage that leads to God.

A Spirituality of Intimacy and Undivided Heart

*As soon as I believe there is a God I know,
I could not do anything but live only for him alone.*
Charles de Foucauld

Chastity is the primary constitutive charism in religious life. It is the heart of our personal dedication to God, who comes to meet us in the Risen Jesus. It is the heart of our love for one another in our community. It is the heart of our dedication to the work of the kingdom of God, a work of freedom, justice, love healing, reconciliation and peace. Chastity liberates the human heart in a unique way and causes it to burn with greater love for God and mankind. (Vat. II Religious Life 12)

1. Expand the Capacity for Love
The object of the vow of chastity is simply to develop our power of love in the soul. By setting a man free from the ties of family life, it sets him free to love with a universal love. Every-instinctive desire, it has been said, must be satisfied; what therefore cannot be satisfied in the flesh must be satisfied in the spirit. This transformation of love from sexual into spiritual love, from Eros into agape, is indeed the very purpose of life.

1.1 Powerful Passion
We have understood celibate love too much as prosaic purity and too little as a powerful passion. Poetry and passion are found in celibate loving, both of which are at the core of wholeness, of holiness. And thus as celibate lovers, we need to be passionate people, fully alive, proclaiming by the way we live that we are about the creation of life, about sharing the life of the Spirit, the life of Christ and about being alive to the beauty of all life, all creation.

1.2. A Healthy Sense of Personal Identity
The foundation of healthy celibate living-as indeed of all living-lies in the achievement of a healthy sense of personal identity. This

consists in a realistic acceptance of oneself as a mixture of light and shadow, a commitment to authenticity and humble achievement. At the psychological level we stress the importance of our community to us in the process of personal growth.

1.3. A Healthy Sense of One's Sexuality

Closely allied to this sense of one's personal identity is the sense of one's sexuality. Fundamentally, sexuality is the expression of one's masculine or feminine reality through one's whole being as an embodied person. Our bodies are the instruments of our relationship with others, of our presence to others and our interaction with others. Our personal wholeness, and thus our happiness and well-being depend on our capacity for living our sexuality in a way which gives life to others.

1.4. Reverencing our Bodies

Chastity is about reverencing our bodies as "temples of the Holy Spirit". Psalm 139 has the perfect response to this attitude in the words: "I give you thanks that I am fearfully, wonderfully made; wonderful are your works" God chose sexuality. God invested sexuality with fire, with energy, with passion and put it in our bodies. Could not the all-knowing God have designed something less volatile to ensure the reproduction of the human species? Would not our creator be capable of thinking of a mating plan that would function only during those times when conception was needed or desired, thus avoiding unnecessary sexual passion? If it has purpose only in marriage, why are healthy infants experiencing its energy? Our arrival was announced with a proclamation of our sexual identity. Before comments were made about our dark curls or ruddy complexions, one announces. "It's a girl!" Our sexual identities were heralded. Before our parents counted our toes, they probably took careful note of our bodies to confirm us as sons or daughters. As males, we might have been born with an erection. As females, we displayed vaginal lubrication at birth. There has been a fear of the body and sexuality, a suspicion of women, and a flight from authentic human intimacy. For the celibate, the expression of sexuality is essential, but it is to be expressed not genitally, but effectively, that is, through the warmth, tenderness, care and compassion of our loving relationships. This, however, is not to deny the existence within our body-persons of genital energies.

1.5. A Capacity for Intimacy

For human beings, the more powerful need is not for sex per se, but for relationship, intimacy, acceptance, and affirmation. The real model for healthy relatedness is, however, that of interdependence. We build our relationship through our sharing, but we can allow each other to be separate." C. S. Lewis explains, "When my friend has a friend, I am enriched. When my friend loses a friend, I am impoverished." Failure to handle the development task of growth in intimacy can manifest itself in unhealthy displacement of intimacy needs, such as over-dependence on superiors, reliance on authoritarian uses of power in work relationships, hypochondria, over-eating, drug addiction, compulsive masturbation, perfectionism and rigidity in adherence to rules and rites.

2 Blessedness of Singleness
2.1 Sign and Seal of the Kingdom

There is a solitude and silence deep in the hearts of consecrated celibacy, a surrender that echoes in the still points of the soul. Religious chastity is still the sign and seal of the kingdom of God among us. There is something indelibly written in the human heart by the vow of chastity. Regardless, too, of our own restless heart, the unspeakable beauty of the three vows is bound up with the essential integrity it sustains, the quest and achievement of an undivided heart.

2.2 Solitude and Tenderness

The monk (monabos) stands as the marginal person, monos-alone. In that desert there is solitude, silence and surrender, but there is also tenderness, joy, freedom and peace, the gifts of the spirit and the happiness of an undivided heart. The reality of celibacy takes us into solitude, not once and for all, but over and over again. Along this way the saints have gone, and we may follow. Our long journey of God is a quest for an undivided heart, stripped of attachment to all that is not God. We do not strive to overcome attachment so that we can be cold, mechanical people, devoid of love. Our consecrated celibacy should make us more loving, more caring, more gentle and tender, compassionate and kind. That is the reality of an undivided heart. To be all things to all for the love of God, unselfishly, with purity of heart, that is the joy of chastity.

2.3 Font of Energy

Our quest for an undivided heart is the journey of courage that takes us into the fullness of God's abiding presence, more and more revealed to us proportionately as we lay aside all that is not God. The whole point of celibacy is union with God, nothing more and nothing less. Chastity is freedom from the pursuit of pleasure and popularity; freedom from encrustations of endless self-adornment for the sake of vanity or sex appeal from self in areas, where self may be the worst enemy. Celibacy is a font of energy in the undivided heart, a directing of the life force to the life giver. We need never be ashamed for having made this choice- indeed, for having been chosen for it.

2.4 The Sea Gull without a Mate

All earthly delights pale beside the effulgence of God revealing himself to those who seek him with a pure heart. Chastity with diligent constancy chips and chisels all the corners of the human heart. As the sea chips and chisels the shore, so does celibacy remove all selfishness as it refines the heart, not without pain, not without suffering, but most importantly, not without joy. I watch a seagull swoop down into the waves, taking his catch from the sea. The small fish is caught, by the powerful beak of the gull, for this is nature's way. Then the lonely sea gull flies up out of the wave and is lost to sight in the evening sky. It reminds me that I, too, fly alone over the ocean of life, single in the world, without a mate, for one great purpose, God.

3. Different levels of Living Celibate Lives

On the physical and emotional level, celibacy is the ability to know oneself as sexual and to experience some considerable comfort with that knowledge. It is the ability to regard oneself as sexual without experiencing the internal or external demand to do something about it – neither the need nor demand to make it go away, nor the need or demand to act it out. It is the choice not to act one's sexuality in a genital or romantic way.

On the level of relationships, Celibacy is the ability to cherish and nurture other people without establishing bonds of mutual emotional dependence with them. It means not to be married, and not to be pursuing the path, which naturally leads to marriage. It is the ability to establish warm and deep relationships with others by loving them and by being loved by them in a non-exclusive and non-possessive way.

On the practical level, celibacy is a way of remaining significantly more available to cherish and nurture other's being and becoming because of the choice not to take on the responsibilities of establishing and maintaining one's own family unit.

On the level of social impact, the prophetic level, it is a way of living, which seriously challenges the hedonistic tendencies in all of us. We strongly assert by choice that self-fulfillment is not the ultimate meaning of life.

On the personal, spiritual level, celibacy is a commitment to stand ready to enter fully and vulnerably into life's moments of loneliness because God can be found concrete in such moments. It is a commitment to face the reality of our separateness and incompleteness and to allow ourselves to experience. We embrace loneliness and pain and become tender and sensitive to the needs of others. We are aware that our own being and becoming is blessed by God and discover the radical all sufficiency of God.

And finally, **on the level of Christian faith,** celibacy is this lifestyle taken up and lived in response to a call or invitation one has received from God. The call to a celibate life is a gift from God. Celibacy as a lifestyle has never been upheld as a value by church. It is celibacy " for the sake of the kingdom" which has always been promoted. It has always presumed that the individual who takes up the celibate life has had an overwhelming experience of God.

Self-awareness Exercise on My Human Sexuality

1. Am I aware of my sexual orientation?
2. How is my self-confidence in relation to men and women? How do I feel in the company of Women/Men? How do I feel in the presence of a mixed group of men and women?
3. Have I been in love/infatuated with a person of the opposite sex?
4. Was I able to share openly with my councilor/guide about this relationship?
5. Is this genital dimension of my sexuality a problem for me? Why?

Morality of Sex

According to conventional sexual morality, sex is morally legitimate only within the bounds of marriage; non-marital sex is immoral. A stable family life is absolutely essential for the proper raising of children and the consequent welfare of society as a whole. But the limitation of sex to marriage is a necessary condition of grooming and maintaining stable family units. The availability of sex within marriage will reinforce the loving relationship between husband and wife. The exclusive availability of sex within marriage will lead most people to get married and to stay married, and the unavailability of extramarital sex will keep the marriage strong. The natural law framework of Aquinas is relevant: "The deliberate use of sexual faculties outside of normal conjugal relations essentially contradicts its finality." "Homosexual acts are disordered by their very nature." "Masturbation is an intrinsically and seriously disordered act."

The Energy of Attraction

In his book *A Brief history of Time*, the world-renowned physicist Stephen Hawking speaks of the "forces" that have been at work from the first moments of the creative fire. The most apparent of these forces is the one that we call "gravity." In actuality, the law of gravity is simply another way of speaking about the "energy of attraction" that can be found at all levels of reality–from quasars to quarks, from the music of the spheres to the longing of human hearts. Cosmologist Brian Swimme calls it "cosmic allurement." We human beings call this "binding energy" love. Love is cosmic allurement as it is revealed in our human lives and relationships.

Healthy Psychosexual Development

Psychosexual development refers to that dynamic interplay of experiences, circumstances, phases, tasks and decisions that lead us toward mature and loving relationships. More specifically, we can speak of healthy psychosexual development as including the following six dimensions:

- **Physical**: the genetic, biological, hormonal factors that influence our sexual response from the first moments of conception and throughout the seasons of our lives.
- **Cognitive**: Accurate and adequate sexual knowledge; the positive perception of our bodies, beliefs that reverence self and others.
- **Emotional**: Being "at home" with our body; being aware of and comfortable with our sexual feelings; having healthy feelings toward others.
- **Social**: Relating to others in unself-conscious ways, having the capacity for self-disclosure, being able to sustain friendship and intimacy.
- **Moral**: Valuing the attitudes and actions that are necessary for ongoing sexual integration; expressions of our sexuality that are faithful, healthy, and other-enriching, behaviors that are congruent with our life commitments.
- **Spiritual**: Affirming the presence of God and the sacred in our sexual feelings and expressions or our recognizing that sexuality and spirituality are not enemies, but friends.

Basic Characteristics of Psychosexual Maturity

- Deepening personal awareness and good self-knowledge.
- Adequate knowledge of sexual anatomy and physiology, as well as current information on sexual issues and concerns.
- Not "over spiritualizing" sexual realities or engaging in emotional/psychic denial in relationship to them.

- Taking responsibility for one's sexual expressions and behavior.
- Awareness of past hurts or traumas around sexuality and the willingness to take steps toward healing.
- The ability to name and articulate our sexual story in an appropriate setting (e.g. with a spouse, close friend, spiritual director, counselor, and therapist support group) and to understand how it has influenced our lives and relationships.
- A psychic and emotional balance between our sexual life and other aspects of living; neither being preoccupied with sexuality nor denying its place in our lives.
- Growing integration between the human and the holy, between our sexual energy and our spirituality.

Celibacy as a possibility is concerned with possibilities for life

1. Development of full humanness is more important than sexual expression.
2. Becoming a loving person is more important than overcoming loneliness.
3. True generativity is greater than sexual potency.
4. Self-transcending is more fully human than self-fulfillment.

We grow in Chastity

1. Each time we say "no" to sexual attractions or temptations.
2. Each time we say 'yes' to loneliness
3. Even in failures, we turn to God in repentance and cry for help.

Failure is attended by following Characteristics

1. A growing carelessness in a person's life in the negligence of and lack of interest in religious life.
2. Uncontrolled self indulgence in food, drink, sleep and inability to say 'no' to one's ease
3. Overwork, nervous tension and unhealthy community life.

The Unfinished Journey

The coming of the kingdom of God brings with it the gift of consecrated chastity. Not all can receive the precept, but only those to whom it is given. (Mt 4:28). It is a charism (1 Cor 7:7). The life of celibacy points to the primacy of God's love. God's abundant love can so grip us that we embrace his love exclusively through a life of celibacy. We anticipate on earth the eternal human condition in heaven where there would be no marriage or giving in marriage. As human persons we will always be, in some sense, unfinished. None of us is exempt from the grouses and wounds of being human. We are all emotional wayfarers. We all have our loose ends, our unfinished business and unresolved issues. "The price of wisdom," writes Robertson Davies, "is the loss of our innocence."

1. **Know** myself (how my body functions and reacts, my affectivity, my moods, my attractions…)
2. **Understand** the reason for consecrated celibacy. Without Jesus Christ it has no meaning whatsoever. As an imposed condition for being an Oblate) package deal) it does not function
3. **Comfortable** with yourself and being alone – not to be afraid of solitude
4. **Learn** self-control (what are the places and situations which are dangerous for me?)
5. **Speak:** prayer, spiritual direction, sacrament of reconciliation, trustworthy friends
6. **Friendship:** have friends who care about me, who are around when I need them; Oblate community
7. **Regularity** of life: rest, physical exercise, hobbies and interests
8. **Pastoral** involvements

Vigilance and Discernment in Spirituality

Thomas A Becket in "Murder in the Cathedral" by T.S. Eliot was tempted by Satan in various spheres, such as wealth, pleasure and power. But when Satan suggests that he would be venerated as a saint and people would visit his shrine, he delayed a great deal before repulsing the temptation.

Everything is Enticing
Our world is said to be a continuous situation of enticement. It is a world of confusion and falsehood, or brutality and terror, of terrors affecting soul and spirit. The psalmist knew this when he wrote:" In sin was I born, a sinner was I conceived (Ps 51). When Peter says, "Lord, depart from me, for I am a sinful man," he was not thinking of particular sins, but of his general state of being a sinner. It is a universal situation in which we find ourselves.

Estrangement Between God and Humans
Firstly there is the state of tension between humans and the cosmos: humans are abusing the powers and resources of the world, of the cosmos, of nuclear energy. Secondly there is a disruption of relationship among humans as seen in broken marriages, discrimination and war. Thirdly there is the interior dissipation in a human being. People suffer from their own limitations, and their propensity to evil. These three spheres of conflict have their roots in the fourth: the estrangement between God and humans. The follower of Christ has to take the devil seriously. We are "not fighting against flesh and blood, but against the sovereignties and powers who originate in the darkness in this world, the spiritual army in the heavens".

(Eph 6: 12).

The good news is that we have not been left alone. We can overcome every human problem. He has delivered us from the power of darkness and placed us into the kingdom of his beloved son" (Col 1:13) "Resist the devil and he will flee from you" (Jn 4: 7) In this world you will have tribulation; but have courage, I have overcome the world'. (Jn 16: 33) As John puts. "Test the spirits, to see if they come from God. (1 Jn 4: 1) Open my eyes that I may see the wonders of you Lord the spirit of wisdom enlightens the eyes. Isaiah describes an attentive devotee. "Each morning he awakens to hear, to listen like a disciple. The Lord Yahweh has opened my ear. (Is 50: 4)

Conditions for Keeping our Spiritual Sense Alert
One requires stillness and silence in life. Contemplation is the ability to listen and behold. Excessive use of television, neglect of monastic silence, pursuit of amusement, attempting to escape from oneself, from being alone, can pose a problem by blunting our senses. The temptation is to prevent us from coming to quietness, to ourselves, to God. "There is no silence in hell says" C.S. Lewis in his Screw Tape Letters. The devils plan to produce so much noise on earth that it will drown man's pricks of conscience". Discernment of spirits is no longer possible for us who have become incapable of silence. We all need desert times and desert places to keep up our strength. Those who seek the desert, solitude, and learn to persevere in it, become men of battle against the powers of evil. They acquire a delicate ear for the voice of the spirit. They hear God's word where others hear nothing.

Life–Giving Silence
The silence referred to is not a paralyzing silence but a wide-awake, living silence. This wakefulness in the Holy Spirit makes the spiritual senses alert and active. This is possible through a regular examination of conscience. We must ask ourselves: have I a taste for the things of God? Can I still linger and contemplate, listen and hear? St. Ignatius said, "It is not the knowledge of many things that satisfies but the tasting and savoring of them from within". It is important that we critically stand aside and watch the moods, inclinations and attitudes.

Opening to Another Evolved Human Being
A further condition for the right use of our perceptive powers is the honest opening of ourselves to another evolved human being, experienced in spiritual life. This throws light into the caverns of

the unconscious and this is indispensable for the discernment of spirits. Both, the one seeking counsel and the one giving it, must endeavor to begin with complete indifference. This detachment of heart produces in us this readiness to accept as coming from the Holy Spirit any verdict that after careful evaluation present itself. In this indifference of heart we desire to be like an empty slate on which God can write what he wishes. Only the spiritual man judge spiritual things (1 Cor. 2:15)

Listen to the Church
We listen to the Church, to her doctrine, to her tradition. Whoever isolates himself is to be distrusted. We need to discern not only between good and evil but also between what is good and what is better, as befits the Christians who is striving for perfection. Our sins, our experience of conversion, our charismatic experience, all need to be evaluated in this way. Do not quench the Spirit! (1 Th 5: 19) but then also say: "Do not trust every spirit (1 Jon 4: 1) A shrewd "money value" is necessary. Peace, joy, calm, selflessness, adaptability, severity, hopefulness and candor are indications, that God's spirit is at work.

The Indication of the Lack of Spirit
Interior depression, sadness, despondency, restlessness, lukewarmness, exaggeration, lack of self-control, the refusal to accept oneself, or the invention of arguments against what has been recognized as right–all these are indications that the contrary spirit is at work. St. Ignatius' fifth and sixth rule for discernment have a special importance here. First, never make any change in an important matter during a period of desolation, but stand steadfastly by these decisions previously made. Secondly, do not give up, but combat the desolation with more fervent prayer and meditation. Discernment must never be made hastily, but in-patient listening to the often hidden movements of this soul. This result of a discernment well made should correspond to the judgment of reason enlightened by faith.

Success
The success of a venture is not a criterion for the discernment of spirits. God's will may well be waiting for us in failure, in risk,

in ridicule. God can expect this from us – but the enemy, never. Worldly failure and the complete bankruptcy of the Cross-was the peak of Christian fecundity. The immolation of personal plans, blind obedience, being led to where one does not want to go, these are constant reminders that the grain should fall into the ground and die, if not itself will remain alone. In darkness or light, in usefulness or uselessness, failure or success, it is ever this same principle: this offer of everything personal, so that God may dispose of it.

The Mind of Jesus Christ
The fundamental criteria for the discernment of spirits is this mind of Jesus Christ. "Let that mind be in you which was in Christ Jesus "There must be no competition among you, no conceit, but everybody is to be self effacing. Always consider the other person to be better than yourself. (Philip 2: 1–11) There is a skilled way of becoming popular, of canvassing votes before elections, of not listening to others in discussion, but trying to force one's own opinion. All this contradicts the mind of Christ and indicates that someone is seeking his own glory. A spiritual man is ready and anxious all his life to be pruned like the branches on the vine. There is an interior detachment while holding office, seeking not his own glory but the glory of God. Do not adapt yourself to this world, to what everyone else does or thinks. Under this guise of brotherly love one can soften these demands of the gospel.

Apostolic Proclamation
Proclaim the good news as Christ did. The Holy Spirit will teach you all things. He will lead you into complete truth. No one may adapt the truth to himself, but he must adapt himself to the truth. Only if this spirit of obedience to the gospel animates our proclamation may we be confident that "he who hears you hears me? We see only half of the moon in the sky. And yet it is as round as ever. Distractions take place when partial problems are taken out of their context. We are being swamped with superficial problems that are becoming ever more intricate because each one acquires a leaden weight by itself which makes it weigh more than the united whole together.

Good Fruit and Bad Fruit

We know that the enemy has enthroned himself in God's sanctuary and claims that he is God" (2 Th 2:4). And Jesus warns us: "Beware of false prophets who come to you in sheep's clothing. By their fruit you should know them.(Mt.7:50) False prophets can be dynamic and seductive, demagogic. Their fruits are disastrous in the community, with ambition and wounding of charity. They are talkers; their effect is loss of peace in the hearts of men. Wherever you find jealousy and ambition, you find disharmony. (James 3: 15)

Charity

All these criteria can be deduced to one, the one thing necessary: charity (1.Cor:13). If I speak... Love is kind and gentle, it is never jealous; it is never boastful and conceited never rude or selfish... Love is ready to excuse, to trust, to hope and to endure what comes. If a teaching, a practice contributes to the growth of charity toward man and God then it is good. It will produce the fruits of the spirit, which will become the criterion for not only discernment of spirits but for our decisive witness to the gospel after the example of Jesus Christ.................

Planetary Spirituality and Globalization

1. Global Village
In 1960, Marshall McLuhan popularized the idea of "The global village." The new electronic interdependence "recreates" the world in the image of a global village where there are no boundaries. Globalization in its most positive sense is an aspiration here on earth to the harmony and unity seen from space. Put most simply, globalization is about a simultaneous expansion and compression of time and space. Globalization makes possible networking politically, economically and socially. It is manipulated interconnectedness.

Globalization as Opportunity
There are two positive dimensions of globalization. The first dimension is the possibility of a more interconnected world. With the communications and transportation technology, which we now have, we have the chance to become genuinely a connected human family. There is the increased opportunity for human development. Communications technology in this new global era has made possible effective protection of human rights. The movement against the deployment of land mines, for example, was conducted entirely over the internet. The televised display of famine and war-induced suffering has mobilized public opinion and forced governments to react to these human tragedies. Globalization in medicine is bringing about campaigns to totally eradicate certain diseases. It has made it possible for human beings to demonstrate sympathy and compassion for the victims of natural calamities and human made tragedies thousands of kilometers away. It has brought to the fore issues such as the rule of law, public accountability, human rights and other canons of good governance; it has globalized Human rights issues; e.g. rights of women, children, refugees, etc.

Negative Dimensions
To value human beings primarily in the light of how much they can consume represents an unacceptable diminution of the dignity

of the human person. We are created in the image and likeness of God. The second negative dimension of globalization is the ever-widening gap between the rich and the poor. The experience of many is that of exclusion or exploitation rather than inclusion in this growing wealth. The third negative dimension has to do with the fracturing of cultures and ways of life, which the homogenizing forces of globalization bring in their wake. Part of human dignity is the right to culture, an authentic but distinctive way of being human. To deprive peoples of their language and way of life, to force them into other patterns of living, is to rob them of a basic dimension of their humanity. The challenge, in short is to ensure a globalization in solidarity, a globalization without marginalization.

2. Global Spirituality

Contemporary writers speak of spirituality as "an exploration into what is involved in becoming human" or an "attempt to grow in sensitivity, to self, to others, to non-human creation, to a God who is within and beyond this totality. We need a spirituality to fight for the human rights, justice and peace, a spirituality deeply rooted in love. Former Buddhist Secretary general of the UN spoke of the four cries of humanity: the cry for physical life, for mental fulfillment, or morality, and for spirituality. Pierre Teilhard de Chardin combined his scientific and religious insights, conceiving the world as a whole and the human community as one single organism. Muller influenced by him wrote in his *Vision of the Past*:

> *In truth it is impossible to keep one's gaze constantly fixed on the vast horizons opened out to us by science without feeling the desire to see men drawn closer and closer together by an ever-increasing knowledge and sympathy until finally, in obedience to some divine attraction there remains but one heart and one soul on the face of the earth.*[1]

3. Shared Ethical Vision

The Swiss theologian Hans Kung in *Global Responsibility: In search of a New World Ethic* states "No human life together without a world ethic for the nations; no peace among the nations without peace among the religions; no peace among the religions without dialogue among the religions [2]." The Russian novelist Tolstoy (1828-1910) influenced Gandhi (1869-1948), who in turn influenced a generation that includes Martin Luther King, Jr. (1929-69), Abraham Joshua Heschel (1907-72), Thich Nhat Hanh (1926-). King nominated the Buddhist Thich Nhat Hanh for the Nobel Peace Prize for his non-violent struggles against the Vietnam War. There emerges an interreligious and international ethic of human dignity, human rights, and human liberation.

Creating a World of Justice: Veil of ignorance
A proposal made by one of leading contemporary philosophers of ethics, John Rawls, can help us understand why this is true. The following story is our own but it is inspired by Rawls's theory of "the veil of ignorance"

> *Once upon a time there were persons in a community who simply looked after their own interests and did not care what happened to others. They said that everyone had a right to choose their own values as long as they didn't interfere with the rights of others. A small group of concerned citizens feared that this would lead to chaos. They all agreed to consult the wisest and oldest person in the city, a person whom everyone admired and respected. They asked: "Are justice and goodness merely subjective i.e., in the eyes of the beholder only. He responded by saying: "If you want to know what justice is, each of you must imagine that you have been granted the opportunity to remake the world in any way you see fit. There are only two restrictions on your freedom. First that you yourself must live in the world you create. Second, that you will not be able to determine or know in advance what position you will occupy in this world you create. The society you imagine under these conditions will be as just as it is humanly possible for society to be."[3]*

The founder of our Global Ethic Foundation, Count von der Groeben kept in his wallet the saying of Mahatma Gandhi about the 'seven social sins in today's world'. .

- *Wealth without work,*
- *Enjoyment without conscience,*

- *Knowledge without character,*
- *Business without morality,*
- *Science without humanity,*
- *Religion without sacrifice, and*
- *Politics without principles.* (Translated by John Bowden*)*

Celebration of the Great Jubilee

Jubilee means in the Bible the cancellation of debt and a new beginning. If authentic globalization is about inclusion and participation, then such inclusion and participation must be made possible by giving the poor a fresh start. The North must write off debts given to the third World.

Our Capacity for Hospitality

What is required today is not the conquest of the world by any one religion or culture but a meeting and sharing of religion and cultural insight. Our common future depends upon our capacity to welcome the stranger, that is, our capacity for hospitality. Immigrant communities should receive equality of treatment. They should be allowed to participate and enjoy the privilege like all other citizens.

Omnipartiality

Ronald Green argues that we require an ethical point of view characterized by "omnipartiality"–seeing one's actions from the viewpoint of all others and a willingness to sacrifice one's own good for the welfare of others. Thich Nhat Hanh's poem, *Call Me By My True Names*, suggested that ethical consciousness requires omnipartiality. One must "become the other"–not only the other of the victim but also of the victimizer.

4. Self Development is a Higher Duty than Sacrifice

The nineteenth century feminist Elizabeth Cady Stanton says that for women "self-development is a higher duty than self-sacrifice." The goal of feminists is not to develop strong male-type egos in retaliation for male dominance, nor to accept the tradition model of subordination, but rather to develop a new model of self–the relational self. In Rosemary Ruether's words, 'Sin exists precisely in the distortion of relationality including relation to oneself'" (1990:

110). Erikson notes that Gandhi describes himself as a "cruelly kind husband" who harassed his wife into seeing the world as he did. The story of Babel found in the biblical writings invites us to abandon the quest for the unity of identity implied in sacred order, and discover what we seek through hospitality to the stranger in a pluralistic world of interdependence. Then we turn to the Christian and Buddhist ecofeminism of Rosemary Ruether and Joanna Macy to discover in their work an integration of audacity and interdependence which creates a bridge not only between masculine and feminine but also between humanity and nature, and religious ethics East and West.

5. The Sacred Center of Society
In a sacred society human beings see the sacred center of society. The Nazis defined "God," and even Jesus, as Aryan. For it is through the stranger that the infinite enters the finite. We must abandon the dreams of domination, the dreams of colonialist, racist, sexist, and religious domination. Ethnocentrism is the most common bias of every culture. Ethnocentrism is just one of many forms of "centrism" (religious bias, racism, sexism, and so on), which focus on one's self and one's group identity without due consideration for the well being of others.

6. Religion is Political
Gandhi wrote: "I can say without the slightest hesitation, and yet in all humanity, that those who say that religion has nothing to do with politics do not know what religion means" (Mehta 1976:69). For Gandhi, to be religious was to be political. The Brahmachari is one who seeks God by transcending all love and hate. If a man gives you a drink of water and you give him a drink in return, that is nothing. If you agitate for water supply for all the people that would be political.

7. Comparative Storytelling [4]
Our approach will be through comparative storytelling and comparative spirituality in response to some of the defining events of the twentieth century: the struggle against colonialism, racism, and sexism and the human capacity to inflict mass death revealed at Auschwitz and Hiroshima. Gandhi did not become a Christian and

King did not become a Hindu, but in each case their own religious identity was deeply influenced by the other. Martin Luther King, Jr. was a different kind of Christian because of Gandhi and Gandhi was a different kind of Hindu because of Tolstoy. Gandhi and King provide us with a model for engaging in comparative religious ethics as a genuine quest to discover wisdom not only in one's own tradition but in that of others.

8. Evangelization

As a Church extended throughout the entire world, the Catholic Church itself is a transnational institution, which brings special resources to a globalized world. In an age when transnational institutions (such as the NGOs) can render a special service to mankind, which no single nation can do, the Church has networks of communication to build solidarity among nations and throughout the human community. The challenge before us now as a Church is to use the network we already have even more effectively. All are called to the banquet table of the Reign of God.

9. Multiculturalism

This interaction of the global and the local has combined with the migration of peoples (both voluntary and forced) to produce cultural interactions unmatched in intensity and scale. Many of the countries of America have long been multicultural. What is new is the intensity of the interaction between cultures. The United States and Canada are now the second and third most multicultural countries of the world (after Australia). The United States is now also the fifth largest Spanish-speaking country in the world.

Reweaving Right Relationships
According to Micah

- With others: Love tenderly
- With all of creation: act justly
- With God: walk humbly with your God

These words contain in germ the spiritual, community and missionary dimensions of the religious vows.

1. **Call to love tenderly**
    - To be instruments of peace and non-violence: we have a responsibility to build and make peace; to be mediators in conflict situations; to promote dialogue and reconciliation between opposing parties and groups.
    - To promote localization i.e. to appreciate and promote cultural diversity; rediscover the significance of the inherent value system in certain local traditional customs.
    - To work for the prevention of conflicts. Where there are sharp inequalities between ethnic and religious groups. Promote healthy and balanced economic development, combined with human rights, minority rights and political arrangements in which all groups are fairly represented.
    - To pursue arms reductions
    - Non-violence in our way of thinking, talking, acting and reacting.
    - Inclusion at every level: women and men, poor and rich, all religions, nationalities, casts, ethnic groups

2. **Act Justly**
    - To collaborate with others to look for the causes of the present injustices and violence, to search for solutions in view of changing the present World Order
    - To globalize a preferential option for the poor and excluded; to globalize altruism and solidarity
    - To build a new ethic of conservation and stewardship;
    - To change our life style; we are being called to resist the consumer culture and to globalize the ethic of enough to make clear option for a Spirituality of Sufficiency
    - To invest in solar-operated and other alternative forms of renewable energy;
    - To appeal to governments, corporations and private organizations to balance economic development with ecologic concerns
    - To promote economic sovereignty; the right of a country

to determine its own economic policies, trading with other countries if and when it comes.
- To promote political sovereignty; the right of a country to govern its own affairs
- To promote legal sovereignty: the right of a country to enact laws
- To promote cultural sovereignty; the right to preserve cultural identity and nationhood.
- Without a strong UN, it will be difficult to meet all these challenges. The UN must act as a catalyst, to stimulate action. It must fully exploit the new technologies, especially information technology.
- A spirituality of sufficiency
- Ecological integrity;
- A journey from greed from material possessions to an abundance of quality life.

3. **Walk humbly**
   - To promote alternative models of democracy, adapted to cultures and contexts. We also need to keep in mind that democracy in the political context is different from the way we envisage it as disciples of Christ
   - To promote alternative models of power and authority. At every level, there is an abuse of power and authority. Religious are being called to develop from within new models of power and authority in the world scene. Religious communities need to be the role models, by giving priority to right relationships in the exercise of power and authority.
   - To promote prudent decentralization. The challenge for us religious is to promote a moderate decentralization, which promotes unity and communion, in diversity. To globalize maximum participation in decision–making. Modern means of communication can contribute to maximum participation in the decision–making process, making it more democratic, open and transparent.
   - To bring about changes in structures and attitudes which

reflect power, domination and authoritarianism. This is possible only if it is accompanied by a certain flexibility in the working of our mental structures.
- To globalize alternative models of teamwork, cooperation and collaboration. Networking is more effective when it is done among "equals".
- Searching with others for God's Will / for God's Plan for our world;
- Living in interconnectedness and interdependence;
- Making discernment a way of life.
- Deepening our total commitment to God's unfolding plan by our obedience in faith to all who mediate his will for us.

A new century, new realities and new problems call for new responses. We are being invited to be clear on God's plan for this world, and on our role as disciples. In a world of broken relationships, the need is urgent to help reweave relationships with Heaven, Earth and Human Beings. Religious life is in urgent need of a new and powerful paradigm in view of an alternative future.

End Notes

1. Robert Muller. New Genesis: Shaping a Global Spirituality Doubleday, New York 1982.
2. Kung, Global Responsibility: In Search of New World Ethic SCM, London: 1991
3. Rawls, John.1971. A Theory of Justice. (Cambridge, MA: Harvard University Press.
4. Darrell J. Fasching & Dell Dechant *Comparative Religion Ethics*, USA: Blackwell Publishers 2001

An Ecological Spirituality

The whole of creation can be considered a garment of God or the body of God. God, man and nature are to be considered one reality according to the cosmotheandric vision advocated by Raimundo Panikkar. Noah is the patriarch of ecology. It was to him that God made the promise that he would never again flood the earth. The Sower went out to sow his seed, and from that moment on, no one has been able to see a field without seeing in it the Sower, the seed, the world, the brambles and the harvest.

Butterfly: An index of Ecological Health
They tell us that a good index to measure the ecological health of a region is the number of butterflies that are seen flying freely in it. The butterflies withdraw because the air is defiled. The grass withers, the flowers depart. Their absence emphasizes the saddened poverty of the air we breathe and the earth we walk on. Retribution will not be long in coming. The day will come when the butterfly will not be there any more to warn us. "All that exists is there to be worshipped," said Claudel.

A Haiku says

> *The Trill of a lone bird; the nightingale does not know that he consoles you.*
> *The trill of the nightingale heals away sadness;*
> *The breeze in the afternoon relieves fatigue;*
> *The color of the rose softens the eyes;*
> *The perfume of the fields widens the soul.*

The Thief cannot Steal the Moon
The greatest gifts of nature cannot be bought; they cannot be stolen. A thief forgot to take the moon framed in the window. The thief took away all that he could lay his hands on. There were not many things in the poor monk's cell. But he could always have found some piece of clothing, some writing utensil, a begging bowl or a walking stick. The monk, always alert to the noises of the night, woke up in time

to see the silent shadow. He noted the missing articles, but then he looked at the window, saw the full moon framed in its background of stars, and smiled to himself. His most precious possession was intact, the white noon was still shining through the square of his window. The monk turned in his bedding and went on with his sleep. His riches were safe.

The Snake changes the Skin

Nature wants change. The snake scans the horizon, waits for safety, chooses a bush, hooks on the end of its sheath over a thorn, and begins to wriggle out, curve by curve, inch by inch, leaving behind the worn-out slough, and emerging bathed in the bright shine of the new suit, after repeated efforts it shakes itself free, and is back on its way with the new found relief of the expanded body. The old covering would not do any more. To grow, one has to change one's skin, even if it hurts.

Open Freedom

You cannot predict too much what nature will do it. There is open freedom. No one knows in which direction the grasshopper will jump. Not even itself. And this happy and free nonchalance makes a chastening example for human life. We need its open freedom. Another jump and a surprise landing, there are even at times little aeronautical accidents, the grasshopper lands on its back or twists a leg. But it straightens itself at once and goes on with its geometric ballet in curves. The grasshopper is nimble, featherweight and therein lays the secret of its liveliness; it jumps, because it is not bound. Few animals – given the size and weight of their bodies –jump so high as the grasshopper.

Work and Rest the Whole Day

> *"How many hours do you give daily to God?" They asked the native of the jungle. And he answered: "the whole day." "And how much time to work?" "The whole day." "And to rest?" "The whole day."*

They explain with unexpected clarity, that he, who does not know how to rest while he walks, will never arrive. Walk in such a way that the walk itself becomes rest instead of fatigue, game instead of duty, relaxation instead of effort. That is the best way to ensure arrival.

The Mountain and the Valley

The valley is lovely, but it has no value without the mountain. The valley is daily life, and the mountain is contemplation, the valley is beautiful in its ploughed fields, its rows of trees its brooks and its byways, its villages and its flocks, but to see its beauty, it has to be viewed from the summit. One has to climb the mountain, gain height, acquire perspective and command the view. In fact the valley would not be a valley without the summit. If two mountain ranges were not there one at either side, there would be no valley. The valley, in order to be a valley, needs the mountain for contrast, for background, for meaning, for personality. Life is life because there is God, in order to understand life we have to reach God.

Heaven at Earth's Boundary

We know that our true homeland lies very far from here, that around here there is only hardship and doubt. To top it all, we have only a pair of worn-out sandals on our feet, how can we reach the goal? Heaven begins where earth reaches its boundary. It is in our defeat itself that victory was hidden. When we sincerely and joyfully acknowledge that we cannot reach, we suddenly realize with a burst of joy that we have arrived. The promise is reality, and the future has become present.

Crow and Partridge

They say a crow saw a partridge walk and was much pleased with her gait. He conceived hopes he too could learn it. The crow is enticed, begins his lessons, tries the steps, feigns the movements, but in the end gets discouraged because he sees by experience that those rhythms are not meant for him, he cannot return to his old ways, because he had publicly repudiated them, and he cannot adopt the new ones because he has not mastered them and never will. Imitation is death. At each step his whole body sways from right to left, with the tail being twisted to alternate sides, as though the bird did not know what to do with the back end of his body. When the crow wanted to revert to his natural walk, he had forgotten how to walk.

> *The goose's legs are too short,*
> *While the cranes are too long.*
> *Still, to lengthen the goose's legs*
> *Or cut short the crane's legs*
> *Could only be the act of a villain or of a lunatic*

You keep your legs, and I'll keep mine, please, do not compare. I like your legs too as they are, they now call that "pluralism". Formerly it was just common sense.

The Carpenter Loves the Wood

Chuang Tzu tells of a carpenter who, on getting an order for a piece of furniture, would go to the forest and start asking the trees, one by one, whether they were suitable and ready for the job, he sensed their answers, weighed them, compared them, and finally chose the tree that was going to be the most fitting to the work at hand. The wood knows better than the carpenter which is the best material for each work. Let us love the wood, so that the wood feels itself loved by us. That is the art of the true carpenter.

> *Tourist to native: 'How is that? Can it be that you speak to the trees?"*
> *Native to tourist: "How is that? Can it be that you do not speak to the trees?"*

The Voice Rings True

A blind man spoke about Master Bankei (1622-1693) and said the best thing he could say: "I am blind, and cannot see the face of the person with whom I speak. I must, in consequence, judge only his sincerity from his voice, and when I hear social condolences, I detect also a secret note of pleasure. When Bankei expresses joy, there is only joy in his voice and when he expresses sadness, it is only sadness that I hear in him."

Still the Noises of the Body

If nature knows how to keep silence, we too can begin to practice those silences in our own body, and learn to still noises so that we may communicate better. That is meditation.

> *A tortoise can tell us more about ways and paths than a hare.*
> (Khalil Gibran).
> *The fish put out its head in the midst of the lake,*
> *And the far shore knew at once of its presence.*

The shores of the lake know everything about the fish in it.
> *When I bestir, I can't help sensation*
> *That I disturb the stars in their station.*

Eddington said:
> *When an electron vibrates,*
> *The whole universe trembles.*

Portrait of a Cat
> *The cats were invented by the Chinese.*
> (Ramon Gomez de la Serna)

The cat is the Zen creature par excellence, the owner of the coziest corners in the house, perpetually relaxed, master of ease, universal pet. It does not need to watch the house like a dog, or to be kept in a cage and chirp like a finch. Formerly they said it had to catch mice, but even that was only a gastronomical sport without any labor contract to force it. The cat moves with elegance, jumps without effort and lives without noise. Its body adjusts itself to the curves of the furniture, and its supple anatomy merges with the human lap. It is always alert and always at rest. It can enjoy profound sleep and wake instantly at any threatening danger. The cat, Buddhist monk, in its unruffled contemplation of the mystery of life and its unfathomable depths is a lesson in attention without tension.

The Congress of the Cats
To explain this situation they tell in Japan, the story of The Cats' Congress of Martial Arts.

Cats boast of their prowess to kill rats,

In the service of humans and of their own stomachs;
But once a huge rat appeared in a house,
And cat after cat failed in their attempts to get rid of it.
At long last an old cat came and sat himself, quiet and restful,
In a corner of the haunted room, and waited.
The rat appeared, was cautious first,
But then it grew careless and made a wrong move.
At the same instant the cat was on it,
Caught it by the neck and dispatched it.
The cats decided to call a meeting
To draw the lesson from that experience
And to learn why one cat had succeeded
Where all others had failed. The old cat explained:
"You all are younger and stronger than I am,
But you were all too keen to overcome the rat,
As it had become a public issue
And the whole community of cats followed it closely.
That is why you couldn't win.
The rat sensed your keenness, you urgency,
Your need to win, and easily avoided
Your hurried moves and violent jumps.
I, on the contrary, simply sat down and waited,
Without a worry on my mind about what was going to happen.
Faced with my utter tranquility, it was the rat that lost its nerves,
And fell a prey to my instant paws.
"And I even know another cat, older and wiser than myself,
Who puts all rats to flight with his very presence
His composure, his concentration,
His absolute motionlessness are such
That he commands respect and obedience,
And, doing nothing, he does everything,
which is the proof of the highest wisdom."

It is common experience that when we try to do things too well, we spoil them. The tension to win hinders victory. The need to succeed prevents success. We have to work with a free mind and a joyful heart.

Let Yourself Be Frightened

> *The Disciple:*
> *"What have I to do*
> *To free myself from the fear of thunder*
> *Which frightens me out of my wits*
> *When the storm rages over my head?"*
> *The Master: "Let yourself be frightened."*

We love the sea and yet we fear it too. "Let yourself be frightened." The advice is unusual, even paradoxical. But it is wise and practical. Allow yourself to feel our own feelings as they come. If the feelings are harmful, the best remedy against them is to look them in the face, greet them civilly, and let them pass. They pass like thunder. Much noise and no harm. Our ears go deaf for a while, and soon return to normal. The storm does not trouble me now. In any case the storm will leave no trace in my soul when it leaves. By giving up safety, I begin to feel safe.

Nature is the sacrament of God. It heals us and restrains us. Yielding and not resisting nature, we gain sanity and wholeness.

PART 2

SERVICE

Burn with Fire Without Burning out

Most of us function as supervisors and maintenance men without the ardour and zeal of an apostle or a prophet. St Paul burned with zeal, overcoming all obstacles, undergoing persecutions for the love of God. The secret of an apostle is that he or she transmits the fire received to all who come in contact, with him. A true apostle follows Jesus who walked the earth. We should have the capacity for delight because we are children of the kingdom. We are Capax Dei, hungry for God. Jesus himself expressed his mission in these words.

> *I came to throw fire on this earth and how much I desire to see it burning.*   *(Luke.12: 49)*

Jesus
Jesus was a man on fire with the spirit. As a man of the spirit Jesus had an intense relationship with God. This relationship was the source of his power, freedom, courage and compassion. The most crucial fact about Jesus was that he was a "Spirit Person" mediator of the sacred.[1] While John the Baptist was filled with the Holy Spirit, (Luke 1:15) Jesus was conceived by the Holy Spirit (Lk.1:35). Jesus experienced God as 'Abba', as unconditional love as endless and forgiving. God is always present with me. He is a wombish God. The Hebrew word 'rahamin' bears the connotation of utter acceptance and security. (Is 49:14-16.) A minister should be able to bear witness to this fact that God's love is unconditional, ever forgiving and ever present. Our defenseless love as symbolized by the cross has greater power to transform others. Our love becomes genuine in fidelity, but it reaches its completion in forgiveness.

The Ability to reach out to people, patients, and their families without being themselves pulled down is pure grace. There are very clear and helpful psychological and spiritual points worth remembering which can often prevent unnecessary stress from taking an inordinate toll. A minister should rely on God and actively seek healthy, psychological and spiritual perspective to remain sane and balanced. The following ten points on "burnout" are offered to help all ministers.

1. Solitude and Silence

Practically every person in ministry can wax eloquently on the value of going off by ourselves to be absorbed in prayer.   (Mk 1:35). Unless this time is taken, our self-esteem, purpose and compassion will all lose their fervour in time.

(a) Set out a time in the morning. Don't worry about doing anything, don't fret over distractions, just be there with God as a good friend. Never vary from it even if you are busy and it will become the central part-of your day. It is not important that you have spent this time most fruitfully, but what is important is that you have dedicated this time to God. God will not be outdone in his generosity.

(b) Be reflective during the day by occasionally imagining yourself in the presence of God. Put God before every circumstance. Real spirituality dawns when God becomes as real as the problems and joys we face each day. Life   becomes more meaningful and fruitful, if we live our day reflectively.

2. Detachment

The whole work is God's work and we are only instruments. We will see the fruit of our labor eventually. We may begin, somebody else will continue and still another will finish it. We need an attitude of aloofness and detachment, of doing our actions without expecting results from them. Bhagavad-Gita   emphasizes the need to pose action without expecting results. Do your action without the consideration for consequences. The opposite of detachment is not compassion but seduction. By that we mean that we are seduced by others' unrealistic expectations and the crazy expectations we have about ourselves rather than being concerned about what God is asking of us. The point to remember is not to try to carry the crosses only meant for God so our arms can be free enough to carry the crosses we are expected to bear.

3. Ongoing Education
Reading, conversation with other professionals and conferences are excellent ways to reignite the excitement and commitment we had when we entered the field originally. With respect to ongoing professional reading, the following is suggested: Read each week from sacred scripture, in psychology, theology and in spirituality.

4. Friendship
After prayer, this is one of most important areas to attend to as a way of preventing burnout. In addition we need healthy friends to visit and relate to, friends who tease, inspire, challenge, support us and help us laugh at ourselves.

5. Physical health
When our physical health is good we can withstand more stress than when we are not healthy. Sleep, regular meals, and exercise are essential. To overcome the temptation of ignoring the need to attend to these areas, we need a regular pattern of rising and going to bed. Take a walk each day and sometimes a long one.

6. Leisure
Leisure is valuable in order to get back energy to be truly available to others if they are in need. Stephen Covey calls this "sharpening the saw". We need quiet times during the day and the week. Many of us are tied to the image of being a "busy, overworked caregiver" and whether we admit it or not, we have difficulty giving up this image.

7. Balance
Each of us has a unique balance in terms of such poles as stimulation and quiet reflection and action, work and leisure, self-care and the care of others, self-improvement and unfolding patience, and involvement and detachment.

8. Effectively Dealing with Negativity
There is a real need to be aware of the negative thinking we are often subject to. If we are to survive in a milieu, which is often filled with depression, sarcasm, despair, and futility, we need stubborn positive attitudes. We need to communicate our own angry feelings in an

effective way. Unexpressed anger can be like a psychological cancer within our personality.

9. Self–Appreciation
We need to reflect on what gifts God has given to us each day and to be grateful for them. Thank the Lord at all times, in good times and in bad. By doing this we set the stage for solid self–esteem and a sensitivity to ourselves, which enables us to best nurture and share our talents with others. To really appreciate ourselves we must have some reasonable level of self-awareness. Anything that can increase such a level: discussions with friends, reflective reading of books on psychology and spirituality, spiritual direction and counseling, is recommended.

10. Be interested in being faithful not Successful
Our success is often intangible and difficult to measure. Moreover, even in those areas that are measurable, we may not be able to see the impact we have had. Be satisfied with your faithfulness even if things don't measure up to others' standards of success.

Burnout Predictors
Behaviorists generally associate the following characteristics with burnout:

1. Obsession with Outside Forces
Individuals who tend to blame others for their burnout do not generally move toward constructive resolutions of their difficulties. They believe that karma (fate), luck and chance play a vital role in their lives if not actually control their lives. They fail to see a relationship between their behavior and work satisfaction, success in their relationships and happiness. They wait with passive resignation for things to happen. Their self-help remedies rely on inactivity, indecisiveness, and giving up. Such individuals are highly burnout-prone in stressful environments and seldom learn from experience.

2. Need for Complete Control
Some people have a compulsive need to control all aspects of their lives and to eliminate all elements of chance. These individuals

seldom achieve a sense of fulfillment. They alienate others by their lack of flexibility and their unbending need to direct. They organize work in such compulsively rigid ways that it rules out unexpected joy or fun. Not only prone to burnout, they also repeat behavior that leads to burnout.

3. Fear of Change
People who fear change tend to choose the safe, predictable and easily understandable. They fear to experience life in its fullness so they reject newness and risk. They continue to operate for indefinite periods of time bearing situations rather than to make changes.

End Notes

1. Gill, j. (1980). " Burnout: A Growing Threat in the Ministry, Human Development, 1 (2), summer, 21- 27.

Wicks, R. (1992). Touching the Holy: Ordinariness, Self-Esteem Notre Dame: Ave Maria press.

_____ (1991). Seeking perspective. Mahwah NJ: Paulist Press.

_____(1990). Self-Ministry through Self-Understanding Chicago: Loyola University Press.

THE CHEERFUL GIVER

"When you give a dinner or a banquet, do not invite your friends or your brothers or your relatives or rich neighbours, lest they also invite you in return and you be repaid. But when you give a feast, invite the poor, the maimed, the lame, the blind, and you will be blessed, because they cannot repay you.   (Lk. 14:12-14)

As it is written, 'He who gathered much had nothing over, and he who gathered little had no lack'... God is able to provide you with every blessing in abundance, so that you may always have enough of everything and may provide in abundance for every good work"
(2 Cor. 8:9ff)

Always giving thanks to God the Father for everything, in the name of our Lord Jesus Christ.   (Eph. 5:20)

Give thanks in all circumstances, for this is God's will for you in Christ Jesus.   (1 Thess. 5:18)

There is a grand flow of energy in the universe. The flow consists the giving and receiving. Gratitude could be expressed indeed in words. While deeds are more authentic, expressing our gratitude in words has its place too. We are obliged to resort to words. Besides we may have to wait a long time to show our gratitude in action. Why deprive ourselves and others of the joy of giving and receiving gratitude.

Three Attitudes
As Robert Rodenmayer says, there are three attitudes toward giving:

> *Grudge giving,*
> *Duty giving,*
> *And thanksgiving,*
> *Grudge giving says, I hate to,*

Duty giving says, I ought to,
Thanksgiving says, I want to.

Do Not Expect Gratitude

Those to whom we do favours will do well to be grateful for their own spiritual and human growth; we who do these favours should not expect any gratitude or reward. As Jesus puts it so strongly:

> *I tell you the truth; they have received their reward in full. But when you give to the needy, do not let your left hand know what your right hand is doing, so that your giving may be in secret. Then your Father, who sees what is done in secret, will reward you* (Mt. 6:1-4)

In the scene about the last judgment, the good people do not know that they were doing anything special or that they were doing a service to the Lord. They did not look for a reward. Hence their surprise is that the Lord rewards them.

> *When did we see you a stranger and invite you in, or needing clothes and clothe you? The King will reply, 'I tell you the truth, whatever you did for one of the least of these brothers of mine, you did for me.* (Mt. 25:37-40)

The magnificent obsession should be that we keep secret when we give. We must not expect to receive from those whom we have helped. Expect your gifts and graces from higher, the giver of all gifts.

Fr. Zucol, an Italian Jesuit, built over 1500 houses for the poor people. Once when he organized a reception for some of his benefactors in a colony of about a hundred houses that he had just completed and distributed, only about thirty families cooperated and attended the reception. To a younger Jesuit who asked him, if he did not feel pained, he replied, "Not really. I built those houses because people needed them and because I had the resources. The important thing is that they have roofs over their heads and not that they are grateful to me." With such an attitude one cannot get disappointed or become resentful. Dag Hammarskjold, the first Secretary General of the UN wrote in his journal:

> *Hallowed be thy name, not mine, Thy Kingdom come, not mine, Thy will be done, not mine.*

We need to cultivate the attitude of serving because people need service and not in order to get a reward. Any reward or salary we get should be considered a bonus. The poor are your strength and fortress.

We Need to Serve Cheerfully
As St. Paul says, "Each one must do as he has made up his mind, not reluctantly or under compulsion; for God loves a cheerful giver" (2 Cor. 9:7). Work done in love becomes lighter. As St. Augustine says, "There is no labor where there is love; even if there is hardship, that hardship itself is loved." As Victor Frankl has put it, the ultimate freedom we humans have is to choose the attitude we want to have. Living joyfully and serving cheerfully makes us gospel people, people who believe in and live the good news. According to Carlo Carretto, one is a hypocrite if one is sad while doing good.

Paul Meyer in hours of thoughtful solitude reads several books and listens to 20 cassettes a month. He treats his yardman and maid with the same respect he treats the president of the United States. The more he gives, the more God entrusts to him. It follows that anyone who gives freely earns lavish applause. Self-sacrifice is accounted noble. "Shall I give to the Lord that which cost me nothing?" asked David in the Old Testament. David, "the man after God's own heart," gave unstintingly.

Giving Time and Energy
The Bible tells us: "He who sows sparingly will also reap sparingly and he who sows bountifully will also reap bountifully. Plant barley, you get barley. Plant grass, you get grass. "Whatever a man sows, that he will also reap" (Galatians 6:7; 1Corinthians 6:9).

> *Bring all the tithes into the storehouse, that there may be food in my house, and prove me now in this if I will not open, for you the windows of heaven and pour out for you such blessing that there will not be room enough to receive it*
> *(Malachi 3:10).*

> *Give, and it will be given to you; good measure, pressed down, shaken together and running over will be put into your bosom. For with the same measure that you use, it will be measured back to you.* *(Luke 6:38).*

The Resourceful Giver

Information, then, is itself a valuable resource. What we know to a large extent determines what kind of job we can do and how much money we make. The information you gain from a contact may be of far greater use to you than the time and energy you invest in befriending him. You may get a better-kept backyard by employing a professional gardener (exchanging money for time and energy) than by going out every Saturday afternoon and doffing the grower beds yourself.

Networking can achieve great results humanitarian, political, business, educational, professional and even spiritual. True, out of a network can come lasting friendships, but that's not the purpose of the network. A net-worker need not invest compassion, heart, soul, and unlimited time. He or she need feel no personal responsibility for other individuals in the network. The network does not invest in the relationships; he merely uses them. The real art lies in exchanging your resources skillfully enough to maximize them to multiply and deepen your relationships, to add constantly to your knowledge and expertise, to eliminate unnecessary activities.

The Giver who Dreams big

But to derive the full benefits from giving, you need a strong sense of purpose. You need to know why you're giving. You need to begin with the dream. You should treat your dream with respect. In saying, "I have a dream," as Martin Luther King once did, you do not necessarily name an unattainable wish: you turn a wish into a direction, a dream into a plan. Nehemiah turned his dream into a plan when he turned his sorrow over the destruction of Jerusalem into a positive agenda to restore the city walls. Making that transition isn't easy. Dream planning resembles sailing. Good seamanship doesn't constantly take new bearings, the uncontrollable factors the winds and currents will force you off course.

The People-Centered Giver

Get into the self-improvement business to help people use more of their God-given potential. Wealth is the sum of what you have spent on yourself and what you have given away after you have provided prudently though not lavishly for our children. In many instances, people have not spent enough on themselves. In more instances, they have not given away enough. Actually, true wealth utilizes money. Never make the mistake of spoiling your giving with condescension.

No Worry

Worry dilutes my strength and diminishes my ability to produce or to be effective. The scripture gives us the best instruction in the following.

> *"Be anxious for nothing, but in everything in prayer and supplication with thanksgiving, let your requests be made known to God; and the peace of God, which surpasses all understanding, will guard your hearts and minds through Christ Jesus".*   *Philippians 4:6-7*

> *"Not that I speak in regard to need, for I have learned in whatever state I am, to be content."*   *Philippians 4:11*

> *Philippians 4:13----"I can do all things through Christ who strengthens me".*

Stewardship

Nothing is mine, including my energy, life, clothes and wealth. Obviously everything belongs to God by right of creation. Out of His love for me, He has let me use some of His riches. The greatest joys and pleasures of my life are giving and sharing. If you give back to Him, He will pour out a blessing that you do not have room enough to hold.

> *Luke 6:38---"Give, and it will be given to you; good measure, pressed down, shaken together, and running over will be put into your bosom. For with the same measure that you use, it will be measured back to you."*

Make it a Fun
George Eastman said, "It is more fun to give money than to will it," Another benefactor, Hugh Roy Cullen, chose to give away 90 percent of his estimated $200 million personal fortune before he died, "so that I may get a selfish pleasure out of spending it." Paul Meyer speaks of his philanthropy as answering a personal "need", and constantly recommends giving as part of his philosophy of the happy life.

Pursue Permanence
Lord Shaftsbury, the tireless campaigner for factory workers' rights in nineteenth-century Britain, once remarked, "When I feel age creeping upon me I am deeply grieved, for I cannot bear to go away and leave the world with so much misery in it". Jesus Christ has altered the source of history more profoundly than any other individual left the world at His death with neither funds nor a definitive text. By contrast, Andrew Carnegie, who liquidated his $250 million business interests in 1901 to devote himself to selecting and supervising objects of philanthropy, soon found his annual income of $12.5 million too large an amount to administer in the time available. It was Carnegie, therefore, who pioneered the solution of creating a series of perpetual trusts for the support of education, scientific research, international peace, and various other causes. D. Rockefeller, Jr. says that giving ought to be entered into in just the same careful way as investing. I must believe that I have the potential to generate a big income and I can afford to give now.

Blessedness
And no doubt Aristotle in his Nicomachean Ethics wasn't the first

to–point out that "The life of money-making is one undertaken under compulsion, and wealth is evidently not the good we are seeking; for it is merely useful and for the sake of something else." "Something else" consists of happiness, fulfillment, peace, or to borrow from the Hebrew shalom. Blessedness is perfect poise and peace, a quality and richness of soul that is unaffected by the wind and wave of adverse circumstance.

Devils of the Apostolate

Our apostolate has to fit into the divine plan must tally with the requirements of the kingdom of God. Let us see some of the common "devils" of the apostolate. In the midst of temptations, the ideal will be revealed to us through contrasts, the way shadow manifests light. The human heart is devious and perverse too.

Messianism
The devil of messianism makes apostles see themselves as the center of all pastoral activities in which they are involved. This temptation subtly penetrates their lives until they feel they are indispensable in everything. Messianism is basically a deficient attitude with respect to God: I am the "pilot" and the Lord is the "co-pilot". Those who fall into this temptation do not stop taking God into account. They do not stop praying to him and going to him during times of problems. But they do so expecting that God will help them in an apostolate, which they themselves direct and plan. In the end, it is incorporating God into their work, not incorporating them into God's work, which is the essence of apostleship: God the "pilot", I the "co-pilot". This attitude to God is shown in an equally deficient attitude towards others who work with us. We become incapable of delegating responsibilities or tasks. We do not have real trust in people around us for the long term. Often, messianic apostles identify themselves with their work to the point that when they leave the scene, or are transferred, the work ends.

Activism
While it is true that humanly speaking, we normally accept the difference between "being" and "living'" there is a sharp gap in this particular case. Activism is expressed in many ways. One is the lack of renewal in the personal lives of apostles. Prayer becomes systematically insufficient and deficient. There is no time for prolonged solitude and rest. Nor is there studying done or any reading accomplished. There is increase in activity without efforts for inner renewal, which leads to the growth in "being". In the final analysis, activism is the excuse

for "escapism". In the process one forgets God, who, in the end, is the one for whom those things are done, planned and carried out.

Not working according to God's pace but to one's own pace is another manifestation of the devil of activism. This can happen by going faster or slower than God. At least during the initial moments the activist usually sins by going too fast. People do not follow the desired pace because their growth follows God's pace and not anyone's vision. People need to wait and be patient, without setting aside studying, developing themselves. Self-sufficiency forgets that "neither he who plants nor he who waters is anything, but it is God who makes the plant grow".

(1 Cor 3:7).

Making God only as a Resource
The temptation here is putting trust in God only as a resource in time of need and for serious and emergency cases, and forgetting him in the ordinary, day-to-day events of the apostolate. By not trusting in God with all our heart, we put our trust in ourselves even though we tell ourselves the contrary. Ironically, true trust in the God of apostolate gives apostles the psychological confidence, which compensates for their evident human limitations. We have known intelligent and well-prepared multi-talented preachers who wielded great magnetism and influence but probably because of their gifts, they have put their apostolic trust in themselves more than in God. "I am with you always until the end of this world" (Mt 28:20).

Diminishing Hope
This devil secularizes the announcing of Christian hope. Christian hope is based on Christ's promises. These promises are the resurrection, eternal life, as well as the certainty of his love and of his grace in this life, which makes it possible for people to be holy in the situation. The temptation in this case is to transmit a message of human hopes, not the fundamental Christian hope. They may also promise success in the liberation people seek today. But although these human hopes are legitimate, and are worth working for, they are not guaranteed on this earth by Christ's promises. To reduce hope is to negate the

announcement of people's vocation to eternal life, to sanctity, to faith, and to love as the prime movers and supreme value of human liberations. We usually mouth empty slogans, quick fix solutions and success ideas. This will only make the apostolate an inspiration to human hopes, to endeavors for a better world, and to good things. But the essence of Christianity, which is the proclamation of Christ as the true hope of human beings, should not be reduced.

Losing Contact with People
This devil turns apostles into pastoral executives. Apostles get absorbed in administrative and organizational matter, in planning and supervision to the extent that they no longer have time, and above all, psychological space, for people they work with. Consequently they are not able to give them the needed time to be close to them. The devil of the depersonalized apostles creates dedicated apostles but their dedication is more to their work and service. In their absorption they forget the people they serve and for whom are the organizations and programs. This temptation can take on many forms. In effect, apostles who become "pastoral executive" can tend to give too much importance to plans, programs and strategies to the extent that they forget the reality of people who are to carry them all out.

Partiality towards People
The temptation of the apostles is usually to take sides not usually manifested in the partiality and discrimination towards people resulting from serious prejudices such as racism, class division, nationalism, different treatments to the rich and to the poor, etc. For the members of the Christian community who have more human gifts, who are more intelligent, more interesting, and more attractive people, their tendency is to subtly set aside those who are less gifted, who are less clean physically and less attractive, who are less intelligent and who are less interesting. This is the most common form of the partiality towards people in the apostolate. The more subtle, deep and widespread it is, the more it is unperceived.

In the apostolate, the love for the poor should not be limited only on the sociological level, which is always considered the essential level. It should also reach out to those "poor" in human gifts, those who are psychologically discriminated upon in terms of attention and acceptance. The apostolate should not be guided by the lone criterion of effectiveness preferring to invest on the more gifted ones and those with leadership potentials. It should also be a witness to the primacy of fraternal love, which is preferably shown to the scorned and to the forgotten.

Sectarianism

The devil of sectarianism leads apostles to limit themselves to their world of work, to their ideas, to their group. Sectarianism has personal and group manifestations. At the personal level, one of the most typical manifestations is isolation. Apostles work on their own, without being a part of a group mission. They do not attend meetings, renewal and training sessions for this purpose. They are not interested in submitting themselves to community standards and plans, or to call for evolution and review. Neither do they relate with other apostles. As a consequence, "sectarian" apostles separate their work from that of the rest. They do "their thing" and have "their people", their own experience and their vision of the apostolate. Anything that is different from their vision and experience is questionable to them.

Enclosing Oneself within One's Experience

Every one sticks to the opinion gained during the mature period of one's life. If one's experience regarding one thing is good, one thinks that will work in every case. Therefore, what did not happen at a certain time with certain people and with a certain set of circumstances does not mean that it cannot happen with different protagonists and circumstances. Wisdom on the other hand, is not letting oneself be conditioned by failures nor by the harsh results of past experiences. It is gained by being open to try other forms of apostolate and opening oneself to the experience of others.

Hoping for Benefits in the Apostolate

The temptation is to keep looking at the apostolate as an ecclesiastical career and to view its deep importance and effectiveness from the position one holds. The devil of the earthly gratifications can offer temptation in many ways. The most vulgar one is when the apostolate is linked to the earning of money, making the apostolate a lucrative profession, being more generous and idealist than others. When this temptation worsens, the apostolate takes on the appearance of a business. This tendency can lead to disinterest for non-paid apostolic tasks. One can lose the sense of free service and evangelization. A more subtle temptation is waiting for recognition and even praises from people and from church hierarchy. Those who fall into this temptation end up needing this kind of human gratification to keep their enthusiasm and spirit high. Similarly, when there is criticism from people the apostles work with, or from the church hierarchy apostles feel rejected and persecuted.

Probably the subtlest devil appears in the desire for position and responsibilities, in thinking that all changes in the apostolate means a promotion. There is a latent hope for "Promotions". All dissent and legitimate opposition to authority are avoided-which in certain moments can be a duty in the apostolate-not so much out of loyalty but out of interests in ingratiating oneself and appearing to have an unquestioning attitude towards authority.

Complacency
The devil of complacency usually happens, but not always, with the passage of time and with the onset of maturity, but they do not want to change and be renewed. They let the younger ones work with them but they do not allow themselves to be questioned. Even if it may not be really serious it curtails spiritual dynamism. They simply say, "This is what I am..." After a certain age, this devil leads to thinking that one has the right to seek compensations and be comfortable. Apostles thus end up getting contented with minimum requirements.

Pastoral Envy
The devil of envy is not a stranger to the apostolate. Its effect on apostles obviously is not as devastating as in politics, arts or in other activities of the "world". Envy within the church is much less grave but subtler. All noble apostles are put down by remarks, jokes, etc. Cynicism is the subtlest expression of envy. It is its best mixing agent. The devil moves among theologians. Not all conflicts or theological

disputes among theologians are inspired by their search for the truth; there are usually personal matters involved.

Losing One's Sense of Humor

This devil tends to dramatize and victimize. Sense of humor in this case is looking at the good side of things, which appears to be negative. It is learning to see things as relative phenomena, to look at situations, which affect us with a "from-the-outside" point of view. Sense of humor also helps attain level-headedness. It stops one from dramatizing and taking things in a tragic manner. Sense of humor is not taking oneself too seriously, nor one's titles, nor one's problems, nor pastoral and ecclesiastical conflicts. It is laughing healthily at oneself, at situations and at the people involved. The devil which takes away or suppresses a sense of humor, slowly leads apostles to automatic criticism and bitterness. Schisms, heresies, dissents, divisions, insoluble conflicts and lack of dialogue and communion are the attitudes of people who usually have lost their sense of humor because they give much importance to themselves and to their ideas. Without a sense of humor, any contradiction, reprobation or questioning coming from the church becomes a drama, a persecution. Thus, apostles without a sense of humor become easily vulnerable and fragile. In the ultimate analysis, sense of humor forms part of Christian strength. It certainly facilitates it.

It's a Matter of Love

In Robert Bolt's play about St. Thomas More, *A Man for All Seasons*, St. Thomas More insists about "a matter of love". It was spoken by a man who was about to be condemned to death for refusing to take the oath supporting the King's divorce. All his friends begged Thomas More to be reasonable, to make compromises, to do what everyone else was doing. Even his wife and daughter begged him to be reasonable and save his neck. But Thomas More answered: "It isn't a matter of reason. It's a matter of love." It sounds very queer, but it is nobler to be true to one's deepest longings and ideals.

To Touch, Help and Heal
Love is two solitudes reaching out to each other-to touch, to help, to heal. My loneliness will no longer be loneliness if I reach out to touch, to help, to heal. The three verbs give us the three stages of love as well as the three reasons for unselfishness and the communication that love represents.

How to Be Real
The Velveteen Rabbit was written in England by Margery Williams, with illustrations by William Nicholson. It was subtitled "How to become real." The most well known part of the book is the passage where the Velveteen Rabbit asks the Skinhorse, "What is real?" The Skinhorse tells the Rabbit that the only way to become real is to be loved. Real doesn't mean that you make a lot of noise, that you are always calling attention to yourself, that you have to be in charge of things. In fact, the most real persons are often the quietest ones, because they are the ones who are most loved. Being real isn't what you do; it isn't what you accomplish. It is what happens to you. Being real doesn't necessarily mean loving. It means being loved, though, of course, no one is going to be loved if he isn't a good lover himself. The philosophy of the Skinhorse shifts the emphasis from loving to being loved. That means you have to become a loveable person yourself. Being real, therefore, is all about being loveable. "You become real", the Skinhorse told the Rabbit, "when a child loves you for a long, long time, not just to play with, but really loves you."

Breakability
The best toys, the most loveable toys, are the ones that don't break easily when they get cuddled; they can't hurt you, and they are not expensive. The same is also true of people. People who break easily are not going to be loved, and therefore, they are never going to become real. People who are too sensitive will never last long enough in a relationship to be loved. That's also true of people with sharp edges: the critical people, the cynical ones, and the ones who are always complaining. People who have to be handled with care, people who are spoiled, are not going to become real, because it is awfully hard to love someone who always has to have his own way. Nobody is going to love you unless you are a loveable person.

Being Loved Off
The Skinhorse says: "By the time you are real, most of your hair has been loved off and your eyes drop out and you get loose in the joints and very shabby. But these things really don't matter at all, because when you are real, when you are loved, you can't be ugly, except to people who don't understand." There is no love without hurt. There is no being real without pain. So most of us never become real because we don't want to be hurt. Lovers give pain to one another. We run away from being loved because it is going to hurt. But the proof that you have become real is that when you are real you don't mind being hurt at all. We don't want to get hurt. We are afraid of the pain. So we end up being unloved because we are afraid.

Recognizing Expressions of Love
There are times when we are timid and shy about expressing the love we feel. For fear of embarrassing the other person, or ourselves, we hesitate to say the actual words "I love you." So we try to communicate the idea in other words. We say "Take care" or "Don't drive too fast" or "Be good." But really, these are just other ways of saying, "I love you. You are important to me. I care what happens to you. I don't want you to get hurt." To express our concern, we say, "I love you". A mother may nag her son constantly about his grades or cleaning his room. The son may hear only the nagging, but if he listens carefully, he will hear the love underneath the nagging. His mother wants him to do well, to be successful. Her concern and love

for her son unfortunately emerges in her nagging. But it is love all the same. A daughter comes home late way past her curfew, and her father confronts her with angry words. The daughter may hear only the anger, but if she listens carefully, she will hear the love under the anger, "I was worried about you," the father is saying. "Because I care about you and I love you. You are important to me".

Sharing Horizons
Khalil Gibran says that marriage is not really two people becoming one. That would mean that one or both of them lose their identity and their individuality. Gibran says that marriage is two people standing next to each other, holding hands and looking in the same direction, "sharing horizons" as the old songs says, although the horizons of each may not exactly coincide. Most people think compatibility means identity. In fact, the Latin root from which the word compatibility comes actually means "to suffer with, to put up with." In fact, it presupposes a lot of differences that you have to suffer with or put up with. Love doesn't mean identity. It means being able to put up with the other's differences, to accept them, to understand them. C. S. Lewis speaks about every man's first friend and every man's second friend. Your first Friend, Lewis says, is very much like you. He is your alter ego, "the person who first reveals to you that you are not alone in the world by turning out (beyond hope) to share all your most secret delights." But if you are lucky, Lewis says, you also have a second friend. He is not like you at all. "The second friend is the person who disagrees with you about almost everything. Of course he shares your interests; otherwise, he would not become your friend at all. But he has approached them all from a different angle". The greatest incompatibility of all is God and Man. How can God possibly love us when He is so different? How can we love Him when we are so full of sin?

Fidelity Is Forever
Love becomes genuine in faithfulness and complete in forgiveness. You should keep your promise forever. Making a promise is like walking through a doorway. Fidelity is the room or the countryside on the other side of the door. It's easy enough to walk through the door, to make a promise in the beginning. But it's often very hard

to find your way around the room on the other side of the door. You can get lost in the land of fidelity. Friendship is a good example of a temporary commitment. Marriage is a permanent commitment. The marriage promise says, "For better, for worse, for richer, for poorer, in sickness and in health, till death do us part." A husband gives his wife everything, and he gives it to her forever. Tell me if a man is faithful in his marriage and I'll know what kind of a man he is. He has not only gone through the door of the marriage ceremony. He also knows how to live in the room beyond the promises of marriage: one body, one mind, and one heart forever.

Leo Buscaglia in *Loving Each Other: The Challenge of Human Relationships* speaks about love, tenderness, compassion, caring, sharing and relating-the most vital forms of human behaviour. On the title page, Buscaglia quotes Luciano de Crescenzo: "We are each of us angels with only one wing. And we can only fly embracing each other." Buscaglia defines a loving relationship as "the dynamic and ever-changing nature of two unique and whole individuals agreeing to emerge and blend in long term commitment." He says "we are not evil, we are inadequate or incompetent when our relationship fails. The poet W.H. Auden says: "We must love each other, or die." Jesus says: "These things I command you, that you love one another." We're all angels. But we need one another to help us fly.

The Ten Commandments of love
These Commandments of Love can be of immense help to all of us in our love relationships.

1. **Take your time**. The creation of anything worthwhile takes patience and energy. You don't build a relationship overnight.
2. **Don't smother each other**. Oak trees don't grow in one another's shade. Don't feel as if you are required to spend every waking hour with those you love. Move aside from time to time and allow them a separate space, too. Never force anyone to do anything for you "in the name of love". Let there be spaces where we can breathe. As Khalil Gibran

says, the pillars of the temple are far apart. If they are strong enough, then we can put a roof over it and make a house. .
3. **Exercise Intimacy.** Feelings have meaning only as they are expressed in action. Increase tenderness and intimacy. They are a powerful source of nourishment for relationships.
4. **Grow constantly.** Forming a relationship takes a lot of looking. But looking can be fun. Grow up together constantly.
5. **Don't be afraid.** Stop all worry. Most of what you are worried about you'll have difficulty remembering a week later. See problems as small miracles, which can bring about knowledge and change.
6. **Don't lose touch with the craziness in you.** Face the rottenness in your soul and face the ugly dragons and salamanders of the heart. Keep the child in you alive. Keep laughing. It exercises your heart and protects you from cardiac problems.
7. **Don't be afraid of disagreements and arguments**. The only people who do not argue are people who don't care-or are dead. In fact, don't have short arguments. Make certain they are thoroughly over and done with. After an argument is over, forget it. Learn to bend. It's better than breaking. Watch out for little irritations. They grow into destructive monsters. Verbalize them at once.
8. **Stop playing games**. A growing relationship can only be nurtured by genuineness. Relationships are not sporting events.
9. **Learn to listen.** You don't learn anything by hearing yourself talk. See all criticism as positive, for it leads to self-evaluation. You are always free to reject, it if it is unfair or does not apply. If you take time to talk together each day, you'll never become strangers. Just Listen! When I ask you to listen to me and you start giving me a lot of advice. May be when I am speaking you are preparing what to say next. When I ask you to please listen to me and you are upset, you are really not paying attention to me. When I ask you to listen to me, and you feel that you have to do something right away to solve

my problem, you have failed me, strange as that may seem. Listen! All I ask you to do is listen, not talk or do anything to help me. I just need someone to listen to me for a while, while I straighten out the confusion in my mind. When you do something for me that I really ought to do for myself, you are only adding to my insecurity and my fear and my inadequacy. And when I talk and you just listen, the answers become clearer for me, my irrational feelings begin to make sense, and I begin to understand what is behind them all. So, please, just listen to me for a while, and then if you want to talk, I'll listen to you."

10. **Affection is non Judgmental** When you criticize me, I feel I am nothing before you. King Lear wanted his daughters to say, "I love you more than anything else in the world" We all need someone to tell us that we're fabulous. We need someone to give us a smile, a pat on the back, a hug. We need the physical manifestations of love and the acceptance that come with affection. We don't like pretence or criticism. If you want to learn how to love, start with affection-the humble, familiar, non-judgmental acceptance of the other person as he is. Put all that into the physical signs of affection. Maybe it isn't as high as the sky, or as deep as the ocean, but it is a very comfortable place to be.

The Three Doors of Love

As John Donne says, sometimes God has to batter our hearts before we reach out in love to others. Growth in love demands that we be ready to walk through the three doors of Love. We can measure how well we love and how much we love by the door at which stand.

The first door is the door of emptiness. Unless we become empty and alone we cannot love, for without emptiness we do not possess the deep self, which is the only gift worthy of love. If our life is cluttered with attachments and selfish emotions and needs, we cannot grab hold of the real self and share it with someone else. And if we do not give the real self, then we are not giving love at all. We are giving presents or tokens, but not love. Children know that they are really loved because we do not give them merely material things. We also give them our time; we give them ourselves. Material things can get in the way of love. If we really want to love, we have to empty ourselves of possessions and give the real self. We have to walk through the door of emptiness.

The second Door of Love is the Door without a sign. Very often when we walk through the door of love, we do not know what lies ahead. It is a door without a sign. It doesn't tell us where we will be ten years from now. All we know is that ten years from now we will still love, for richer, for poorer, in sickness or in health. We really do not know what lies ahead. But at this moment we promise love in the years to come, no matter what lies beyond the door without a sign.

The third door of Love, and the highest degree of love, is the door without a wish. Not to know what is ahead is a great challenge to the promise of love. But to want whatever lies ahead, to leave behind our own dreams and our own hopes of love, to wish whatever lies ahead, even if we may not want it, is the greatest challenge of all. "Que sera, sera. Whatever will be, will be." Married couples tell us that the greatest challenge of love, and the highest degree of love, is the door without a wish. How hard it is to desire not what we want in our selfishness or pride, but to want whatever love demands. It is the greatest act of love because it is total surrender. The most beautiful part of love is that there is always another door. It is a frightening thing to go through the door of emptiness, the door without a sign, and the door without a wish. Love drives out fear. We can march boldly through the doors of the unknown because we are truly in love.

The Qualities of Love
St. Augustine, in one of his sermons, said: "I really don't know what love is. All I know is that God is Love". Erich Fromm in his book, *The Art of Loving*, says that it is impossible to define love, but we can list down a number of qualities of love to help us understand ourselves better. This checklist can help us evaluate our own sense of loving. Erich Fromm suggests four qualities of good loving.

First, he says, love is **caring.** When we care, we are loving. But Fromm uses the word in its technical sense. To care, he says, is to be supremely concerned with what is good for the other person. When you care for a person, you always do what is good for the person. If you feel that the other person's life is as important as yours then you truly love. You don't always do what the other person wants. The mother cannot say "Yes" when the baby wants to play with a knife. Parents who spoil their children don't always love them. God loves us because He cares for us. He doesn't always give us what we want, but He gives us only what is good for us.

Second, love, Fromm says, is also **"respond-ability**," the ability to respond to the other person's needs. It means to think of the other and not only of ourselves. Marriages begin to fall apart when husband and wife no longer respond to each other. Martin Buber has a definition of love which underlines this essential element of responsibility. "Love," Buber says, "is the response of an 'I' to a 'Thou'". The personal pronouns and the use of the more personal form "Thou" for the second person pronouns emphasize the personal and intimate nature of love.

Third, love means **respect**. Fromm again uses the word in a technical sense based on its Latin root which mean "to see," or "to look at." In our use of the word, respect often means, "to look up to," but Fromm uses it to mean, "to look at." This means to really see the person we love with reverence. Romanticism and emotion make it hard to look at a person and really see him. First impressions are so deceptive. We look at a person and we "fall in love." But it is often no more than a crush or an infatuation. When, after a time, we begin to really see him for what he really is, the infatuation disappears. You don't fall in love with a pretty face. You fall in love with a person.

Commitment is at the core of the mystery that every person is. Commitment comes from a Latin word meaning "to bring, join or to combine into one whole; to join or put together, to connect or to unite." Commitment means we have to find the person or the thing that will make us whole. First, always keep your promises, especially the little ones. 'The Little Prince' in Antoine de St. Exupery's story says, it is very important to keep your promises. A promise links the present and the future. It assures me that you love me today, but that you will also love me tomorrow. The commitment of marriage is built on a promise: you will love me tomorrow, for better, for worse, for richer, for poorer, and everything else in between. One is reminded of an old Chinese proverb that has often been quoted: "In order to be happy, you have to have a job to do, someone to love and a dream to hang on to." The secret of happiness is that we have to go outside of ourselves. We have to find something bigger than we are. Confucius always emphasized the importance of making our actions beautiful. Yet it takes great love to make an action beautiful the dominant motive of every action must be love and any other motive will soil it.

Reconciliation: Celebrating Forgiveness

The sacrament of reconciliation also called the sacrament of penance celebrates the unfailing forgiveness that God extends to us. In his public ministry, Jesus communicated that forgiveness of God over and over to those who approached him with sincere faith: "Your sins are forgiven." The sacrament of reconciliation also provides a way for us to heal our spirit by telling the story of our own brokenness and failings.

Once there was a man from Iceland, a great poet and storyteller named Ivar. He won fame for his storytelling in the court of Istine the king of Norway. Ivar and his brother lived in the court of the King. One day, Ivar's brother decided to return to his native Iceland. Before Thorfin left, however, Ivor asked him to bear a message to Adney a young woman whom Ivar had loved and who had loved him since childhood. Ivar asked his brother to tell Adney that he would return in the spring to marry her. When Thorfin arrived in Iceland, he himself fell in love with Adney and she with him. And so they married. Thus, when spring came and Ivar arrived in Iceland to marry Adney, he was heart-broken. Filled with sadness and bitterness, he returned to the court of King Istine in Norway.

Everyone at the court noticed a change in Ivar especially the king noticed and bitterness cast a cold shadow over the entire court. The king guessing the problem might concern a woman asked, "Is there a woman, Ivor, someone back home, perhaps? Ivor finally nodded yes. The King said I shall take you to the your countryside and you can find any woman you like best to satisfy your deepest longings. Ivor shook his head " No my lord, for every time I see a beautiful woman I am reminded of Adney, and my grief is deepened. "The king said I will give you land and estates which will keep you preoccupied and busy. But Ivar said, "No Lord, I have no wish, no desire, and no ability to do such work".

The king offered money to travel wherever his heart desired to go, to the farthest corner of Europe. Once again Ivar refused, saying he had no desire, no wish and no ability to travel anywhere. The king offered to give time everyday after supper to listen to the story of his love for his woman Adney. You may do as long as you need. Ivor told his story for days and even months. And at the close of the meeting, the king gave Ivor a small but meaningful gift. In this process Ivar found that his old joy returned to him, and once again Ivar began to sing. In the following year he met a young woman with whom he fell in love. Ivor was once again a happy man, but he was now also a wiser person. Thus Ivor soon gained even greater fame as a storyteller whose tales had wise and happy endings. Ivor needed to forgive Thorfin and Adney for the pain they had caused him, even though they had not intended to hurt him by failing in love. Istine gave Ivor the chance to lay his burden down.

Telling Our Stories: Passing the Hurt

Life can present heavy burdens and we may react in ways that add to life's burdens. Acknowledging and then examining our own human weaknesses is one step in laying our burdens down. Sometimes our response to the hurt in our life is to pass it on to others, causing even further hurt. Sins often result from carrying around a legacy of hurt that we refuse to lay down.

Healing: Bringing the Darkness into the Light

We all have our dark side--weaknesses that cause us to do things we would rather not do or things we know we should not do. All of us are in need of healing. The story of Ivor points to the truth that our healing comes from bringing our dark side into the light. Maturity is marked by the ability to admit that we have a dark side, and by the determination to bring that dark side into the light. The best friend is someone with whom we can be ourselves and even make mistakes without fear of embarrassment or rejection.

Confession as a Ritual of telling our Stories
In the sacrament of reconciliation, the sharing that happens in everyday life, the sharing of one's weakness and woundedness, is ritualized in a process called confession. In confession, the priest listens and offers acceptance, guidance, and forgiveness on their behalf.

Turning Around
Recall that in the story, the younger son turns his back on his parents, taking his inheritance and going off to spend it in reckless living. But when his money runs out, he is left with feeding pigs, his only means of survival. We know that the father in the story welcomes his son back with open arms, so delighted is he that the young man has returned. He throws a big party for his son, insisting that he be treated specially. The point of the story is to demonstrate God's unconditional, all embracing forgiveness of those who wander away, but note how the young man opened himself to experiencing forgiveness. In a journey that was both spiritual and physical, he came to his sense, acknowledged his mistakes, made a turn around and travelled back to his parents' home in order to make things right.

The Ripple Effects of our Actions
The pain we cause by our wrongdoing goes beyond those whom we have hurt directly. We also add to the climate of negative expectations. Creating more barriers for everyone to overcome more tension, mistrust, and hostility. We damage our ability to live freely and fully. Just as a pebble tossed into a pond disturbs the entire pool of water, so our actions both for good have far-reaching effects.

> *A wealthy merchant happened to share a compartment on a train with a poorly dressed old man whom he treated rudely and disdainfully when they arrived at their common destination, the merchant saw in the railroad station a throng of people waiting in ecstatic joy to greet the arrival of one of the*

> *holiest rabbis in all of Europe. The merchant then discovered that the old man who had traveled in the compartment with him was himself (the great rabbi.) Embarrassed at his own disgraceful behavior and distraught that he had missed a golden opportunity to speak privately with a wise and holy man, the merchant pushed his way through the crowd to the old man, when he reached him, he begged the rabbi's forgiveness and requested his blessing. The old rabbi looked at him and replied," I cannot forgive you. To receive forgiveness, you must go out and beg it from every poor old person, in the world* [1]

When we sin, we need to ask forgiveness not just from the person or persons we have harmed directly but, in a sense, the whole community. The whole world is worse off because of our sin.

A Tale of Forgiveness: Al and Adele

On the outskirts of a quiet village housing a few small businesses and shops stands a farm with freshly painted buildings. Al owned a farm there. Al is a proud, honest man of few words. Tall, slim, with a pointed chin and aquiline nose, he is as much feared as respected by the locals.

Adele, his wife, always has a warm smile and welcoming words. People feel good in her presence. Adele suffers silently, enduring a husband who is miserly, both with words and caresses. Deep down, she regrets having married this "hard-working man" whom her now-deceased father so admired. Certainly, Al provides well for her and is faithful, but his total absorption in his work leaves little time for intimacy and pleasure.

One day, instead of working until dusk, Al comes home early. To his great dismay, he finds Adele in bed with a neighbor. The man flees though the window, while Adele, distraught, throws herself at Al's feet to beg his forgiveness. He remains unmoved, face white with indignation, lips blue with rage. As he faces this betrayal, his feelings range from humiliation through deep pain to anger. Soon he realizes, showever, that the silent treatment he is inflicting on Adele tortures her far more than any words or acts of violence.

No one really knows how the story of Adele spread through the village, but the gossip mill is in full swing. Everyone expects that Al will ask for a separation. But Al beats the gossips at their game. He appears, head held high, at Sunday Mass, with Adele at his heels. In true Christian style, he appears to have understood the words of the Our Father: "Forgive us our trespasses as we forgive those who trespass against us." But the forgiveness on which Al prides himself secretly feeds on Adele's humiliation.

At home, Al continues with silence and furtive, disdainful glances at the sinner. Yet, in heaven, this virtuous posturing fools no one. An angel is sent out to redress the situation. Each time Al casts his harsh and somber gaze on Adele, the angel drops a stone the size of a button on his heart. Each time, Al feels the tinge, his face contorting with pain. One day, while Al is swathing his wheat, he notices a radiant personage leaning against the fence, and hears him say: "Al, you seem rather overburdened." Surprised to hear his name on the lips of a stranger, Al, asks who he is and how this is any of his business. The angel answers: "I know your wife cheated on you and that the humiliation is torturing you. But the subtle revenge you are inflicting on her is depressing you." Knowing that he has been found out, Al lowers his head and admits: "I can't chase this miserable thought from my mind: how could she have betrayed me – me, such a faithful and generous husband: She's nothing but a slut; she has defiled our bed!" At these words, Al grimaces in pain. The angel offers to help him but Al is convinced that no one can relieve him of his burden. "As powerful as you may be, stranger, you will never be able to erase what has happened."

"You're right, Al. No one can change the past, but you have the power, at this moment, to see it differently. Recognize your hurt, accept you anger and humiliation. Remember how indifferent you were towards her. Put yourself in her shoes". Al does not really understand, but he trusts the angel. He asks his visitor how to change his outlook. The angel instructs him as follows: "Before you look at Adele, smooth out the wrinkles on your forehead, around your mouth and the other muscles in your face. Instead of seeing Adele as a mean woman, look at the wife who needed tenderness; remember how coolly and harshly you treated her; remember her generosity and her warmth that experienced at the beginning of your relationship. Each time you look at her with these new eyes, I will remove a stone from your heart." Al accepts the deal but not without protesting that he feels awkward. Little by little, slowly and with great effort, he works at

seeing Adele though new eyes. Little by little, the pain in his heart eases. Adele seems to change before him: from the unfaithful wife, she becomes the gentle and loving person he had known when he first fell in love. Adele feels the change. Relieved, she regains her high spirits and her smile. Al, in turn, feels completely different. He lets his heart, still battered by the burden it had carried, be filled with a profound tenderness. The new emotion that overcomes him still scares him. But, one night, he takes Adele into his arms. The miracle of forgiveness has just taken place.

Forgiven by God and the whole Community

Although God can forgive us whenever, it's our humanness that demands visible, audible, tangible signs. We need a time and space when we can put our sin behind us and know that God "remembers not the sins of the past". The sacrament of reconciliation provides for our need to be forgiven, not only at the one-to-one level but also at the community level. Reconciliation highlights its community focus. If sin can be understood as things or actions that break a community apart, then reconciliation can be understood as the processes or actions that rebuild community. In the sacrament of reconciliation, community members come together to admit their weakness and celebrate their return to God and one another.

> *I will give them a new heart and put a new spirit within them; I will remove the heart of stone from their flesh and give them a heart of flesh, so that they may follow my statutes and keep my ordinances and obey them. Then they shall be my people, and I be their God*
> *(Ezekiel 11; 19-20)*

An Examination of Conscience
Relationship with God

- Have I developed ways to make God's presence active in my life?
- Do I take time for God by participating in Sunday Eucharist, for setting aside moments to pray or read the scriptures?
- Do I bring Jesus' perspective to bear on my decisions

about my relationships with others, my use of money and other materials, and my view of myself?
- Do I speak of God and my faith with reverence?

Relationship with Others

- Do I love and respect my parents and other family members and try to resolve my differences with them peacefully.
- Do I treat other people with respect, not with abuse, prejudice, or manipulation?
- Do I share what I have with those in need and reach out to suffering persons with support?
- Am I truthful, fair and genuine in my dealings and with others?
- Do I work honestly at my job or studies?
- Have I hurt others' reputation by speaking falsely about them or spreading gossip?
- Have I honored the sacredness of sexuality by not using another person sexually and by reserving full sexual expression for marriage?
- Am I a faithful friend? Do I waste resources?

Relationship with Self

Do I try to develop myself as a person, making full use of my strengths and talents?

- Do I explore my own motivations and attitudes about things to become more honest with myself?
- Do I let fear stand in the way of doing what I think is right?
- Do I take care of my health as well, exercise, and get enough rest and relaxation?
- Am I respectful of my own sexuality?
- Do I seek the help of other wiser persons when emotions or problems are causing me a lot of distress?

End Notes

1. "Adapted from Cavenaugh, The Sower's Seeds, page 2.

The Eagle in You

"But now ask the beasts, and they will teach you; and the birds of the air will tell you."   (Job 12:7)

The eagle is the symbolic of the prophet and thus the sudden great interest and relevance in our ministry. The prophet is a "seer", who sees what others cannot see. The Church without the prophet is blind. The eye of the Eagle is a wonder in itself. The Eagle can look at the sun for long periods and not be blinded. It can fly at a speed of more than a hundred miles an hour and the wind and dust do not damage its eyes. The maturing of the Eagle in many ways parallels the making of a true prophet of God. There is an eagle in all of us and we be willing to pay the price to soar the heights.

The Prophet
The prophet in his day was fully accepted by God and totally rejected by man. In a day of faceless politicians voiceless preachers, there is not a more urgent national need than that we cry to God for a prophet! The prophet is God's detective seeking for lost spiritual treasures. The degree of his effectiveness is determined by the measure of his unpopularity. Compromise is not known to him. He is totally "otherworldly." He is unquestionably controversial and unpardonably hostile. He marches to another drummer! He is a "seer" who comes to lead the blind. He lives in the heights with God and comes into the valley with a "Thus saith the Lord." He lives in "splendid isolation." He is forthright and outright, but he claims no birthright. His message is, "Repent, be reconciled to God or else…! His truth brings torment, but his voice is never void. He is villain of today and the hero of tomorrow. He is excommunicated while alive and exalted when dead! He is friendless while living and famous when dead. He is against the "establishment" in ministry then established as a "saint" by posterity.

Let him be as plain as John the Baptist.
Let him for a season be a voice crying in the wilderness
of modern theology and stagnant churchianity.

Let him be as selfless as Paul the apostle.
Let him say nothing that will draw men to himself,
but only that which will move men to God.
Let him cry with a voice this century has not heard
Because he has seen a vision no man in this century has seen.
God sends us this Moses to lead us from the wilderness of crass materialism,
Where the rattlesnakes of lust bite us and where enlightened men,
Totally blind spiritually, lead us to an ever-nearing Armageddon.

When the Bible refers to an eagle, it is mainly referring to two particular types of eagle found in the Middle East. The first kind is the Imperial Eagle, named because of his kingly lifestyle. The other is called the Golden Eagle because of its divine nature. And this fine bird is golden in colour. The eagles can grow so large to have a wingspan of fourteen to fifteen in feet and an average weight of thirty pounds. Because of its immense size, the eagle has been widely used as a symbol of power, freedom and greatness. It also represents beauty, grace and confidence. The eagle is the king of birds. Here, it is seen to master its surroundings where it soars gracefully and flies above lofty mountains through scorching sun and turbulent storms. The eagle speaks of someone who is the master of his environment and who is in control of his situation. He is someone who has the ability and power to rule and live above his circumstances even in the midst of storms and trials.

Matting Patterns of Eagles
It is interesting to note how eagles fall in love. The two birds begin their courtship way up in the heavens. The female will pick a stick with her talons and fly over the hills and mountains looking for a prospective mate. As soon as she spots a male eagle that she likes, she will drop that stick to where he is. If this female eagle wants to respond to the female, he will then fly into the sky and stretches out his feet to seize the stick. He will glide towards the female eagle and return the stick to her. He then dives down and resumes his place. The female will continue circling the air with that stick and drops it again. The male will see that stick falling and if he is interested in her, he will once again reach out into the sky, catches that stick and

sends it back to her. They will both fly high into the sky and grapple with each other's talons. They will enfold each other and from miles up in the heavens, they will come tumbling down. And just before they hit the ground, they let loose of one another and again soar upwards. This is a picture of how eagles mate. They do not mate on the ground nor up in the trees. They mate in the sky. And their love making, their fulfillment, their flight and joy are abound in heaven and not on earth. Eagles mate for life. A change of mate takes place only at the death of one or the other. They are faithful until death.

The Eagle's Nest Preparation and Lamb Sacrifice

The eagle will always choose a lofty place, usually a tall tree or a steep rock ledge. He does not make a nest on the plains or steppe preferred by the crows. Rather, he chooses mountainous country, away from distractions, noise and away from the crowd. The eagle will soar and find a site that is high, different and distinct and there he will build his nest.

> "Does the eagle mount up at your command, and make its nest on high? On the rock it dwells and resides, on the crag of the rock and the stronghold. From there it spies out the prey; its eyes observe from afar." (Job 39:27-29)

The eagle in its effort to build his nest will make thousands of trips to select choice sticks to furnish his nest. Other materials include stones, twigs and bark which make the nest crude and uncomfortable. Once the major framework is done, the female leaves the toting of the building materials to the male while she stays with the nest arranging and rearranging until the nest becomes a virtual fortress in the rocks. The nest is extremely deep with a shallow eighteen inch brooding area on top. The diameter of the nest will vary from six to ten feet, depending on the wingspan of the eagles.

The nest will be composed of many things when completed. The frame, which is made of wood so that it will last for many years, may be constructed with limbs measuring four inches to eight feet in diameter. Building on up, the limbs will get smaller until the nest is ready for the final cabinet work. The limbs are now reduced in size to one inch in diameter to allow some flexibility in positioning. Now the finishing touches of the nest will include vines, which may be used to weave the upper layers together; leaves which create the soft home effect, and perhaps the fur of some recently devoured dinner, to make warm and soft enough for the baby eagles.

In extreme contrast to the eagle, the vulture is not a committed spouse. The male will offer no help in locating or building a nest. The responsibility rests solely on the female. Vultures would rather eat than nest, and so the house building continues to be put off until one day the female realizes it is too late. Frantically she seeks out an old tree, perhaps a fallen log or if the worst comes to the worst, a grassy field, to lay her eggs.

Once the nest is completed, the eagle will begin to glide through the air searching for a lamb. An eagle has great muscular strength and is able to carry in his talons prey equivalent to his weight. After much searching and hunting, the eagle begins to sight a lamb and determine its weight. He then swoops on his prey, seizes it and kills it with his talons. He carries this lamb to the nest and tears it up. He will eat its flesh and drink its blood. He will then spread the lamb's wool in the nest to make it comfortable.

Creatures of Faith
After painstakingly building their nest, the eagles are now ready to start their first family. Although there is still snow on the ground, the eagle lays her eggs. She must remain in the nest until the snow melts. The responsibility for the food now rests on the male who will in the next few months spend all his time hunting and preying on fish to feed the family. This is not an easy task when the snow is still on the ground because much of the food supply has disappeared during the winter months. The beauty of this part of the eagle's life is not found in many other birds. The eagles have not flown south for the winter but instead they have endured the winter months.

Each year the eagle's nest is remodeled. Materials that are soiled or dirty will be discarded. As he continues refurnishing, the nest becomes bigger and could weigh up to 200-2000 lbs. Because of its enormous size, other weaker birds that are unable to build their own nests will find shelter beneath the eagle's nest. Your life will be such that as you build your nest, the feeble ones will draw (spiritual) strength from you. Because of its high location, the eagle's nest inevitably exposed to the sun and rain. Hence, the eaglets without shelter, may by burnt or drenched. The parents birds spread their wings and provide shelters. This is where we see God as our protector, our assurance and security. Just as it is written,

> *"He shall cover you with His feathers, and under His wings you shall take refuge…"* (Psalm 91:4).

Love for Solitude

The eagle is a solitary bird. He loves to be alone. He has chosen a lofty dwelling above the turkeys and crows, where the environment is lonely. This setting allows him time to care for his mate and to skillfully train his young. It is said you become and act like those you mingle with. If you spend your time with the turkeys, you will gobble. If you spend time with the ducks, you will quack. If you spend time with the eagle, your voice will seldom be heard but when it's heard, it will be a cry of victory.

At thousands of feet above sea level, the mother just throws her eaglet off balance and expects him to fly. But the eaglet keeps falling at very high speed. He is still struggling for dear life. Doubts begin to fill him. He begins to question why his mother is doing this. But just before he crashes onto the ground, or just before some predators seize him in mid air, the mother comes to his rescue. And what a relief it is to the young eaglet.

> *"As an eagle stirs up its nest, hovers over its young, spreading out its wing, taking them up, carrying them on its wings."* (Deuteronomy 32:11)

The eagle actually chooses his diet for the day and then goes to find it. Once he finds his meal, he dives down and lays hold of it, crushing the life from it with his strong talons (claws). He then ascends to his nest and tears the prey apart while it is still warm. This bird will not devour decomposed animals of any sort. If we are (in the spiritual sense) what we eat and if our strength lies in our diet then what are we to eat? Our spiritual life, (our inner man) has a great appetite, and hunting and pecking in the dirt will not satisfy this great desire. We must learn to discern the spiritual nutritional value of everything which we allow enter into our spirit.

Spiritual weakness is the direct result of a poor diet. A sick or weak eagle will not reproduce, he will not be able to discern the truth, nor will he able to contend with these enemies. The vulture builds his nest in dead trees or even on the ground. His head and neck are featherless and hairless so that he can more readily stick his head into a rotting carcass. The diet of this bird is a diet of leftovers. After circling over his meal for hours to make sure it's dead, the vulture descends, usually accompanied by other scavengers which do not want the solitary lifestyle of the eagle. The vulture will eat until he becomes intoxicated with blood by overeating and then is unable to fly, often becoming the prey himself. But the food of a free eagle is fresh and this food makes him clean.

The Eagle's Unique Eyes
Food is scarce in the lofty heights. Because of this, the eagle instinctively develops binocular eyesight to search for food. He can accurately determine the exact location of his prey and his eyes can detect small movements. The reason for such powerful and keen eyes is his hunger. And God has put hunger and thirst within us. As you hunger and thirst after God, your spiritual eyes will be developed and you'll be able to see clearer and deeper into the things of God. The eagle has a unique pair of eyes in that double lids are set on his forward-facing eyes. With one blink, he can look into the glaring sun and not be blinded. With another blink, he is able to view the land below him. He looks up and he looks down and yet his vision is not affected. God wants you to have the eyes of an eagle so that you would be able to see far and clear. If he can carry only 12 lbs of weight, he knows he must not catch a fish heavier than that. If the eagle catches a fish that is right in size, he will be able to fly away and enjoy the fresh fish. But if he lunges his talons into a fish that is 30 or 40 lbs in weight, that bird will not be able to take off. Instead,

he will struggle with the fish and will be pulled into the water and drowned.

The Eagle Renewed

Now the parent eagle have grown a little old. Their feathers begin to shed. Their eyes have grown weary. Their beaks have become blunt, and their talons no more sharp and strong. The eagle which was once powerful has now lost his splendor. And we see this eagle flying to a lofty location and finds himself a rock to perch on. Here, he faces the sun and focuses his eyes only on the sun. He stops drinking and he stops eating. He will be still and not give into distractions around him. Rain and snow will fall but the bird will not move. Storms will rage but he remains motionless. For days and weeks, he is immovable. As the sun shines upon his face, all the ugliness, blindness, deafness and bluntness begin to shed from that eagle. That eagle does not give up. He waits and he waits…God says if we would just learn to wait on Him and hear His heart's desires, we shall exchange our weaknesses for His divine strength. We shall exchange our human frailties for divine enablement, and exchange our human failures for God's success and victory, if only we will wait upon the Lord. And one day, new feathers begin to replace the old ones with a shine more brilliant. His beak is now sharpened. New talons begin to grow. He becomes far sighted. His ears begin to clear. And there standing on that same Rock is a renewed and dignified eagle. Are you willing to focus your eyes on the Lord and attune your ears to the moving of the Holy Spirit? Do you want to be that renewed eagle?

Part 3

Prayer

Mystic Journey

Oneness and Peace
Relationship, oneness, harmony peace and justice are superior values than the limited values like "economic growth" "efficiency" "patriotism" "nationalism" etc. When one stresses one culture, one goes to the extent of rejecting others belonging to other cultures. One is so obsessed with one's religion that one hurts the people of other faiths. One is so territorially obsessed that one is prepared to treat the nation state as a sovereign God which for its sustenance requires the sacrifice of humans.

Religion
What is necessary is insight, relevant image or metaphor for meaningful action. The mystic and sages have revealed that everything is one. Multiplicity is illusory. This message is extremely relevant. We humans can contribute a great deal by going about creating oneness, peace and harmony. In this light, planetary community is a better metaphor to work on. This mystic from the beginning of time have bestowed us insights and metaphors such as brotherhood, equality, and oneness. They did not mean to create structures as we have now. Structures stifle the spirit. The structures of religion, as we have now, will no last long. They will give way to inner directed, mystic paradigms, free from dogmatic and ritualistic preoccupations. Everything will have his own value system, world view, philosophy of life and code of conduct. Those who look secular, may be in reality more religious than those who appear and profess to be religious.

Nation State and Globalism
From the beginning of time, structures of power have not repeated themselves. It is very unlikely that empires and colonialism will repeat themselves in the same from. They may appear in different forms. You may have economic empires and cyber colonialism. If we envisage a planetary community, new communities cold emerge, drawing inspiration form already existing ethnic communities.

Communities will cater to culture, while retaining openness with other communities. Global government will not interfere in the usual administration of communities. They are to function automatically, as self sufficient entities. The planetary government will concentrate on the common good of the planetary community and the preclusion of anti-social elements among communities. The communities can also assert themselves because of their anti-social instincts.

Globalization needs more management to open opportunities for the poorest countries, not close or restrict them in order to create employment and avoid greater economic disparities. The whole world looked at as a while has all the characteristics of the third world such as inequality, unequal distribution and disparities of income. Globalization and culture do not contradict each other. Cultures need not necessarily suffer in the process of globalization.

Let us adopt a detached view and a mystic view it will be a great service if we contribute to expansion and readjustment of our world view.

Co-Creative Consciousness

There is a creative intelligence operating in the universe. Nature tends towards greater consciousness, freedom and order. Human being experience themselves as "co-creators". The intelligence, individuality and intuition fuse to form a higher stage of consciousness, called "Co-creative consciousness".

The basic structure of the Universe is consciousness. As actualizes oneself, consciousness too rises in the same proportion. When consciousness breathes through human intellect, it is genius, when it breaths through his will, it is virtue; when it flows through his affection it is love.

To gain higher consciousness one must free oneself form security, greed and power addiction. Addictions and compulsion keep one from loving oneself and others. Individuals and international actors must become aware of these obstacles to perceive and discover the finer energies that enable one to intuitively merge with everything around one.

Demons of Prayer

Prayer is one of the essential foods for a seeker of God. Its weakening or extinction affects all aspects of life. A fervent Christian will turn mediocre, if one surrenders to the "devils" of prayer. If that Christian is apostolic, he or she will become an empty activist. The "devils" of prayer are extremely varied.

Lacking Sufficient Motivation
There are too many praying people who fall into this temptation: they pray because of psychological needs, not because of faith. If no fervor or devotion is felt, if God is not "needed" for something, if the value of prayer is not "felt", there is no interest and motivation to pray. Here is where the temptation lies. We have to become motivated through the word of God and through reality of faith, and not through "psychological needs". We do not pray to obtain something, or to be comforted, but to put on Christ continually and participate in his life. Overall, the supreme motivation and cornerstone, which make prayer solid and determined in the face of any temptation of the devil, is the belief in the love God has for us.

Depersonalized Prayer
This devil makes prayer an experience, certainly a religious experience, but an impersonal one. This temptation affects many praying people. They pray to a "divinity", to a "Supreme Being", to someone religious and powerful. They even sometimes pray "to the wind". But Christian prayer is essentially a personal relationship, the meeting of two beings, oneself and God, the meeting of absolute misery and absolute mercy, which through the grace of God's united in friendship. In prayer, we have contact with a person, not with a power or religious principle. The old advice of spiritual people is a wise one: when praying, one should start by putting oneself in the presence of God even though that takes time. Time spent this way is already prayer.

Secularizing Prayer
This devil consists in losing trust in the effectiveness and influence of prayer in our day-to-day life. That is precisely the temptation of

secularization. Human beings are thought to be knowledgeable in manipulating the laws of nature, of science, as well as of history (economics, demography, politics) and of the human mind (psychology) to the point that everything is more or less scientifically predictable. Yet on the other hand, they do not trust the power of praying in daily life. True Christian prayer however experiences God in everything. It experiences God who is active in everything and who directs everything both extraordinary and ordinary. The temptation is presenting God as one more factor among other competing factors in the affairs of the world. God is the "divine mean", a transcendental one, of the march of history and scientific laws. All the visible world is subject to those laws. At the same time, everything is loved and allowed by God. Prayer is always effective and influential during times of need because it penetrates our life.

Not Deeply Surrendering Oneself

This devil deceives when it brings the praying person to habitually utter a lukewarm and self-hearted prayer. A meeting between two people is not intimate when either one or both of them do not really seek out one another intimately. It happens when one enters into prayer without separating oneself from worries, images, distractions which one brings from the outside. Surrendering oneself deeply in prayer is surrendering to God the foundation of one's life. The essence of life, that point where we decide between selfishness and love, sin and grace, mediocrity and sanctity, is the freedom of the will. To surrender oneself in prayer means to surrender oneself to God, surrendering to him what we can, our free will.

Not Nourishing the Faith

It is common knowledge among praying people that in times when prayer is difficult, going to the Word enables prayer to happen. Therefore, to maintain and deepen a life of prayer an assiduous contact with the word of God whether read or heard but always internalized, is absolutely necessary. The temptation is not so much setting aside prayer but in giving less importance to going to the word and making oneself its disciple.

Neglecting the Humanity of Christ

This devil suggests to praying people that they should leave behind the memory and relationship with the humanity of Jesus of Nazareth. Praying people should become contemplative and attain the purely spiritual and loving experience of the Trinity. As traditional doctrine, the great spiritual masters remind us continually that we have the access to the mystery of God solely through the humanity of Christ. All reference to intimation of Christ slowly disappears. Prayer is turned into an illusion, which becomes impossible to prove through Christian practice. From that incarnation, prayer and all aspects of Christian life should take root. It is the only way and model of all true experiencing of God.

Separating Prayer and Coherence in Life

How does one know that prayer is improving in quality? It does when prayer penetrates one's life and when it tends to extend itself beyond prayer time. If God has not been sought for, he will not be found in prayer. If one has gone after "idols" in prayer, the presence of those idols will persist in prayer. One lives as one prays. It is impossible to deepen the surrender of self, if this surrender is absent in one's life.

Separating Prayer from the Good of Others

This is the devil of the self-oriented praying person. Christian prayer is never self-oriented. It is based on the needs of the world, of others, and of the Kingdom of Christ. Christians never pray only for themselves, for their good and well being. They also pray as representatives of their brothers and sisters, and above all, of those who do not pray and who need more prayers. They pray in solidarity with the condition of all people. The apostolic nature of Christian prayer means that prayer liberates the heart for love and apostolic service.

Discouragement

This devil seduces one to abandon prayer through discouragement in the face of difficulties. Ironically, these difficulties are usually normal in prayer. The temptation is to apply perfectionism in one's prayer life. It is thought that prayer will be more perfect if circumstances surrounding it are better and if we have a "perfect experience" in prayer at a human level. The response to this devil should always be the same: persevere in prayer whatever the circumstances without ever being discouraged.

Associating Prayer with Good Feelings

The temptation puts excessive value on sensibility. In this case, it is thought that prayer goes well when there is affection, devotion, and good feelings of consolation. Prayer is said to be going wrong when none of these is present and when dryness, obscurity and boredom are experienced instead. One tends to abandon prayer if it does not give us emotional gratification. We are ready to accompany Christ in his splendor in the Mount of Olives, but not in his nakedness and agony in the Garden of Gethsemane. God is never so present as when you feel God is absent.

The real effectiveness of God is not measured by the experience of good feelings or by the results we see; the effectiveness comes through what God does in us, from the depths of our heart, from the roots of our freedom and faith, hope and love. Prayer makes us take on Christ's character. In the final analysis, the Lord is not interested so much in external perfection as in identification with Christ. "Incompetent praying people" should persevere with humility, without "measuring" their prayer but trusting in the effectiveness of God who works in them.

Sometimes God gives consolation to encourage us and help our fragility; sometimes he takes it away to help us mature in prayer and purify and augment our faith, hope and love in God. The great mystics' answer is unanimous: the quality of prayer is seen outside the prayer itself. It is seen in one's life and in one's faithfulness to God through prayer. If in day-to-day life there is persistent desire and effort to imitate Christ, if there is more freedom and inner poverty, if one grows in community life, love and apostolic spirit, these are solid proofs of quality and progress of prayer even if one's prayer may seem dull and less exciting.

Wrongful Discernment in the Use of Methods

This temptation belittles all methods and believes that prayer is sufficiently mature in itself as not to need a method. Disinterest in a method is seen sometimes among those starting to pray, which is worse. Another temptation is using a method, but without looking for an appropriate and personal one that helps one to pray. There are different methods of prayer, some are well known, but not all are appropriate for every person. One must use the method that suits oneself, whatever it is, and not other methods no matter how interesting they may be. The spiritual masters tell us that a method should be used in as much as it helps develop a more intimate contact with God. We should like to feel that "we are producing". Renouncing methods in favor of the action of the Spirit becomes a waste of time for us. The temptation is in persisting in our plans, ways and method, and not letting ourselves be led by the spirit.

Confusing Prayer with Human Contemplation
This devil leads the praying person to replace Christian prayer with listening to music, reading an inspiring book, viewing of landscape, and reflecting philosophically. All these are good and should have their place in the life of people. Even then, they usually prepare the soul for prayer. One's time is used in listening to religious music, reading a book on Christian topics, preparing for a celebration or a preaching. All these have to be done, but at their proper time, not during prayer. The temptation to do two things at the same time, such as beholding beauty and praying or studying and praying, in the long run leads to abandoning true and intimate prayer.

Disregarding Lifestyle
Once again this devil separates what should be joined together in the authenticity of prayer. The progress of prayer requires certain conditions in the person's way of life. Prayer requires a minimum organization of life, of contemplative discipline. If scholars and researchers, athletes and writers should impose on themselves personal discipline and control, all the more should that be done by anyone who seeks to experience God in prayer.

Not Being Helped By Other People
This is the devil of self-sufficiency. The saying that "one is not the judge of one's own cause" is especially applicable here. It is a rule

in Christian spirituality that the person during the long period of learning above all, needs the guidance of another competent and experienced person. The advisor, consultant, spiritual director, confessor is a factor of prime importance for education and progress in prayer. Every praying person needs to be assiduously stimulated, helped, assured and warned of the failures and temptations of his or her prayer.

The Essentials of Prayer

Prayer is Essentially Loving Attention[1]

Prayer begins and ends with a loving attention to God, without making specific acts. He should conduct himself passively, as we have said, without efforts of his own, but with the simple, loving awareness, as a person who opens his eyes with loving attention.[2]

Attention animated by desire is the whole foundation of religious practices.[3]

I shall not dwell upon this because I want to say something about the way in which I think those of us who practice prayer may profit, though everything is profitable to a soul that loves the Lord with fervent desire, since it instills into it courage and wonder.[4]

Two essential elements of authentic prayer are contained in the definition of prayer as loving attention: awareness of the presence of the other and a heartfelt concerned response. Distractions within consciousness and indifference of the heart are obstacles to meaningful communication with God. If, on our part, we are called to love with attention, this is consequent upon God's loving attention towards us. The Father's loving attention has been revealed in Jesus, the Word incarnate. Further verification is found in the sending of the Spirit into our lives, the Spirit of love and knowledge. Because of this personal Grace we are enabled to pray.

The Spirit too comes to help us in our weakness. For when we cannot choose words in order to pray properly, the spirit himself expresses our plea in a way that could never be put into words, and God who knows everything in our hearts knows perfectly well what he means, and that the pleas of the saints expressed by the Spirit are according to the mind of God.[5]

Prayer is Proportionate to the Quality of One's Love[6]

> *Farewell, farewell! But this I tell*
> *To thee, thou Wedding Guest!*
> *He prayeth well, who loveth well*
> *Both man and bird and beast.*
>
> *He prayeth best, who loveth best*
> *All things both great and small;*
> *For the dear God who loveth us?*
> *He made and loveth all.*[7]

He knew that without prayer true love was impossible and he learned from living that without love prayer became self-centered and barren.[8]

God grant that nothing worse than this may happen-for, as you know, anyone who fails to go forward begins to go back, and love, I believe, can never be content to stay for long where it is[9]. The Spiritual life demands balance. How one relates to God in prayer is intimately related to how one encounters his neighbor. "He who says that he loves God and at the same time shows hatred to his neighbor is a liar".[10] The person who spends an hour in prayer while neglecting the obvious needs of people close at hand must seriously examine the authenticity of such prayer. Indeed, the reality check for one's prayer life is fraternal charity[11].

Genuine Prayer demands some self-control of Body and Spirit [12]

> *We shall not fail to observe the fasts, disciplines and periods of silence which the order commands; for as you know, if prayer is to be genuine it must be reinforced with these things-prayer cannot be accompanied by self-indulgence.13*
>
> *Oh, who can tell how possible it is for a man with appetites to judge the things of God as they are?14*
>
> *We shall have overcome a considerable obstacle when prayer and penance condition each other, for their unity*

> *will be able to become the guarantee of their orientation. If it is necessary to deprive oneself of food and sleep, it is not to establish a performance or glorify oneself over an exploit, but to allow the spirit to give itself freely to prayer, since, if it is less strongly captivated by the things of earth, it will be able to give attention to what is above it.*[15]

Prayer is premised upon the ability to say "no" to one level of reality so as to be able to say "Yes" to the workings of the Spirit. If the farmer wants the full harvest, then he must willingly do the spring plowing and planting; if a person wants to listen and respond to the Lord, then time and space must be created for the encounter to happen. Strong and determined desire lies at the root of such discipline.

Waiting for God is at the heart of prayer and is already a deep form of prayer; self-control makes that waiting possible and grace makes it sacred. Although not speaking of prayer, C. S, Lewis describes well this aspect of what is, after all, part of the human condition; "Then came the worst part, the waiting."[16]

In Prayer, I Must Bring This Me to the Living and True God[17]

> *I enter the presence of God with all my load of misery and troubles. And he takes me just as I am and makes me to be alone with him.*[18]

> *If you're approaching him not as the goal but as a road, not as the end but as a means, you're not really approaching him at all.*[19]

> *I can testify that is one of the most grievous kinds of life, which I think, can be imagined, for I had neither any joy in God nor any pleasure in the world. When I was in the midst of worldly pleasures, I was distressed by the remembrance of what I owed to God; when I was with God, I grew restless because of worldly affections.*[20]

One of the greatest causes for sterility in prayer stems precisely from a misconception of God and a failure to be in touch with our identity. God says to us, "Come as you are" – no need for formal dress here. C. S. Lewis remarks that God cannot be captured by our finite reason:

> *" My idea of God is not a divine idea. It has to be shattered time after time."*[21]

Authentic prayer demands authentic, real persons, our real self must be continually ferreted out; our real God must be longed for and awaited in silence and solitude.

Prayer's Primary Focus Is on God, Not Self or Events [22]

> *It is not my business to think about myself. My business is to think about God. It is for God to think about me.*[23]

> *This is the curious nature of Mister God: that even while he is at the center of all things, he waits outside us and knocks to come in. We open the door. Mister God doesn't break it down and come in, no, he knocks and waits.*[24]

Prayer deals directly with centering. Our experience indicates how easily self-centeredness moves in or how daily anxieties and worries can become so strong as to exclude any awareness of a loving, caring God. Only in grace can the obstacles blocking encounter with God be removed. Jesus' Prayer and life were centered on the Father and the doing of his will. The lives of the saints are the records of people who struggled to center on God in spite of their own selfishness. Teresa of Avila admitted that for years her prayer was superficial. John of the cross speaks of the constant challenge to mortification lest the self dominate. All these experiences reveal the eternal conflict between the ego and divine love.

Silence, Solitude and Surrender are Conditions for Prayer
The beginning of integrity is not effort but surrender; it is simply the opening of the heart to receive that for which the heart is longing. The healing of mankind begins whenever any man ceases to resist the

love of God. This SSS Principle (Silence, Solitude, and Surrender) establishes the dispositions allowing for union with God. Simply by looking at their opposites, we realize how important they are. Constant chatter impedes prayer ("In your prayers do not babble as the pagans do." Mt. 6:5); crowding our lives with activities and people stifles the inner agenda; clutching desperately to our own wills thwarts the realization of the Father's will.

The Tone of Prayer is one of Reverence and Awe [25]

> *Then prayer is a witness that the soul wills as God wills and it eases the conscience. And so he teaches us to pray and to have firm trust that we shall have it; for he beholds us in love, and wants to make us partners in his good will and work.*[26]

Earth's crammed with heaven
>   *And every common bush afire with God;*
>   *Only he who sees takes off his shoes-*
>   *The rest sit around and pluck blackberries.*[27]

First, therefore, I invite the reader
>   *To the groans of prayer*
>   *Through Christ crucified,*
>   *Through whose blood*
>   *We are cleansed from the filth of vice-*
>   *So that he not believe*
>   *That reading is sufficient without unction,*
>   *Speculation without devotion,*
>   *Investigation without wonder,*
>   *Observation without joy, work without piety,*
>   *Knowledge without love,*
>   *Understanding without humility*
>   *Endeavor without divine grace,*
>   *Reflection as a mirror without divinely inspired wisdom.*[28]

A personal attitude toward a particular person or object is known as tone. Hostility, lack of openness and prejudices are negative attitudes creating an atmosphere (tone) of fear and discomfort. Gentleness, respect and affability are positive attitudes promoting a climate (tone) of warmth and joy.

Julian of Norwich writes that, when one is comfortable in coming to the Lord, deeper experiences of prayer are possible:

> *And so prayer makes harmony between God and man's soul, because when man is at ease with God, he does not need to pray, but to contemplate reverently what God says.*[29]

Love's cousins are reverence and awe. Julian of Norwich shares her experience of God's tonality: Of everything, which I saw, this was the greatest comfort to me that our Lord is so familiar and so courteous, and this most filled my soul with delight and surety.[30] When gifted with these gentle attitudes, our prayer takes on an entirely different quality. Without these gifts our hearts are stifled and our service cool. The reverent feel deeply and serve generously; the awe-filled see with wonder and hear with trembling.

God's Activity in Prayer is Far More Important Than Our Activity

Prayer is a personal response to God's presence. It is more something that God does to us, rather than anything we do. This means that God first makes himself present to us. Prayer is our awareness of and then response to God.

> *In the first place it should be known that if a person is seeking God, his Beloved is seeking him much more.*[31]

Self-sufficiency is a trait much admired by our culture. We like to be in control. With such a mentality, it is not surprising that God's invitations and graces fall on deaf ears and are unseen because of our blindness. The consequence of such disposition is tragic: "A person extinguishes the spirit by wanting to conduct himself in a way different from that in which God is leading him."[32]

> "Our task is always the humble and courageous one of listening obediently and acting boldly."[33]

There is no One Way of Praying: Pluralism in Prayer Must Be Carefully Safeguarded [34]

God leads souls many ways, but those who are unable to take this road should not be condemned or judged incapable of enjoying the great blessings contained in the mysteries of Jesus Christ our God. [35] God does not lead us all by the same road, and perhaps she who believes herself to be going along the lowest road is the highest in the Lord's eyes.

> *God leads each one along different paths, so that hardly one spirit will be found like another in even half its method of procedure.*[36]

A popular expression states: "Different strokes for different folks!" During certain periods of faith development, vocal and formal prayer may well be the best form of prayer for that time.

> *"As soon as God's word makes its impact, we must leave all the rest and follow it."*[37]

Prayer is a means to an end; it is union with God. The paths to union are multiple. The principle to be followed in personal, private prayer is that of freedom. Only the individual knows the context of his/her own life; it is the context that sets the parameters for the form and style of prayer.

Prayer Leads

Prayer Leads to Intimacy with God and to Solidarity With all Creation.[38]

> *In prayer, I can enter into contact with the God who created me and all things out of love. In prayer, I can find a new sense of belonging since it is there that I am most related.*[39]

> *We are put on earth a little space. That we may learn to bear the beams of love.*[40]

The end of the spiritual life is union with God and by means of this unity we are mysteriously united to all of creation. Oneness is attained by love; prayer is a central love act in our lives. The Lord stands at the door knocking and a choice has to be made. Following our "Fiat," God comes to dwell with us and our homes are never the same. The experience of love comes alive when we move from the map to the land it describes.

End Notes

1. Rom 11:33-36.
2. *The Collected Works of St. John of the Cross*. (Tr., Kavanaugh and Rodriguez, Washington, D.C. ICS Publications, Institute of Carmelite Studies, 1973). p. 622.
3. Simone Weil, *Waiting for God*, Introduction by Leslie Fiedler (New York: Colophon Books, 1951). p. 197.
4. *The Complete. Works of St. Teresa of Jesus*, translated and edited by E. Allison Peers (London: Sheed and Ward, 1944), Vol. II p. 363.
5. Rom 8: 26-27.
6. I John 2:9-11; Lk 4:42-44.
7. Samuel Taylor Coleridge. "The Rime of the Ancient Mariner."
8. Murray Bode, Francis; The Journey and the Dream (Cincinnati: St. Anthony Messenger Press. 1972). P. 64.
9. St. Teresa, 11, p.347.
10. I John 2.
11. Spiritual Renewal of the American Priesthood (Washington, D.C: Publication office United Sates Catholic Conference, 1973), p. 48.
12. Gal 5:16-26; Mt 4:1-17.
13. St. Teresa, 11, p. 16.
14. *The Collected Works of St. John of the Cross*. p. 364.
15. François Roustang. S.J., Growth in the spirit, (New York: Sheed and Ward. 1966). p. 232.
16. C.S. Lewis. *The Last Battle* (New York: Collier Books, 1956), p.13.
17. Jn 6:13; Rom 7:14-25.

18. Raissa's Journal, Presented by Jacques Martian (Albany, N.Y: Magi Books, 1974), p.225.

19. C.S. Lewis Surprised by Joy (New York: Harcourt, Brace & world, 1955), p.21.

20. St. Teresa, I. p. 48.

21. C. S. Lewis, *A Grief Observed* (New York: The Seabury Press, 1961), p. 32.

22. Ps 23; Gal 2:17-21.

23. Simon Weil Waiting for God. pp. 50-51.

24. Fynn, *Mister God, This is Anna* (New York; Holt, Rinehart and Winston, 1974), p. 174.

25. Is 6:1-9; Ps. 118:5-7

26. Julian of Norwich: Showings, translated by Edmund College, O.S.A. and James Walsh, S.J. (New York: Paulist Press, 1978), p. 353.

27. Elizabeth Barrett Browning, " Aurora Leigh."

28. Bonaventure: *The Soul's Journey Into God*, translation and introduction by Ewert Cousins (New York: Paulist Press, 1978), pp.55-56.

29. Showings, p. 159.

30. Ibid.p.136.

31. *The Collected Works of St. John of the Cross*. P. 620.

32. Ibid. p. 232

33. Romano Guardini, The Life of Faith, translated by John Chapin (Westminster, Maryland: The Newman Press, 1961), p. 106.

34. Col 3: 12-17;Lk 4:42-44.

35. St. Teresa, 11, pp.307-308.

36. *The Collected Works of St. John of the Cross*. P. 633.

37. Hans Urs von Balthasar, Prayer, tr., A V. Littledale (New York: Shed and Ward, 1961). p. 108.

38. Ps 139; Jr. 31:31-34.

39. Henri J.M. Nouwen. The Genesee Diary: Report from a Trappist Moastery (New York: Doubleday &Company, 976).

p.51.40. George Herbert, "The Little Black Boy."

How to Pray

If you are too busy to pray, you are too busy-
Anonymous.

With me, prayer is a lifting up of the heart, a look towards heaven, a cry of gratitude and love uttered equally in sorrow and joy in a world, something noble, supernatural, which enlarges my soul and unites it to God.
St. Therese of Lisieux.

Prayer will continue to exist, as long as there will be humans on earth. All religions espouse some kind of prayer. Baltimore Cathechism defines prayer as "the lifting up of our mind and heart to God". This does not emphasize the role of God sufficiently. Some define it as a conversation with God. Catherine de Hueck Doherty says, "Prayer is love. It is love expressed in speech and love expressed in silence. To put it another way, Prayer is the meeting of two loves: the love of God and our love'.[1] A prayer is being in the presence of someone I love and who loves me. Prayer is our "time out" from our busy life to reflect on our deepest needs and desires. One reason why we pray to an all-knowing God then is this: to discover what is really on our mind and in our heart. Henri Nouwen has defined in the following words. Prayer is to descend with the mind into the heart, and there to stand before the face of the Lord, ever present, and seeing, without you [2]. When we pray, we give our all-knowing God a chance to communicate with us. By wanting God to speak to us we risk being changed. We risk having our attitudes altered, our perspectives broadened, our plans modified.

1. Pray as you can and do not pray, as you can't. Take yourself as you find yourself; start from that. (Dom Chapman)
2. God walks amid the pots and pans (St. Teresa of Avila.) There are certain places such as church, park or a retreat center. Any place can be a good place for prayer. God is everywhere, prayer can be everywhere too.
3. Of all things, we do, the prayer is the least practical (Abraham

Heschel). No immediate results. We pray to love someone and to become someone. Ordinarily we become that person not by dramatic leaps and bounds, but by taking barely noticeable baby steps.
4. The only way you can fail at prayer is not to show up (Thomas Keating). If we keep showing up for prayer, we have not failed. If we persevere in prayer, that in itself is a wonderful grace. Jesus teaches – perseverance.
5. A lot of trouble about prayer would disappear if only we realized – that we go to pray not because we love prayer, but because we love God. (Hubert Van Zelles) Prayer is only a means. The end of prayer is love of God and the fulfilling of God's will. The end is meeting of two loves.

Sharing in the Divine Power

Blaise Pascal says that God created us to be sharers in the divine power, not spectators of it. God distributes his gifts though those who pray. A special way we share in the divine power is prayer. Prayer is the most powerful energy one can generate. Prayer is a prayer as real as terrestrial gravity. I have so much to do today that I must set apart more time than usual to pray. (Martin Luther) Satan trembles when he sees the weaker Saint upon his knees. (William Couper)

God-Centred Prayer

Jesus teaches us to begin not with ourselves but with the Father; not with our interests and needs but with his kingdom and his justice before everything else, and all the rest will come to you as well" (Matt 6:33). The one great obsession in Jesus' life was not mankind, but his Father. His food and drink was to do the will of his Father. "Father, take this cup away from me; I do not want it; but if you want it for me I shall take it " (John 14:31) He teaches us to begin with God: to be concerned about the coming of his kingdom, about his name being glorified. We must become humble, accept the fact that we have needs, even material needs, and beg God to fulfill these needs. Jesus bids us ask for three things for ourselves: for our daily bread (for need, not luxuries!), for spiritual strength, and for forgiveness of sin.

Petitionery prayer

Jesus' prayer from start to finish is petitionery prayer: "Father, may your name be glorified, may your kingdom come, may your will be done" The kingdom of God is going to come even more surely than the sun is going to rise. And yet Jesus bids us ask that it may come. And so I say to you ask and you will receive; seek and you will find; knock, and the door will be opened. For everyone who asks receives, he who seeks finds, and to him who knocks, the door will be opened." Everyone, no distinction between saints and sinners, no 'ifs' or 'buts'. Every one who asks will receive." "Is there a father among you who will offer his son a snake when he asks for fish, or a scorpion when he asks for bread. If you give your children what is good for them, how much more will the heavenly Father give the Holy Spirit to those who ask him!" Luke 11:1-13. Mark 11:22-14. Matt 21:20-22. Luke 18:1-8. John 14:12-14. John 15:7. John 16:23-24. Jam 1:5-8. John 3:22. 1 John 5:14-15. Phil 4:4-7. 1 Tim 2:1ff).

The Laws of Prayer

If you have not succeeded in prayer it is not because prayer does not work. It is because you have not learnt to pray well. An engineer may complain that engineering doesn't work because every time he builds a bridge it collapses. The truth is that engineering works very well; but he is a bad engineer. If we fail in our prayer, it is because we are bad prayers. We have failed to master the laws of prayer that Jesus clearly enunciated, for prayer has its own laws just as much as engineering.

The First Law of Prayer: Faith

Jesus always insisted on faith in his power to heal and cure and work miracles. We are told that in his hometown, Nazareth, he could not work many miracles because of the lack of faith of the people there. You need only say to this mountain, "Be lifted from your place and be hurled into the sea," and what you say will be done. And whatever you pray for in faith you will receive. Has it ever struck you that every time Jesus sent his apostles out to preach, he gave them the power to heal and to work miracles as if he linked the two ministries inextricably together, the ministry of healing and the ministry of preaching? Jesus somehow linked the charism of healing and working miracles with the ministry of preaching. (Acts 4:31) If in our own lives we never or hardly ever experienced God's miraculous interventions, it is either because we are not living dangerously enough or because our faith has grown dim and we hardly expect any miracles to occur. Prayer must be accompanied by an unshakable faith. Those problems of yours that seem like enormous mountains will yield before the power of your faith.

Believe That You Have Already Achieved

Jesus adds a very interesting detail in (Mark 11: 24); "I tell you, then, whatever you ask for in prayer, believe that you have received it, and it will be yours." When someone gives you a cheque, do you first wait to have it cashed in the bank before you thank him? When you realize that God is going to give you what you are asking for, that is the moment to begin to thank him. A woman prayed to be cured of arthritis. She began her thanksgiving three whole years before this cure came, because she was convinced that the cure was on its way. Could this be what St. Paul meant when he told the Philippians to blend their petitions with thanksgiving?"The Lord is near; have no anxiety, but in everything make your requests known to God in prayer and petition with thanksgiving. Then the peace of God, which is beyond our utmost understandings, will keep guard over your hearts and your thoughts, in Christ Jesus". (Phil. 4: 6-7)

The Second Law of Prayer: Forgiveness

In Mark 11, Jesus tells us of the need for faith if our prayer is to be effective. In that same passage, he insists on the need of something else: forgiveness. "And when you stand praying, if you have a grievance against anyone, forgive him, so that your Father in heaven may forgive you the wrongs your have done." (Mark 11: 25) This is a fundamental law of all prayer. If you do not forgive, you will not be forgiven; it is impossible for you to be united with God. "If, when you are bringing your gift to the altar, you suddenly remember that your brother has a grievance against you, leave your gifts where it is before the altar. First go and make peace with your brother, and only then come back and offer your gifts."(Matt 5: 23-24).

How to Forgive through Prayer
There are some effective ways of obtaining the grace to forgive and to get rid of resentments:

1. Pray for the welfare of the people you dislike. This is what Jesus recommends in the Sermon on the Mount. As you keep praying for them, your attitude towards them undergoes a mysterious change. You begin to care, to be positively inclined, even to love them. It is easier to forgive people we love and pray for.
2. See every injustice done to you as planned and controlled by God for some mysterious purpose and for some good in your life. It is not enough to say, " God permitted it." God does not just 'permit' things; he plans them, he controls them. The passion of Christ, that enormous act of human injustice, was not just permitted by God. It was planned and willed and foreordained. (Acts 2: 22-23)

The opposite of love is not anger or even hate, but coldness and indifference. To rid yourself of grievances and resentments, stand in spirit before the Crucified Christ and keep your eyes fixed on this great Victim of injustice. "How blest are those who have suffered persecution for the cause of right; how blest you are, when you suffer insults and persecution and every kind of calumny for my sake. Accept it with gladness and exultation." (Matt, 5: 10-12).

Crying out in Childlike Confidence
When a child calls his daddy, the daddy comes. Many people never learn to pray, because they have never learnt to make effective use of petitionery prayer .The hand outstretched to beg obtains what the hand pressed against one's head to think does not. You will realize the truth of Paul's words to the Philippians: "The Lord is near: have no anxiety, but in every thing make your requests known to God in prayer and petition with thanksgiving. Then the peace of God, which is beyond our utmost understanding, will keep guard over your hearts and your thoughts, in Christ Jesus" (4: 6-7). Even a baby, too weak for anything and unable to walk to his mother on his own little feet, can yet roll about and scream and cry because he wants

her. Therefore, as he cannot come to her, she, moved by his longings and by her own love of her child, takes him up and sweetly fondles and feeds him. Thus also deals the loving God with those who come to him and long for him.

The Power of Prayer
Jesus replies to Mary "Woman, my hour has not yet come". Then, mysteriously, his hour did come and he worked the miracle of changing water into wine. Didn't Mary change destiny? "A good man's prayer," says James 5:16-18, "is powerful and effective. Elijah was a man with human frailties like our own; and when he prayed earnestly that there should be no rain, not a drop fell in the land for three years and a half; then he prayed again, and down came the rain and the land bore crops once more". One story from the Indian literature serves as illustration of Jesus' doctrine.

Ezechias fell sick, and was at death's door; indeed the Prophet Isaias visited him with this message from the Lord: put thy affairs in order; it is death that awaits thee, not recovery. At his Ezechias turned his face towards the wall, and prayed to the Lord thus: Remember, Lord, I entreat thee, a life that has kept true to thee. And Ezechias wept bitterly. Whereupon, before ever Isaias reached the middle of the courtyard, the word of the Lord came to him: Go back and tell Ezechias, the ruler of my people, here is a message from the Lord, the God of thy father David. I have granted thee recovery. Within three days thou shalt be on thy way to the Lord's temple, and I will add fifteen years to thy life. (4 Kings Ch.20)

The prophet Amos says. "This was a vision the Lord God showed me; here were locusts a-making. Ah, Lord God, said I, "be merciful! How should Jacob survive, the puny creature he is? And with that, the Lord relented; "Happen it shall not", said he. And a second vision the Lord God showed me, how he would summon them to ordeal by fire; fire should devour the waters below the earth, and devoured some part of them were. "Ah, Lord God", said I, for pity! How should Jacob survive, the puny creature he is"? And with that, the Lord relented again; happen it shall not, said he (7: 1-6).

Moses has a lengthy argument with God in Exodus 32. And finally succeeds in making God change his mind.

> *"The Lord said to Moses, I know them for a stiff-necked race; spare me thy importunacy, let me vent my anger and destroy them; I will make the posterity into a great nation instead. But Moses would still plead with the Lord his God. So the Lord relented, and spared his people the punishment he had threatened. Genesis 18: 16-32 shows us how Abraham attempts to do the same thing with God by interceding for the cities of Sodom and Gomorrah. So the Lord told him. The ill repute of Sodom and Gomorrah goes from bad to worse; their sin is grievous out of all measure. Abraham drew close to him, and asked, Wilt thou, and then sweep away the innocent with the guilty? Suppose there are fifty innocent men in the city, must they too perish? Wilt thou not spare the place to save fifty such innocent men that dwell there? And the lord told him, if I find fifty innocent citizens in Sodom, I would spare the whole place to save them. Then he said, Lord, do not be angry with me for pleading thus; what if thirty are found there? If I find thirty, he said, I would not do it. I have taken it upon me, he said, to speak to my Lord, and speak I will; what if twenty are found there? If I find twenty, I will grant it life, he said, to save twenty. I entreat thee, for making one more plea still; what if ten are found there? I will spare it from destruction, he said, to save ten".*

Simone Weil said that the trouble with the Marxists is that they expect to mount up in the air by dint of marching inexorably forward. All your marching, no matter how vigorous, will not succeed in raising you even one foot up into the air. For that, God's intervention is needed. And Jesus made sure we are always kept aware of this by insisting that we ceaselessly ask God for everything.

Unworldliness

James 4:2 ff. says, "You do not get what you want, because you do not pray for it. Or, if you do, your requests are not granted because you pray for wrong reasons, to add to your pleasures. Have you never learned that the love of the world is enmity to God? Jesus advocates a life that is simple, uncluttered by luxuries and wealth, he bids us ask for our daily bread, our daily sustenance, not for the superfluities that glut our consumer society markets.

Generosity

Any man who expects God to be generous with him must be generous with his fellow men, "Give," says Jesus, "and gifts will be given you. Good measure, pressed down, shaken together, and running over, will be poured into your lap; for whatever measure you deal out to others will be dealt to you in return" (Luke 6: 38). If you are tight-fisted and calculating with the poor, the needy, how can you expect God to be generous with you?

Pray in Jesus' Name

If you ask anything in my name I will do it, so that the Father may give you all that you ask in my name. In very truth I tell you, if you ask the Father for anything in my name, he will give it to you. So far you have asked nothing in my name. Ask and you will receive, that your joy may be complete." (Jn. 14:12-14; 15:16; 16:23-24). It is from these words, no doubt, that the Church developed her practice of addressing her prayers to the Father "though Jesus Christ Our Lord" and "in the name of Jesus Christ your Son." Praying in Jesus' name means relying on his influence with the Father, on his intercession, on the Father's love for him and eagerness to please him and give him all he asks for.

Practical Rules for Praying according to St. Vincent de Paul

These "rules" are simply a group of practical rules that according to experience are helpful for those who want to pray.

1. **Faithful prayer requires discipline.** Saint Vincent alluded to this when he spoke of mortification as a prerequisite for prayer. It is important to fix a prayer time and to have a place. Likewise, it is most helpful to go to bed at a reasonable hour if one is to rise early to pray. Today it is advisable when there

are many diversions that can easily distract us from prayer time (e.g., television, radio, films, etc,).

2. **Mental prayer demands quiet.** One should choose a prayer time when noise and interruptions are unlikely, when telephones and doorbells will not be ringing. That is one of the reasons why communities have traditionally chosen to pray early in the morning before the busy pace of the day's activities begin. Dietrich Bonhoeffer states: "Silence is nothing else but waiting for God's word"[3].

3. **It is important to be acquainted with various methods,** by having, so to speak, a "prayer repertory"[4]. Different methods will be appropriate at different times in life. We may find ourselves, at later stages in life, returning to methods we used earlier.

4. **The prayer needs to be nourished.** Some of the main elements in the diet are the reading of sacred scripture, good spiritual reading, and, especially in an apostolic spirituality, live, reflective contact with Christ in the person of the poor.

5. **Prayer should result in renewed self-definition**[5] Through it, our values should become redefined and take on an increasingly evangelical character. Prayer should lead to continued conversion. It should result in acts of charity and justice. This is why Saint Vincent insisted on "Practical resolutions ".

6. **What God is communicating is more important.** In the long run, prayer is a relationship. Those who are deeply in love can often spend significant periods of time together while saying very little. "Mere" presence is a sign of fidelity. Jesus, in fact, warns us against the multiplication of words in prayer (Mt 6:7)[6].

7. **Prayer must also take on the other biblical "moods":** praise, thanksgiving, wonder, confidence, anguish, abandonment, resignation. Typically Christian Prayer is filled with thanksgiving.

8. **As Jesus recommends, we should often pray to do or accept God's will.** This is what Saint Vincent meant when

he recommended indifference as a predisposition for prayer. This is especially important in times of discernment.
9. **Physical and environmental conditions can help or inhibit prayer.** Images, candles, incense, the beauty of the setting, tabernacle, lighting, and music-all can be aids to our praying.
10. **Distractions are inevitable,** since the mind is incapable of focusing on a single object over long periods of time. When distractions are persistent, it is often best to focus on them rather than flee from them, and to make them a topic of our conversation with the Lord.
11. **Sharing prayer can be very useful.** Each of us has limited insights. We can profit very much from those of others. The faith-witness of others can deepen our own faith.
12. **Faithful praying demands perseverance.** Saint Vincent encourages the Daughters of Charity by telling them that Saint Teresa spent twenty years without being able to meditate even though she took part faithfully in prayer. Sometimes we may feel that we are "wasting time" in prayer, or we may experience long-lasting "dryness" and be tempted to quit. We should resist the temptation and the journey will bring great rewards.

The Ultimate Criterion Of Prayer Is Always Life: "By their fruits you shall know them" Unfortunately, experience demonstrates that some of those who pray quite regularly may be very difficult to live with. Ultimately, one cannot judge, in an individual case, what is really going on between God and a person in the depths of his or her being? But one can surely conclude, in general, that there is something very much wrong with prayer that does not result in change of life. St. Vincent's contemplation of God's love overflowed into practical love for the poor.

End Notes

1. Melanie Svoboda. *Traits of a Healthy Spirituality*, USA: Twenty-Third Publications. 1998

2. Henry J.M. Nouwen. *The way of the Heart*, London: Dartan, Lougman, Todd, 1981.

3. Bonhoeffer, *Life Together*.

4. Wilkie An, *By Way of the Heart, Toward a Holistic Christian Spirituality* (Mahwah: Paulist Press, 1989) p.92

5. Margaret Miles. *Practicing Christianity* (New York: Crossroad. 1988. 142.

6. Cf. SV XII, 328, where, in the context of praying the office, Saint Vincent, following Chrysostom, compares mindless rattling of words to the barking of dogs!

Meditation

The best way for one to change is by "Working on oneself" from within by meditation. Although the cultural religious trappings may vary, the core experience of meditation is an altered consciousness in which the ordinary sense of the ego is diminished. Although enlightenment is the ultimate goal, many (perhaps most) meditation will not reach this fulfillment. Nevertheless, the following are the worthwhile benefits.

Effects of Meditation on Life

> *Freedom from the feeling of pressure in day-to-day affairs.*
> *Freedom from what is generally called "that tired feeling".*
> *Minimal recurrence of chronic nagging pains such as headache, arthritis, indigestion, and colitis.*
> *Reduction of insomnia.*
> *Greater tolerance and love for others.*
> *Greater satisfaction from one's religious affiliation, if there is one.*
> *Greater desire to be helpful, either in public service or in one's own private life.*

Awareness

Meditation is the means to reconnect the individual with the whole i.e., to make the individual conscious of his universal origin. This is the only positive way to overcome the ego-complex, the illusion of separateness, which no amount of preaching and moral exhortation will achieve. Meditation might be described as a technique for developing attention without tension. The common core of all meditation experience is an altered state of consciousness, which leads to "relaxed attention," "non-anxious attention," and "passive volition".

Techniques of Meditation

Meditation involves coming to a stillness of spirit and a stillness of body. The real work of meditation is to attain harmony of body, mind and spirit. The psalmist puts it well: "Be still and know that I am God". In meditation, we turn the search light of consciousness on ourselves. In meditation we are not thinking or imagining about God at all. We seek to do something immeasurably greater; we seek to be with God, to be with Jesus, to be with his Holy Spirit. In meditation, we go beyond thoughts, even holy thoughts. Meditation is concerned not with thinking but with being. The task of meditation, therefore, is to bring our distracted mind to stillness, silence and concentration.

To meditate, we seek a quiet place, and find a comfortable upright sitting position. Close your eyes gently. Sit relaxed but alert. Silently, interiorly begin to say a single word. We recommend the prayer phrase of "Maranatha". Say it in the following manner, ma-ra-na-tha. Four equally stressed syllables. Some people say the word in conjunction with their calm and regular breathing. The speed should be fairly show, fairy rhythmical. Maranatha is in Aramaic, the language Jesus himself spoke. It means, "Come Lord". It is probably the most ancient Christian prayer. St Paul ends Corinthians with it, and St John ends Revelation with it. Listen to the mantra as you say it, gently but continuously. You do not have to think or imagine anything, spiritual or otherwise. Meditation has nothing to do with quiet reverie of passive stillness, but with attentive wakefulness. Don't use any energy in trying to dispel a distraction. Return with fidelity to meditation each morning and evening for between twenty to thirty minutes. Meditation is a pilgrimage to your center to your own heart. To enter into the simplicity of it demands discipline and even courage. However, if one is patient and faithful, meditation will bring us into deeper and deeper realms of silence. It is in this silence that we are led into the mystery of the eternal silence of God. That is the invitation of Christian prayer to lose ourselves and to be absorbed in God.

The silent forms of meditation center on three-technique concentration, contemplation, and the mental repetition of a sound .The sound called 'mantra' may be a single syllable such as

Om. It may be a word phrase or verse from a Holy Scripture. The Tibetan Buddhist *Om mani padme hum* ("the jewel in the lotus," or enlightenment) is an example. So is the simple prayer in the book called *The Way of a Pilgrim* praying "Lord Jesus Christ, have mercy on me." Many Christians use the Lord's Prayer as a basis for meditation. Saying the decades of the Rosary is likewise mantric meditation. The Indian sage Kirpal Singh taught his followers to silently repeat five names of God, which he gave then in a ceremony. Zen Buddhism has a variety of meditative techniques, which involve the use of a koan, an apparently unlovable riddle that the meditator silently examines, such as "What is the sound of one hand clapping?" Another inquires more directly about the basic nature of self-identity: "Who am I?" In contemplative forms of meditation, the eyes are open so that the meditator sees what is called in Sanskrit a mantra, a form on which he centers his attention.

Concentration

Concentration is generally considered the most difficult form of meditation. In concentration techniques, an image is visualized tidily in the mind. The mind may be held free of all imagery and mental chatter. Some disciplines combine different aspects of several meditative techniques. For example some steps of the martial arts uses meditation in their training regimen. The Russian mystic Georges Gurdjieff taught his students to combine movement and meditation. Psychotherapist author Ira Proof guides people through therapeutic sessions using techniques called process meditation.

Experience of Love

Meditation leads us into the experience of love at the center of our being, it makes us more loving people in our ordinary lives and relationship. Not only is meditation the necessary basis for contemplative action, but also it is the essential condition for a fully human and Christian response to life. The wonderful beauty of prayer is that the opening of our heart is as natural as the opening of a flower. It is for this we have been created.

Experience and Enlightenment

Historically the goal of meditation has been a transformation of the whole person. Throughout history teachers of meditation and spiritual masters have emphasized, "Right living" to support one's meditation. By that they mean a healthy mind, a healthy diet, an honest means of income, kindness and humility in relations with others, a social conscience, giving up egotistical desire for power, fame, prestige, wealth, psychic powers and so forth. The true aim of meditation is to bring the meditator more fully into the world, not to retreat from it. A religious retreat may be appropriate for some in the course of their meditative training and discipline. The great possible result of meditation is enlightenment. Through direct experience, people can reach a state of conscious union with ultimate reality and the divine dimension of the universe. In that, state all the long sought answers to life's basic questions are given along with peace of mind and heart.

When learning and living are integrated in spontaneous proactive moment-to-moment living, the meditation becomes what has been called meditation in action. Meditation is no longer just a tool or device or mental exercise, no longer just a visit to that state in which the larger sense of self as cosmos emerges. The gains from meditation become integrated in a manner of living best described as enlightenment. The meditator has so completely mastered the lessons of meditation that his entire life is a demonstration of the higher consciousness, which can be experienced if sincerely sought. People who attain this state have been recognized through the ages as special persons for whom attention and reverence is proper. For them, the alteration of consciousness called meditation has led to a transformation of consciousness.

The Social Dimension of Meditation
The two deepest and most pervading dynamics in the human person are inward towards transcending and outward towards relating. The first draws us irresistibly towards the source of all consciousness, all being and all energy, beyond ourselves, towards the Creator, whom we name God. The second attracts us towards building up relationships: towards unity of person with person, of person with nature and with the cosmos.

Love is the Measure of our Sanctity

We do not meditate in order to experience unusual phenomena. Such experiences can result from a sudden and extreme release of stress. The great Christian mystics teach that spiritual growth is a gift of God and develops through a growing relationship with God and an awareness of his presence in 'the center of our being'. It is not something we can produce by our own effort—by meditating for longer hours, for instance. We can only open ourselves to God's Spirit acting in our depth. There is just one way to measure our sanctity, our closeness to God, and that is the measure of love: the degree to which we love God expressed by our willingness to do the will of God and by our love of our neighbour and a care for creation.

Expanding the Heart

The regular, twice-daily practice of meditating causes us to become more open, more loving, more compassionate because we are gradually becoming more whole. The fruits of meditation are those listed by St Paul (Gal 5:22) as the fruits of the Holy Spirit: love, joy, peace, patience, kindness, goodness, faithfulness, gentleness, self-control—all of which have a relational value. It is a common experience of meditators to enjoy a sense of the oneness of all humanity. Being an experience, it is difficult to describe. But it could be said that we increasingly feel that our own essential being is part of the very essence of humanity, so that other people's sadness becomes our own, their joy is our own joy—at a very deep level. In fact, meditating draws us out of ourselves and makes us more open to the other.

The Effect on the Field of Consciousness

There is a scientific, social dimension: the influence meditation has in the field of consciousness. Our brains are like radio transmitters and receivers and like these instruments the more finely the mind can be tuned, by passing into deeper states of consciousness, the greater the potential for having an effect on the surroundings. It has been observed that if a number of people in a given area regularly meditate, they influence the field of consciousness in that area in such a way that there is a decrease of stress. Scientific studies made by independent researchers over the last couple of decades in cities throughout the world have shown that when as few as 1% of the population of these cities practices meditation over a given period, the decrease in stress becomes manifest in such phenomena as a drop in the number of accidents and traffic fatalities, a lowering of the crime rate, less violence, a fall in the number of hospital admissions. The reason for this is that people meditating produce brain waves of the same frequency thus sending out a concentration of mental energy. This is particularly evident when they meditate as a group together. The effect can be compared to a platoon of soldiers marching over a suspension bridge. Thirty separate individuals crossing the bridge will have no special effect on the structure, but the same number of soldiers marching across in step will cause the bridge to start swinging. The physical effect of the rhythm they produce when in step is far greater than that of their total foot power.

Meditators are Kingdom Builders
The core of Jesus' message during the all-too-short three years in which he went public was not, as is often thought, about founding a new religion but about a new way of living. The kernel of his kingdom teaching is about a new way of living relationships. This plan, which God will complete when the time is right, is to bring all creation together, everything in heaven and on earth. (Ephesians 1: 8-10) God's plan for his creation—the Kingdom of God—is already fulfilled in the Eternal now of the Godhead but it is still to be worked out by us in partnership with God in the dimension of time.

Zen Meditation

Zen masters themselves often give little help in understanding their elusive discipline. When one puts questions to them about it, they often smile and remain silent. This is because they see Zen not as a doctrine but as an activity – and thus an experience –so simple and immediate that, when one attempts to conceptualize it, he only abuses it, as when one tries to define the experience of love or life. It suffices to say it has been practiced for more than 1400 years. Concerning the question of its place of origin – whether India, Tibet, China, or Japan – let us concede simply that it developed in the East, probably in a pantheistic culture. To do Zen, one follows a series of seven conventions, so that our efforts remain not an exercise in looking only but also translate into a creative experience. Let us observe successively these conventions as we set them forth.

Having chosen carefully the place for our meditation-as free as possible from distractions, harsh lights, sounds, and drafts—we assume the Zen position. In this position we join our hands and bow from the waist in the traditional oriental gesture of courtesy which here means, "Now I begin my meditation". A similar bow at the end will mean, "Now I end my meditation." If we must stand to attend to something—best disconnect the telephone beforehand—or a cramp we simply cannot ignore, we bow as we break off meditating, then again as we resume it. This puts parentheses around each session of our meditation, separating it from interruptions coming to us and from our world around us.

We try to keep our backs as erect and comfortable as possible: the base of the spine is the key. We do not worry if at first it tires quickly. After a couple of weeks of daily meditation, it will surprise us by its new toughness, even during longer sessions of Zen. Our legs should be crossed comfortably, making allowances for bad knees and general decrepitude. We strive to keep faithful to the time we agree with ourselves to meditate daily. Twenty-minute sessions are good to begin with. As we go on longer, circulatory pain in our legs can force us to take a break. For this, we bow, stand, join hands before us, pace the room for two minutes; then, taking again the Zen positions, we bow, and resume meditating.

Our hands and wrists should rest comfortably on the insides of our thighs-left four fingers on top of right four fingers, the fingers underneath press dynamically against those above, while the tips of the thumbs touch together ever so lightly and delicately. Here aim to combine a relaxed and stable dynamism of our fingers with an alert delicacy in touch of our thumbs. Our head should be erect, titled slightly forward comfortably, and with chin in. Our tongue should rest relaxed in the base of our mouth, and we avoid all nervous movement of tongue and jaw. Lips should be relaxed and slightly parted to permit exhaling through the mouth.

Our eyes should remain half closed and out of focus. If we close our eyes, we will go to sleep; if we focus them on anything that will become a distraction. Our breathing should be not from the chest but from the diaphragm. We loosen our belts, allowing our lower abdomen full freedom to expand and contract. We inhale, knowing the air we take in through our nostrils will heal and give peace, and the air we exhale through our mouth will carry out those things that rob us of peace. This breathing is indeed the key to both traditional and Christian Zen because, once we are in observance of these conventions, the conscious listening to the sound of our breathing becomes the central continuous deliberate activity during the entire time we are meditating. We strive to make this breathing more and more regular, more deeply from the diaphragm.

Even the pain we will feel in our legs after thirty minutes of continuous meditation can be turned to our advantage. As this pain grows, we seek to enter it, to enter within it to find in it a certain rest. Thus our concentration upon our breathing will become more complete and more central, and foreign thoughts will be more completely excluded. The above conventions are, curiously, the essentials of Zen as it has developed over the past millennium. Being in essence nonverbal, non-conceptual, and non-imaginative, Zen does not lend itself to being systematized. To those practicing Zen, it is the experience that matters whereas the conflicting ways one tries to describe or analyze this experience are then secondary at best.

The partial suspension of our bodily and mental activities for a set period daily is the objective of Zen. As we strive for this disengagement, and achieve it in a growing degree, we are actually inducing our physical and mental powers into a daily, deep repose. Not only the member of our bodies, but also the thoughts of our hearts are put to rest during our meditation: our conflicting values competing for dominance such as our desires, both ordinate and inordinate, our ambition and passionate longings; and grievances. We acquire a deeper understanding of our own best values, of how to bring to bear our nobler motivations.

What is Christian Zen, which we will now call centering prayer? Will an attempt to use Zen in prayer, contrary to what Zen masters maintain—that one cannot accommodate true Zen to any ulterior purpose—render it ineffectual? To answer, let us consider an analogy of a ballet apprentice who works daily on her techniques. She may give little thought to what ballet grammar—the body language she is learning—might be saying or to whom; she meticulously strives only to perfect every move, every step of it. For the present, the immediate benefits of her efforts—pride in pleasing a respected teacher, satisfaction in mastering an art—are sufficient reasons for striving for self-discipline; and she grows daily in pose and beauty. But one day a certain impresario discovers her and offers her a part in a new production. Now she has two things lacked before: a role, a 'dramatis persona' to live within, and an envisioned audience. These give form and finality to her efforts. Just as this ballerina can adapt her previously acquired skills to this new orientation, so also, as many Christian contemplatives have found, the skills and the strength of traditional Zen, with little change in its dynamics, can be fitted into the larger synthesis of Christian prayer.

When the prophet Samuel was a small boy sleeping in the temple, he was awakened repeatedly by a voice calling, "Samuel, Samuel!" Each time he got up and went to his master, the elderly priest Eli asked what he wanted. Each time Eli replied, "I didn't call, my son; go and lie down again." Again Samuel heard the voice calling, and again he went to the old priest. But this time Eli, perceiving it was the Lord calling, instructed him, "The next time he calls, you must respond, 'Speak, Lord, for your servant is listening.' It is the reality from which the call came that makes the difference between an obedient child and the prophet-to-be. We must listen continuously to the voice of the Lord who seeks us when and where he chooses. If we find traditional Zen apt for putting us in contact with the healing and peace-giving powers of our human spirit within, how much more will we find centering prayer apt for opening our beings to the Spirit of God within us, to surrendering ourselves to this Healer?

Centering prayer is not in contrast to the Ignatian Exercises but ancillary to them. Many of Ignatius' instructions can be applied with profit to Zen mediation: making preparation before meditation by spiritual reading and acts of self-denial; cultivating honesty and sincerity in evaluating our efforts at praying; making from time to time reviews of moments of joy or of sadness; and, with the retreat master's help, using carefully Ignatius' instructions on the discernment of spirits. With no more than a bow of adoration and a word to greet him by name, such as, "Jesus, have mercy on me, a sinner," we surrender ourselves with total passivity to his Spirit within us who will shape our minds and hearts according to his holy will.

GOD HUNGER

Falling in Love with God[1]
"A Mystic," Peers wrote, is a person who has fallen in love with God. The entire humankind loves a lover. They attract us by their ardor, their single mindedness, their yearning to be one with the object of their love. Mysticism is nothing more or less than a love driven way of knowing God's presence-or absence-as contrasted with the efforts of our minds to think through, capture and describe the object of our belief in clear language, theological subtlety, or scientific precision. "To the questing soul no mere message from God suffices. She cries out for God himself". The God we seek is not the first cause, the chilly abstraction of the best our minds, but the subject of a passion that overwhelms us even as it releases the very heart of our fallible and finite humanity. One of the most profound themes of the western spirituality is that the God we pursue is also our pursuer, that what keeps us apart is not God's distance but our flight, that we need perhaps more than anything else, to stop running and let ourselves be caught.

Surrender and Darkness
In the end, searching for God is not a journey of the mind but of the soul.

> *Moses' vision of God began with light.*
> *Afterwards God spoke to him in a cloud.*
> *But when Moses rose higher*
> *And became more perfect,*
> *He saw God in the darkness. Gregory of Nyssa*

The exploration, if it is to lead anywhere, must be conducted prayerfully from that place within all of us which Dag Hammarskjold calls *"a center of stillness surrounded by silence"*. What you seek on your journey is not a solution to a problem, not the answer to a question, but an encounter with mystery that will by very definition far exceed the best efforts of your mind, the uttermost limits of your imagination.

Our Situation of Nostalgia

We live, as C.S. Lewis reminds us, with a "lifelong nostalgia, a longing to be reunited with something in the universe from which we feel cut off". It is the "old ache" that will not go away. It's meant to be life long. It must be life long, because its object will forever exceed our grasp. The emptiness, the hunger at its core is too great to be attempted by comprehension

> *Our lifelong nostalgia,*
> *Our longing to be reunited*
> *With something in the universe*
> *From which we feel cut off,*
> *To be on the inside of some door*
> *Which we have always seen from the outside,*
> *Is no mere neurotic fantasy,*
> *But the truest index of our situation.*
> *What does not satisfy when we find it,*
> *Was not the thing we were desiring.* C.S.LEWIS.

Big Dreams

We dream too small. We are forever chasing after a thousand things that masquerade as the desire of our souls, as God. So many sirens call us, if not to destruction, at least to distraction and frustration. We need to look them in the face and say: "No, you are not it. You are not what I desire. You are not what you long for.

> *Stir in my soul dreams as big as the love offer,*
> *For even the impossible dream is too small*
> *For those you have created in your image.*
> *Let me see through the impostors*
> *That knock forever at the door of my soul*
> *Promising what you can give.*
> *Replace my small dreams with your invitation*
> *This hunger is better than any other fullness;*
> *This poverty better than all other wealth.* C.S.LEWIS

God as Hunger

God comes to us not as food but as hunger, not as presence but as distance felt, not as fulfillment but as longing, not as love consummated but as desire enkindled. God does not take away our loneliness but intensifies it. God does not answer our questions but floods our souls with ever-expanding mystery. God does not soothe that "old ache" but deepens it. God does not open the door but prompts us to go on knocking. For our hunger is a joyful longing. Our hunger is made present.

> *God gives his gifts where he finds the vessel empty enough to receive them.*   -C.S.LEWIS.

God "gives", says *St. Augustine*, "where he finds empty hands". "A man whose hands are full of parcels", adds Lewis, "cannot receive a gift." Only the uncluttered emptiness of the uncluttered hands, our unashamed longing leaves room for God. Our whole being by its very nature is one vast need incomplete, preparatory, and empty yet cluttered. -C.S.LEWIS

God is where we are and where we are not

It is one more temptation to reduce the terrible mystery of God to the "familiar" to live where we have already been, to avoid the upsetting truth that the spiritual quest will take us into the unknown and the unknowable, that to live in God we will have to die to much that is familiar. If God does not show himself, nothing we can do will enable us to find him. Dramatic moments come and go. We return from the sea to the city. We exchange serenity for the confusion of our homes, classrooms and workplaces. The quite prayerful end of the day gives way to morning. God is not bound by our limitations. God is where we are and where we are not. We can expect to be surprised by God,

> *I insist on tying you down*
> *To special times and places,*
> *To where I think I should be.*
> *But the whole world is your world,*
> *Not just the tiny part of it that I inhabit,*

Not just the familiar neighborhood of my soul.
Surprise me, lord,
Where I least expect to find you.

(C.S. Lewis)

A Journey Home

The desire to find God and to see him and to love him is the one thing that matters. There are always those who believe that God's soft, sweet invitation to rise up now, to come away is an invitation to leap beyond the human condition into an exotic spiritual world where citizenship is restricted to those who have shaken off their humanity. But the great mystic poet of Islam, Rumi, is here to remind us that God's invitation is not designed to separate us from our humanity. It is on the contrary, an ongoing call to all of us to rediscover our human roots, to come here, to return to our natural habits.

Fly away, fly away bird to your native home.
Home is where my heart
Is meant to be.
Take me home.
Let my heart speak
My mother tongue,
My soul rediscover
Its native land.
Borrow the beloved's eyes.
look through them and you'll see
the beloved's face   Rumi

They asked the lover, "where do you come from?"
He answered, "from love."
"To whom do you belong?"
"I belong to love."
"Who gave birth to you?" "Love"
"Where were you born?" "In love"
"Who brought you up?" "Love."
"How do you live?" "Love"
"What is your name" "Love"
"Where do you come from?" "From Love"

> *"Where are you going?" "To love".*
> *"Where do you live?" "In love."*
> *Have you anything except love?" "Yes",* he answered,
> *"I have faults and have sins against my beloved."*
> RAMON LULL

Giving and Dying

So to accept the word of Francis, it is better to give than receive. To convert the center of our lives from receiving to giving is a kind of dying, a kind of conversion from a life of accumulation and consumption to a life where things are put in their place. But our calling is to console, to give the gift of hope, when no other gift is enough, to share the hope that is in us with some one who is in danger of losing it.

> *Be prepared to let go, to die a little everyday.*
> *He is what I or we,*
> *Or any other creature*
> *Has never come to know*
> *Before we were created.*   ANGELUS SILESIUS

> *Help me*
> *Not to settle*
> *For what I have,*
> *For what comes to easily*
> *To my heart,*
> *But to seek*
> *In every passing moment*
> *The "more" you have promised.*
> *O beauty ever ancient,*
> *It is in giving that we receive*   Francis of Assisi

A Leap into the Abyss

From the earliest centuries there has been a mystical tradition that is called the negative way. Briefly, it means that no human words, any concepts however subtle, no images however searching are up to the task of describing God. The best we can do is to approach God in what is not.

> *God is the purest naught,*
> *Untouched by time or space;*
> *The more we reach for him,*
> *The more he will escape.*   ANGELUS SILESIUS

Our spiritual quest is an exploration of our likeness to God-a case of mystery courting mystery. We are in search of only reality worthy of our efforts, the only truth large enough to satisfy deepest needs.

> *The abyss that my soul*
> *Invokes unceasingly*
> *The abyss that is my God.*   ANGELUS SILESIUS

Abyss is such a strange, unexpected word for our souls and for our God. It conjures up images of the land dropping suddenly away from where we stand secure and certain of our footing. Abyss is a synonym for what lies in wait for us beyond what we know. The spiritual quest invites us to surrender the security of what we know, what we can measure, and what we can exhaust for the deepest, unknown reality of our mysterious being and the even more mysterious reality of God.

> *It would be easier, lord,*
> *To stay with what I know,*
> *To take only well-marked paths*
> *To familiar places*
> *In my heart and soul.*
> *But if I am to come to you*
> *Then I must leave behind*
> *The comfort what I already know*
> *And accept your invitation*
> *To journey into your infinite mystery.*
> *Take my hand, guide my steps,*
> *Give courage to my heart and soul.*   ANGELUS SILESIUS

Meet me where I am. Lead me beyond the limitation of my words and the poverty of my spirit. Let nothing but you satisfy me. Draw me step by step closer to you and deeper into the mystery of your life without end. None of the words we use about God-even the word God, even the word divinity- define God, but acts only as so many arrows pointing to a great mystery that defies all our words. But we must go on forming words in which to search for you.

The Way of Nothing

> *If we are attached*
> *To the material*
> *Nature of the world–*
> *If we think of ourselves*
> *As something,*
> *Then God cannot clothe his self in us,*
> *For God is infinite,*
> *No vessel can contain God,*
> *Unless we think of ourselves*
> *As nothing.* The Kabbalah

The spiritual seeker soon discovers that she is not exploring something "up there," but rather the beyond that lies within. Letting go of traditional notions of God and self can be both liberating and terrifying."

> *What we can do is to strive to pursue true knowledge.*
> *True knowledge begins where knowing ends.*
> The Kabbalah.

> *There is no paying our way into the presence of God, no qualifying for divine acceptance. The slightest taste of God is a gift. No amount of finite virtue can earn the infinite love of God. Holiness is always a gift. We become a dwelling place of the divine.* The Kabbalah.

The goal of our journey is to become the dwelling place of our God. But there is a test, the condition, the paradox of what we seek: we can never become the dwelling place of God so long as we think of ourselves as something, then God cannot clothe himself in us

Unsettled and Uncommitted

> *We have not surrendered our lives to bloodless evil,*
> *But neither are we in fiery pursuit of goodness.*
> *We stare into an abyss*
> *So deep that we cannot glimpse its bottom,*
> *And at the same time raise our eyes to mountain tops*
> *That are unreachable. And we stand between them*
> *Wavering, unsettled and uncommitted.*
>   HILDEGARD OF BINGEN

Like the lovers all the world over those who have fallen in love with God, the mystics are passionate, ardent, single-minded in their yearning to be at one with the object of their love. They do nothing by halves. We spend our days and drain our energy, as Hildegard says, wavering, unsettled and uncommitted." Only a passionate heart can overcome our fear of heights, our preference for solid, familiar ground beneath our feet. Passion should be the characteristic virtue of our spirituality, a passion that is never a synonym for warm sentimentality but always a word for courage, risk, and adventure, for full-heartedness, for living with burning intensity.

Our Lack of Passion

We are children with our noses against the bakery window. Even though the door stands wide open and the baker is beckoning, we stay where we are, dissuaded by our lack of passion, our petty fears of the unknown, our preference for who we are, our fears of who we might become. We are not yet hungry enough, passionate enough for God alone.

> *God never says: "enough." Above all God never dismisses*
> *us as hopeless cases, unworthy of further attention. The*
> *note we end on is and must be the note of inexhaustible*
> *possibility and hope.*   Evelyn Underhill

The mystics are the realists of spirituality. They know all about the living lives of blind faith, of dark days and nights, when God hides his face and the soul cries out for just one moment of warmth of reassurance. The invitation to "come follow me" may always be the same but it is never delivered twice in the same way, certainly never in the same context. With the mystics as our companions we choose to pay full price, to hear the truth and desire more than anything else to live it. "Keep walking, keep at it, you won't regret a step of the way." Spirituality is about achieving a pound of self-esteem, that is, coming to see ourselves as God sees us, the object of infinite love, unremitting solicitude, the bearers of God's greatest dreams for humanity. We need them to remind and reassure us that it is okay to dream of the spiritual best. It is after all not a question of our qualifications but of our willingness to let God have his way with us.

End Notes

1. John Kirvan, Sorin Books. Notre Dame.1999 U.S.A

The Art of Creating Affluence and Resourcefulness

Affluence is a quality of our mind. It is a product of the positive and magnanimous heart. All the events that take place are the dramatic manifestations of the internal phenomena of our souls.

Integrity
One of the essential ingredients of affluence is integrity. Integrity requires consistency between your public statements and private thoughts. If you consistently do the best you can, with integrity, you will regret less and move forward with greater ease. If people don't see what they hear, they will automatically mistrust. Mistrust destroys relationship. Your integrity is at stake when your actions don't match your words. Moreover, your reputation, credibility and relationships are at stake too. When an organization has integrity, it can more easily attract and keep competent, talented people. When an organization lacks integrity, competent and talented people will leave.

Breaking your commitments always results in frustration to the people dependent on you. Never break your commitments, unless you responsibly communicate your change in commitment to everyone depending on you. Always take the most ethical and moral course. Never do anything that will make you lose sleep. In the long run, you will benefit more by doing what is right, even if the immediate cost of doing so is higher. Any unethical or immoral behaviour or attitude is self-sabotaging and repels people. You will attract more success by eliminating it, even the small transgressions that nobody notices. Get rid of anything less than excellent in your life and your integrity will increase. You will always know a person's true intentions when you see their results. Integrity exists when the stated intentions and results match. Never lie to anyone. Lost credibility is too costly and too difficult to regain. Above all else, practice what you preach. Highly effective people never blame circumstances for their lack of results. Instead, they accept responsibility and recommit themselves to the actions necessary to produce the intended results.

Focus on Giving
Focus on giving rather than getting, and you will ultimately attract much greater success. Giving helps the flow that God intends. It is absolutely true that nothing is truly mine and everything passes through my hands. In reality giving is receiving. Imagine a line of people forming a circle and you as one of them gives with your right hands and if everyone passes it and it will reach your left hand.

Be Non Judgmental
Treat people without judgment, and they will more readily support your dreams. Never judge or underestimate people by their physical appearance. When you judge, you separate and create a division between you and the other. Successful people who may be willing to invest in you come in all weights, heights, shapes, sizes and colors. The more you judge people, the more you will push them away.

Trust is the foundation of all good relationships. Being passionate will increase your magnetic field which attracts others. Often times, it is the primary reason that relatives, friends and associates will invest in you. Your staff and customers will not be more enthusiastic than you are. Partnerships will attain the greatest success possible, if the partners share a common vision. The most needed, wanted and powerful activity in which you can engage is to authentically recognize, acknowledge, and appreciate others. A bad attitude is toxic to any organization. Practice making other people "right." They will feel validated, become more productive, expand, and take more risks. The more people you influence, the more power you have. One way to really know if you are excellent is to look around you and see if all of your close relationships are excellent. The one person all of these relationships have in common is you. The more you respect another person, the more they will trust you. The moment you blame anyone for anything, your relationship and your personal power will deteriorate.

Avoid Negativity

Never commiserate with fellow workers. Negative people have no chance of survival in a proactive and profitable company. The more your confidence outweighs your doubts, the more people will believe in you. Attitude can be changed in a nanosecond. People with a positive attitude will attract opportunities more easily, earn more, and have better relationships with their peers. The art of getting customers to buy is much more effective than the art of selling. Take a genuine interest in your customers, and they will be more likely to want to buy from you. Be generous with your humanity, compassion and gratefulness. You will attract more people to you if you act and speak from abundance rather than scarcity. Accept your weaknesses instead of resisting them and you will gain more credibility and move forward with greater velocity.

Improve your Standard and Earn Your Reputation

Each time you shop for clothing, upgrade the quality of your wardrobe. People have a tendency to lend more credibility and respect to a person wearing fine clothes. Deliver more than you get paid for, and your reputation will bring you more business. Promise what you can deliver and deliver more than you promise. There is no advertisement as powerful as a positive reputation traveling fast. If your reputation is that you subscribe to the "status quo" opportunities will avoid you. Once you say something, it can never be taken back. The busier you get, the more important it is to remain calm. Never make negative comments or spread rumors about anyone. It depreciates their reputation and yours.

The only way to keep a good reputation is to continuously earn it. A strong reputation leads to authority and influence. Authority and influence are the foundation of power. The degree to which people will be inclined to present opportunities to you is often proportionate to the reputation that precedes you. You risk your own reputation when you surround yourself with people whose reputations are at a lower standard than yours. One way to evaluate your own reputation is to think about what would be said of you at your eulogy. If you are spending time defending your reputation, you have problems. To rebuild your reputation, it is often necessary to go back and finish those things you left incomplete. Your reputation can and will travel faster than you.

Negotiation

When negotiating, always listen to the other person's point of view and interests first. He or she may be willing to give you more than you expected. Never make a proposal-written or verbal- until you know what the other person wants and why. This knowledge will vastly increase the effectiveness of your proposals. Often, the easiest way to move a negotiation forward is to remove some of the risk for the other party. The best way to make a good deal is to have the ability to walk away from it. The best time to ask for a raise is when you are given additional responsibilities.

When negotiating, it is often easier to ask for more and take less than it is to take less and return later to ask for more. Remember, it is almost always easier to buy than it is to sell. Therefore, the buyer has more leverage in most negotiations, even when it doesn't necessarily appear that way. It is important to note that in any negotiation, the issues less meaningful to you might be the ones most meaningful to the other party.

Listening

Listening is a matter of hearing a communication, detached from the filters of our beliefs, judgments, and assessments. When actively practiced, listening enables us to hear and validate someone else, without his or her communication being filtered by our own internal dialogue or agenda. This results in deeper comprehension between the listener and the speaker. You will always learn more by listening than by speaking. Most people need and want someone who will listen to them with undivided attention. If you spend more time asking appropriate questions rather than giving answers or opinions, your listening skills will increase. Showing people you sincerely care about them can often be as easy as listening to them. Reacting includes an emotional component that will often impair your ability to listen and cause a loss of objectivity. Opportunities are everywhere. Listen first, before speaking, and you will hone your personal radar.

Begin practicing your listening skills much like an artist would practice a brush stroke. When you take listening to the level of an art form, your ability to hear things and your effectiveness will increase. Always listen to people as if they are speaking 100 percent truthfully. Whether you agree or not, most people will speak what is true from their standpoint of reality. Listen 85 percent of the time; speak 15 percent. Your whole world will shift, and you will learn more, too. People value a good listener.

Most of the listening we do is rather selfish. We listen to our internal dialogue more than we listen to others. You can shift your internal dialogue and become a more effective listener by immersing yourself in daily positive input from positive people, tapes, and books. People will feel safer around you and speak truthfully to you when they feel you are listening intently to them. The best people to listen to are those who have already been successful accomplishing exactly what you are seeking to accomplish. If you listen carefully, you will hear that most people are crying out for love.

Entrepreneurialism
Mastering your work includes mastering the ability to replace yourself. This frees you up for greater opportunities and self-fulfillment. The fastest way for you to attract more opportunity is to consistently outperform expectations. Use your free time for self-development. Listen to motivational or educational cassettes, while driving to work. Read an inspirational book before bed. Always nourish your brain cells with positive input. What distinguishes an entrepreneurial company is its ability to innovate, respond, change, and adapt at an astounding rate. Highly successful people, however, spend a great deal of money and effort risking what they already have to get what they want. Your personal capacity to handle more valuable projects will go up when you appreciate yourself more. All success comes from a combination of implementation and knowledge. Knowledge alone is meaningless without action. The most common cause of insufficient results is insufficient action.

Money
The very first step to building wealth is to spend less than you

make. Invest 5 to 10 percent of your income every year in your own business training and development. If you work for a company, ask them to subsidize or pay for your training. If your organization is not interested in your self-improvement, leave it. The more you increase employees' rewards and reduce their risks, the more they will perform. Fear of risk or providing inadequate rewards often causes employee paralysis.

Always communicate promptly with your creditors regarding any inability to make payments on your debts, or they will sue you, and will have bigger problems to consume your scarce resources. If things often seem too expensive, either you are not earning enough income or your standards are too high. It is much easier to increase your income than it is to lower your standards. The more people you can positively influence, the higher your earnings. Bear in mind that it is always easier to lend money than it is to get it back. If you believe that wealth is attracted to you, you will attract more opportunities and money. You must be mentally prepared to be wealthy or your wealth will be temporary at best.

Time

Most people connect their results with the amount of time they have invested. If you change your thinking to "results have no relationship to time," this new perspective will give rise to previously unforeseen possibilities. Do not waste your precious time being occupied with what you think other people are thinking. Not only is it an ineffective use of your time, it will also result in misguided assumptions.

Make a habit of having a place for everything and putting everything in its place. Make a list of everything that is holding you back. Then handle each task or issue one at a time until you are free. If you nurture your mind, body, and spirit, your time will expand. You will gain a new perspective that will allow you to accomplish much more.

The central concern is to facilitate, enable and support the flow of energy in the universe. Wealth is our farm of energy. The greater attention should be paid to be dissemination of knowledge and creation of skill. The most important element is service. Concrete expression of love is service. Let us seek to serve and every wealth and resourcefulness will be added unto us. Service is the rent we pay for being allowed to live on this earth.

Part 4

Religious Life

Obedience in Religious Life

In Religious Congregations Obedience is primarily understood as a community experience within the corporate mission of the congregation. We are learning to search together for God's will, to share wisdom, to listen to one another, to reverence the gifts each brings to the decision–making process. As disciples of equals we are all responsible for actively seeking the will of God. To act according to the Gospel is an essential part of that self-surrender. (Rom 1:5; Acts 6:7)

Stewardship of Self in Obedience
The vow of obedience in the context of the vision of Jesus is unremitting fidelity to His mission of proclaiming the Father's love through the power of the kingdom, set free in human hearts to transform, to heal, to reconcile, and to draw them into communion. Obedience calls us to stewardship of the gift of God that is ourselves. We open ourselves to being.

Sister Daniel defined authority as the capacity of a person to author a life vision. Obedience is fidelity to that vision and power, as the energy, which is released when one authors a meaningful vision and remains faithful to it. This power is a positive thing, not a negative manipulation but a liberation of the person to make choices or decisions in line with a vision. Having emptied our hands through poverty and surrendered our hearts in celibacy, we receive from God through obedience the assurance that all is done in accord with the divine plan. Every peacemaker must be obedient. Obedience calls us to stewardship of the gift of God that is stewardship. How much more should we value ourselves and hold ourselves in stewardship. We are a gift of God to be treasured and used according to the plan of God. Obedience encourages us to take seriously this call to stewardship of self.

Authority and Obedience
To speak and act without authority is authority. Jesus' speech has the ring of a prophet's authority. (Mt 16:14) He made truth his

authority. Deeds of Jesus had an enticing persuasive power of their own. Something can and will happen because it is good and because it is true that goodness can and will triumph over evil. He is the truth and the life. (John, 14:6). Faith in God gives genuine experience and thus he becomes the way. His words based on truth carry conviction. Two images of authority are child and shepherd. (Child MK 9:33-36; Mt 18: 1-4; Lk 9:46. Shepherd' John 10: 11-18.) The kingdom of heaven does not belong to those who make their authority felt, but to those who make their service felt in carrying out the will of others

Prayerful Discernment
Prayerful discernment is central to religious obedience even though we may not be practicing it in accordance with any formal structures. It is not restricted to merely giving and taking orders. I may fail by backing away form decisions if I withdraw from the local or congregational decision-making process in which all have been invited to participate. I could fail in my obedience, my creative fidelity to my vision, if I do not accept the corporate mediation of my community in my decision-making. Obedience is submission to authority, full compliance without questioning motives.

As a disciple of equals who are in a love covenant with one another, we are all responsible for actively seeking the will of God and fulfilling it wholeheartedly. We need attentiveness to all relevant mediations of God's word as well as listening to the word of God in Scripture, we learn to listen to human mediators, whether in designated authority roles and events and institutional expressions of community wisdom in laws and rules. We seek the will of God within a specific context of mediation of community, which comprises the persons, the rules, and the designated persons in leadership positions. Obedience is to the community. There is always a person or group to whom every individual is accountable. In their actions for non-violent resistance, Gandhi and Martin Luther King taught their people to begin with prayer and fasting. Plans for action are submitted to the reflection and discussion of the community.

The Vow of Obedience

1. The vow of obedience is undertaken in a spirit of faith and love in order to follow Christ who became obedient even unto death.
2. It demands the submission of one's will to superiors
3. A religious is not bound to submit his mind, opinion, experience and insight
4. A religious is not bound to intellectually agree with the decision of the superior.
5. A religious however is bound to carry out the decision of the superior, who acts in the place of God where they command according to the constitution (Cf con. 601)
6. Superiors don't replace God; it rather means that superiors becomes human instruments or representatives through whom God communicates his will

Mistakes

a. Backing away from making decisions and expecting others to make choices.
b. Not accepting the consequences of one's choices.
c. Not accepting the corporate mediation of ones community in the decision-making.

Leadership.

In order to author a life vision in the community and to play the leadership role effectively one should adopt the following lifestyle and habits

1. Reading. One should be alert to truth and remain connected to the suffering of people. Create new road maps and paths
2. Friendships. Without healthy relationship we wither and die
3. Prayer and contemplation. One should gain total perception and remain connected to the life source.
4. Spiritual Direction and mentoring. Constant discernment and guidance is necessary to see things in proper perspective.

5. Support from peers. People in a similar field and experience can give us encouragement and support.

Obedience is the queen of all virtues. All virtues obey obedience. By obedience one merges and attunes one's heart and mind to the grand purposes of God's design in our regard. In his will is our peace. Merging our will with the maker we become perfect co-creative instruments and species in the Kingdom of God.

References

1. Sister Mary Daniel Tuner. *"On Becoming Religious"* Six Essays based on the Experience of U.S Women Religious.
2. Dorothy Soelle *Beyond Mere Obedience*, Theological Manual 1997
3. Barbara Fiand. *Refocusing Religious Life into the Future* New York A Cross Road Publishing Company, 2001.

HOLY INDIFFERENCE AND OBEDIENCE

Indian Spirituality sees a grand order in the universe and in the affair of the humans called 'Rta'. The Christian spirituality would call this order the grand plan of salvation. The Chinese will call this the harmony or Tao. According to the Buddhist spirituality "whatever will happen will happen and whatever will not happen will not happen".

Effective Love of God

Effective love consists in the conformity of our will with the will of God made known to us in a two fold way by his commandments, counsels and inspirations, and by his good pleasure. The conformity of our will with God's commandments, counsels is the ecstasy of action, whereas the conformity of our will with God's good pleasure is the ecstasy of holy indifference. Holy indifference is a total self-surrender to whatever is pleasing to God, especially in sufferings, disappointments and afflictions, and is, therefore, the highest expression of our love of God.

> *To love God's will in his commandments, counsels, suffering and affliction out of love for God is the summit of most holy charity. In it nothing is pleasant but the divine will alone.*[1]

Resignation and Indifference

In resignation we reluctantly accept events as coming from God's will, whereas in holy indifference, we fully embrace them as an expression of God's good pleasure. Indifference therefore goes beyond resignation, in that it loves nothing except God's will.[2] "The indifferent heart is like a ball of wax in God's hands ready to receive all impressions of his eternal good pleasure." De Sales tells us to "to leave off doing some good when to do so pleases God, and to return after going halfway when it is so ordained by God's will.

God's Good Pleasure as Expressed in Events

In many ways God's good pleasure is made known to us in events.

As long as it is unknown to us we are bound to do God's will as manifested or signified to us especially in the duties. However, when it becomes evident that sickness overcomes us and finally should lead to death, then, in holy indifference, we are called to accept this event as coming from God's good pleasure.

Apostolic Work
We often feel so frustrated as to give up, to lose all hope. De Sales distinguishes between two possibilities: failure in our apostolic work either because of our own fault or without our fault. In either case we are called to practice holy indifference. Sometime we are inspired with lofty plans, which do not succeed. Then just as we must confidently begin and pursue the work as long as possible, so also we must humbly acquiesce in whatever outcome God is pleased to give to the enterprise. We are commanded to have great care about things that pertain to God's glory and are in our charge, but we are not responsible for or charged with the outcome since it is not within our power.

Francis de Sales cites the example of the Good Samaritan who told the innkeeper "to take care" of the man who lay half dead between Jerusalem and Jericho, and not "to cure him". He takes the example of the apostles who did all they could to convert the Jews, but were forced to leave them and to turn to the Gentiles. In all our apostolic endeavors, we must keep in mind, "It is our part to plant and water carefully but it is God, who makes this grow," but sometimes it happens that our apostolic activity fails because of our own fault.

Practice of Virtue
A second area, where we are called to practice indifference, is our advancement in virtue. This does not mean that St. Francis favors quietism, because he makes it perfectly clear that God has ordered us to do all we can to acquire virtue. After we have planted and watered, we must realize that it is for God to give the increase to the trees that are our good inclinations and habits. For this reason, we must wait to obtain the fruit of our desire and labors from his divine providence. If we do not find our soul's progress and advance in the

devout life to be such as we would like, let us not be disturbed, let us abide in peace, so that tranquility may always reign in our hearts.

Even if we know that it is by our own fault that our progress in virtue is delayed, we should not be upset and disturbed. With regard to the sins of others, we must have the same attitude of holy indifference. We must try to prevent with all our power "the birth, growth, and domination of sin." When it is committed "we must do all in our power to have it wiped away" and "never lose courage in aiding and serving them" but at the end we must leave it to God. The main characteristic of this holy indifference is that we unite our will with God's pleasure so as to establish a union between our will and the will of God, which has as its main effect tranquility and peace of mind.

Holy Will Desired in the Our Father
Holy indifference, therefore, is the same as the liberty of the spirit and consists actually in living the first three verses of the our *Father*. "The first things we ask God is that his name be hallowed, that his kingdom may come and that his will be done on earth as it is in heaven. What else can this be but the liberty of the spirit? For as long as God's name is hallowed, his majesty reigning in our heart, his will be done we do not mind anything else."

The *Our Father* has a liberating effect; it liberates us from all attachments to our plans and their success, and makes us accept failures and disappointments with all the meekness possible. A person not attached to his inclinations does not get impatient when he cannot have his way. Liberty of the spirit is freedom from enslavement and freedom from our over-attachment to our plans and projects. De Sales mentions Ignatius Loyola who "ate meat on Wednesday in the Holy Week because the doctor ordered it for some little trouble he had. The indifferent and truly free man is always ready to follow God's will in whatever events it is made known to him.

Pleasing Not Ourselves but God
Sometime we act like little children who, when one gives them a piece of bread with honey on it, lick and suck out the honey and

then throw the bread away. We love God not because it is pleasing to him but because it pleases us. If good feeling could be separated from love, we would leave love and take only good feeling. Another possibility is that, at least, we find pleasure in pleasing God. De Sales compares this spiritual condition to a deaf musician who, although he cannot hear his own song and music, finds pleasure seeing his prince listen and take pleasure in it. Pure love of God consists in loving him without knowing whether it pleases him or not. This is exemplified by the musician who keeps singing even when the prince goes hunting. This is what is called spiritual anguish "which renders love exceedingly pure and clean. Being deprived of all pleasure, such love joins and unites us immediately to God, will to will, heart to heart, without any intervening comfort or further expectations.[3]

Commend Our Spirit
The only thing the soul can do is to let its will die in the hands of God's will in imitation of Jesus. Jesus' very last words on the cross were: *"Father into your hands I commend my spirit."* When convulsive spiritual torments deprive us of other kinds of relief and means of resistance, let us commend our spirit into the hands of the eternal God who is our true Father; and "bowing the head: of our acquiescence in his good pleasure let us consign our entire will to him

De Sales refers to the queen who accompanies King Louis as he embarks and sets sail to travel overseas. She is not concerned at all where the king is going and only desires to be in his presence. The places to which the king is going are all a matter of indifference to her except that he will be there. Just as a man on board a ship does not move but lets himself be moved solely by the motion of the vessel in which he is, in like manner, the heart that is embarked in the divine good pleasures should have no other will but that of permitting itself to be led by God's will. In such case, the heart no longer says, "Your will be done not mine, as though it did not have its will at its own disposal but only at that of divine providence.

Just as master and servant are two persons, so also the master's will and that of the servant are two wills. But the will of the servant is dead to itself so as to live in God's will. St. Francis further illustrates the difference between the first degree of holy indifference and the death of the will by using the image of a father who walks with his little child. We ourselves, little children of our heavenly Father, can walk in two ways. In the first way, we can walk with the steps of our own will, which conform to his, holding always the hand of his divine intention and following wherever it leads us. But we can also walk with our Lord without having any will of our own.

As the liquefaction of the soul is the highest form of affective love, so is holy indifference, the summit of effective love. Both have the same degree of passivity and, at the same time, the same degree of receptivity for the working of God's goodness. In both instances therefore, de Sales quotes the same Pauline texts, (Col. 3:3 and Gal. 2:20), to show their ecstatic nature. "[The will] 'is completely hidden with Jesus Christ in God,' where it no longer itself lives but God's will lives in it." He compares both liquefaction of the soul and the indifference with the light of the stars "ravished and absorbed into the sun's supreme lights." This unity is one of total trust, of filial affection and confidence in God's goodness itself, who knows and wills and we could will or ourselves. To demonstrate this condition of the soul, De Sales tells the beautiful story of a daughter of a physician who is in pain, but does not ask for any remedy, because she has total trust and confidence in her father.

Waiting
This highest form of indifference of the human will is true ecstasy. It is a going out of oneself, which consists in the greatest possible passivity of the will. In this kind of ecstasy, the will is not active at all, neither by acquiescing, nor by accepting, or by permitting. To wait is neither to do nor to act, but only to remain subject to some event. If you will examine the matter, this waiting on the part of the soul is truly voluntary. Nevertheless, it is not an action but rather a simple disposition to receive whatever shall happen. This disposition of the soul in holy indifference is a simple and general state of waiting so as to be disposed to trust and have confidence in God who knows and wills what is best for us. This is what De Sales means by "asking for nothing refusing nothing," by which we "hold ourselves in readiness to receive" whatever God wills. As far as the passivity of the will is

concerned, it lasts only until the will of God is clearly known. "As soon as the events take place and are received, the waiting changes into consent or acquiescence."

Stripping

De Sales further demonstrates the meaning of holy indifference in the last chapter of book nine of the *Treatise*, there he presents the same doctrine by means of a new image: the despoliation of the soul united with God's will. During his passion, Jesus was stripped of all his garments, his skin, and finally his soul was stripped of his body. In his passion and death, Jesus suffered total despoliation but in his resurrection he put on a new and immortal body. Holy indifference, as an ecstatic form of love, makes the soul "die to itself and live again in God." This dying is a stripping "of all human desires and self-esteem which is as closely fixed to our spirit as akin to flesh. At length it denudes the soul of its dearest affections, such as those it had for spiritual consolations, devout exercises, and perfect virtue which seems to be the very life of a devout soul."

In a letter written to Dom. Jean De Saint Francois, St. Jane De Chantal writes, God's will was the only mainspring of all his actions, and as it says in his holy book, he longed for nothing on earth and in heaven except to see the accomplishment of God's will. "Ask nothing, desire nothing refuse nothing': this excellent and little known saying of his, which he himself so faithfully practiced to the very end of his life, could only have come from someone completely indifferent and dead to self. Holy indifference is the purest form of love of God. And a man in love with God is "the end, the perfection, and the excellence of the universe."

End Notes

1. James S. Langelaan O.S.F.S., "Ecstasy of Action, "Review For Religious, 36 1977: 1977, p. 266.
2. Saint Francis de Sales, Treatise on the Love of God, tr. by John K. Ryan, 2 vols. Rockford, Tan Books 1975.
3. Ibid. Vol. II, p. 127.

INNER FREEDOM

To love God and others we inner need freedom. A successful College Principal was asked what would be the one thing that he would ask God as the fruit of the retreat he was about to make. He replied, "Freedom, freedom from compulsions to succeed, to please others, to control, to overwork, to prove my worth to myself and to others, to live up to the expectations of others, in short, to be inwardly free." Two old people were seriously ill in a hospital. While one was relaxed and cheerful, accepting death calmly, the other was frantically looking for any straw he could get hold of to cling to life.

Inner freedom means the inner facility or the ability to do the right thing. The one with inner freedom can choose between right and wrong and accept the right calmly and with ease. This is what St. Ignatius means by 'indifference'. Ignatian indifference is not apathy or inertia, but an active alertness, unfettered by anything that could prevent one from seeking and doing what is right. It is similar to the attitude of the fireman all set and ready to rush to the next call. St. Ignatius points out that the goal of all spiritual exercises is to prepare and dispose the soul to rid itself of all inordinate attachments, and, after their removal, to seek and find the will of God in the disposition of our life.

It is the attitude, which Krishna asks Arjuna in Bhagavad-Gita to have, "Plunge into battle, but keep your heart at the lotus feet of the Lord." It is 'Nishkama Karma' (Desireless action), laboring enthusiastically, without expecting to get the fruit of one's labor. The Bhagavad-Gita teaches the doctrine that we should pose our action without concern for consequences and duty should be done with detachment. It is the dropping of 'desire' that Buddha taught his disciples.

Freedom from our compulsions that enslave us is what Christ came to give us:

> *The Spirit of the Lord is on me, because he has anointed me to preach good news to the poor. He has sent me to proclaim freedom for the prisoners and recovery of sight for the blind, to release the oppressed.*   *(Luke. 4:18)*

St. Paul says that those who are filled with the Spirit are inwardly free:

> *Now the Lord is the Spirit, and where the Spirit of the Lord is, there is freedom*   *(2Cor. 3:17)*

> *It is for freedom that Christ has set us free. Stand firm, then, and do not let yourselves be burdened again by a yoke of slavery.*   *(Gal. 5:1)*

A person who is not inwardly free is like a boy who cannot pull out his hand from a jar because its mouth is too small for his fist filled with nuts. It is enough if he lets go of the nuts to get free; but he doesn't, as he wants the cookies badly. Once philosopher Diogenes was eating lentils for supper. His friend Aristippus, who was living comfortably by flattering the king, told him, " If you would learn to flatter the king you would not have to live on such garbage." Diogenes replied, "If you had learned to live on lentils you would not have to flatter the king."

Christ asks his disciples to deny or to bring under control that part of self which stands against their doing what is right. Again he says:

> *Anyone who loves his father or mother more than me is not worthy of me; anyone who loves his son or daughter more than me is not worthy of me; and anyone who does not take his cross and follow me is not worthy of me. Whoever finds his life will lose it, and whoever loses his life for my sake will find it.*   *(Mt. 10: 37-39)*

St. Paul tells us how he put into practice the teaching of Christ:

> *I am not saying this because I am in need, for I have learned to be content in whatever circumstances. I know what it is to be in need, and I know what it is to have plenty. I have learned the secret of being content in any and every situation, whether well fed or hungry, whether living in plenty or in want. I can do everything through him who gives me strength.* (Phil. 2:11-13)

What matters is not fasting or not fasting, or being rich or poor, or enjoying good reputation or ill-repute, but being inwardly free from any attachments that prevent us from doing God's will. There is only one thing that counts and that is, to be ready to do God's will. Hence St. Ignatius in his "Spiritual Exercise", writes:

> *Man is to make use of them (all created things on earth, except man) in so far as they help him in the attainment of his end, and he must rid himself of them in as far as they prove a hindrance to him (in attaining his final goal). Therefore, we must make ourselves indifferent to all created things. Consequently, as far as we are concerned, we should not prefer health to sickness, riches to poverty honor to dishonor a long life to a short life.*

Here is a beautiful story that tells us of the inner peace and unruffled joy of one who is truly inwardly free.

> *A girl in a fishing village became an unwed mother and after several beatings finally revealed who the father of the child was: the Zen master who meditated all day in the temple outside the village. The parents of the girl with a large group of villagers marched to the temple, rudely disturbed the Master's meditation, abused him for his hypocrisy and told him that, since he was the father of the child he should now bear the burden of bringing it up. All that the Master said in reply was, "Very well, Very well." He picked the baby up from the floor, when the crowd had left, and made arrangement for a woman from the village to feed and clothe and look after it, at his*

> *expense. The Master's name was ruined; no one came to him for instruction any more. When this had gone on for a whole year the girl who had born the child could stand it no longer and finally confessed that she had lied. The villagers were most contrite. They prostrated themselves at the feet of the Master to beg his pardon and to ask for the child back. The Master returned the child. And all he said was, "Very well, Very well."*

A sister in charge of an orphanage told of an incident about herself with utmost simplicity. One of her benefactors, an American lady, once paid a visit to the orphanage. After going round the institution, she said to her "Sister, I pity you people. You have to sleep without a cot and a mattress." The sister replied, "Madam, I pity you very much. I can sleep on a cot with a mattress on, or without a mattress, or on the floor with or without a mat. You need all that just to sleep."

> *St. Paul warns us of this possible misunderstanding:*
> You, my brothers, were called to be free. But do not use your freedom to indulge the sinful nature; rather, serve one another in love. The entire law is summed up in a single command: Love your neighbor as yourself.
>
> (Gal. 5:13-14)

Freedom from Rules

> *"In a particular desert land, peaches were very scarce. Some holy people of the land had a revelation, which they put down in the following code: 'Thou shalt not eat more than two peaches a day.' Later some found the means to convert the desert into a garden. Trees started flourishing, peaches grew in plenty, so much so that they were falling from the trees and rotting on the ground. The young people began to rebel against the law on peaches, but the holy people were determined to maintain the law as they claimed God had revealed it. There were some people who ate more than two peaches a day and they were feeling guilty. Others who ate more than two peaches' didn't feel guilty. Those among the young people who proclaimed*

"It is all right to eat more than two peaches a day' were punished".

Think of Death and Become Free
"A grateful heart can never be unhappy. If you do this, you will enjoy each day. Think of death and you will start to live. We never think of death; so, we cling to things and persons, and end up leading a miserable life, afraid that we may lose them. Don't get attached to things in life, enjoy them while they are there, remember one day you have to leave them behind, you cannot take them with you. Is it worth all the misery we go through trying to keep them?" "If I die tomorrow and if I knew I was going to die, the thing that would make me very happy is that I have helped so many people. My being on this earth has been of some use to humankind. We always have everything we need to be happy. It is what we want and cannot have that we concentrate on and we are therefore miserable."

Fear leads to Cruelty
Anthony de Mello on one occasion instead of giving a devotee an exercise chose to give him the following explanation: "Whenever you encounter a troublesome person, do not identify her as cruel, stupid, etc. Instead, see her as a frightened person. This is exactly what the cruel or rude person is. All negative emotions have a foundation in fear. Her angry aggressiveness is the only method she presently knows for releasing her tension or fear. If you take the wrong view of seeing her as cruel or hateful, this will have a definite effect on the way you try to deal with her. It makes you afraid of her, for negativity in one person arouses negativity in another. So if you turn negatively to this person you cannot deal with her wisely and tactfully. See what happens when you understand. The process is reversed. Instead of her negativity transferring itself to you, you transfer your positiveness to her. Try this miracle method for yourself on a specific situation. It is remarkable what changes it makes."

According to him "when you see clearly that a position you have adopted, a judgement you made is clean, uninfluenced by the ego, then you will have also the strength to act accordingly." He wrote once: "At the moment you don't experience the strength because you don't see yourself clearly. Truth will make you free. Knowing yourself, as you are without the admixture of lies you will become steady. And then you can stand up to anything or anyone."

Inner Freedom and Saying Goodbye

Inner freedom implies the ability to say goodbye to what is lost or cannot be got back. Thus one has to be able to say goodbye to a son, a daughter, a husband or a wife who dies suddenly; to one's family, when a girl marries a man; to one's youth, health and soft skin as one grows old and finally to life itself. In fact our whole life is an adventure in saying goodbye, beginning with our first goodbye to the comfort and protection of the mother's womb and ending in death. Those who have learned to say goodbye are happy, as they grow older; those who have not, will be weeping over the spilt milk all their lives. That which you cannot let go of, you do not possess. It possesses you.

A Self-test

Let us look at a few concrete things that will tell us how free we are.

If I have a tendency to hurry up with my work in spite of having sufficient time, so that I get unduly tired at the end?

If I feel very bad when I make mistakes, more so, when others notice them?

If I find it difficult to forgive?

If I find it hard to take the initiative to go and talk to one who has hurt me?

If I easily laugh at the mistakes of others?

If I'm the only one who seems to enjoy and laugh at my jokes?

If I have a tendency to criticize?

If I have the habit of cracking cynical, poking jokes?

If I have a tendency to argue, quarrel, cry, and be sad or moody?

If I am afraid of meeting strangers, men or women?

If I am afraid to ask what I need, for fear that my request may be refused.

If I feel uncomfortable whenever I do a less than perfect job?

If I have an urge to tell others when I see them making a mistake, or doing a sloppy job, even though I am not their boss nor have I any responsibility over them?
If I have strong likes and dislikes about food?
If I have a hard time to listen to a remark, criticism or feedback? Do I get defensive on such occasions?
If I am obstinate about my views?
If I have a tendency to do certain things always the same way or at the same time and I get unduly upset if I cannot do them, as I want to?
If I have irrational fear to see blood, dead people, to travel by bus/boat/plane?
If I grieve over my mother's/father's spouse's/child's death even after a year or more?
If I feel comfortable with only certain types of people and try to avoid, if possible, others?

We need to go counter to our compulsions consciously, gently, and with humility. Thus one who is too dependent on others needs to attempt to make decisions by oneself, beginning with comparatively minor matters, and becoming slowly, more and more independent. One who is inwardly free has only one goal: to seek and do God does will. With Dag Hammarskjold he will say:

> *For all that has been, thanks.*
> *To all that shall be, yes.*

Dialogue:
The Path to Community

If God is one, the structure that reflects this unity is community. It will be a minor miracle, if people can live in harmony in community. Any attempt to build a life together, which can be called "community" and not simply a group of "religious living in common," cannot neglect the need to deepen the level of communication within the group. Communication is the lifeblood of community. Without it there can be no unity of hearts in a religious community.

1. Levels of Communication
In our everyday contact with people, we relate at different levels. The most frequent and at the same time the most superficial is the neutral level. It might equally be called the business level. We relate to people because of their role, because they can provide us with our needs. Our only reason for relating to them is to achieve a task.

The next level communication is between persons as persons, but it is still superficial. It is the sort of conversion that takes place at a party, or even in the community dining room. It is a social exchange. We chat about the day's news, the weather, all very safe topics because we give away nothing of our feelings or ourselves.

Among close friends a deeper or interior communication is possible. It is more personal. We are able to share opinions and feeling, because trust has been established. They are getting to know us rather than just to know about us.

The next is the intimate or deepest level and this is only possible between a few very close friends. We give and receive as we are. We feel free to express our joy, our anger, and our sorrow. We can be free with them and know they will think no less of us. We feel safe in their company to be our real selves. We do not have to pretend with them that we are other than we are. This is the most beneficial context for personal growth. Between people at this level there is a deep communication in which few words are necessary. There is no embarrassment in long periods of silence.

Finally, of course, there is the level of our communication with God in which nothing is hidden. It is the union of the core of my being with the core of God's being. There will be always a decreasing number of people with whom we can relate as we go to deeper levels.

2. Truth and Love level of Dialogue

The most useful word for understanding human communication is 'Dialogue'. St. Paul in the letter to the Ephesians refers to 'Speaking the truth in love' (Eph.4: 15).

Speaking the truth in love implies wishing for each other's growth. This concerns the attitude and the willingness with which we enter into dialogue. We have to be prepared to accept others without any conditions, allowing them the freedom to be themselves according to their gifts, their prejudices, their way of relating and communicating, their wounds, their failures and their masks, but always believing in their sincerity, their honesty, their desire for truth, their goodness. A loving attitude to dialogue also means accepting myself and asking the other to accept me as someone different. It demands that I share who I am, not just at the level of ideas. It means sharing without any attempt to change the other or to win the other over to my point of view. It requires that I choose the appropriate language, gesture and moment. In this exchange I take a risk. It is a risk to be my real self, to lower my mask, to lose my feeling of superiority or inferiority. I risk feeling rejected, misunderstood. Above all, I risk hearing God speaking to me through the other and allowing God to speak to the other through me.

3. Five Forms of Dialogue

In order to enter into dialogue as a tool for community building, we need some form, in which to practice it. Here are five exercises that can be used in community.

3.1. Shared Prayer

Through shared prayer we enter into a new dimension of relationship with others, because we reveal something of our inner selves. We do not gather to recite prayers, but to pray from our hearts, as we feel inspired. We share in this prayer as much by accepting the prayers of another as by praying aloud ourselves. We are allowing the Holy Spirit to speak to us through another person. It is action listening. The best example we have is the way Jesus opened his heart to his Father in prayer, during the Last Supper in the presence of his closest friends. In these sessions we can feel comfortable with periods of silence.

3.2. Communication of Life

There is so much around us that communicates death and negativity that this is an exercise in which we can be life giving to one another. We share now how each is experiencing life at this point in time: our joys, worries, sadness, and encouragement. What we are sharing is the common fund of human experience that the community experiences right now. Our listening to each other is respectful and not judgmental. We do not enter into discussion; still less do we express a contrary view. It calls for trust in each other's good will. And of course it presumes the confidentiality of the group: what is said goes no further than the group. In receiving this communication we are receiving these persons through their body language as well as through their words. The community will become deeper as trust deepens and the community matures.

It is often good to launch this sharing around a particular theme or question. It might be as simple as: "How do you feel as a member of this community at this moment? Any response that begins with 'I feel that" is not the expression of a feeling but of thought. We receive people, as they are. This is not a time for offering consolation or advice. Needless to say, plenty of time should be allowed for such session. Nothing is more cramping than pressure to finish before the clock strikes.

3.3. Revision of our Work

Since we are people with a common apostolate, this form of dialogue should not be infrequent. It is not to be confused with the regular house council at which the practicalities of the community are discussed. It matters not whether the whole group has the same apostolate or whether each member is different. There is a constant need to evaluate what we are doing: to take a fresh look at what we are achieving – or not achieving-and ask why. Besides being an occasion for preplanning, it allows a clarification of and a sharing upon the different visions that the group might hold. It makes room for the gifts and charisms of each. We have to ensure that the common good is our yardstick for decisions. This demands that we each have the courage to give up personal whims and hobbyhorses.

3.4. Revision of our Community Life

This is similar to the above except that it concerns the internal life of the group. It is easy for each and the whole group to get into a rut, despite the frequent change of circumstances and personnel. But it is almost impossible for a community to exercise this level of dialogue unless members feel at home with the previous exercises. It calls for great delicacy and sensitivity. It provides a chance to deal with some of those hidden agendas. It can be helpful to have particular questions to share upon, especially if the opportunity has been allowed for each one to reflect upon each questions as:

> *What does community life means to me?*
> *How do I see myself as a member of this community?*
> *What do I expect from this community?*
> *What do I expect to give this community?*
> *How much time do we need together?*
> *What kind of social, cultural and recreational sharing and support do I need?*

3.5. Mutual Support and Encouragement

This is the most difficult but the most fruitful level of dialogue. It is not to be confused with fraternal or sororal correction. That was given one to one and was usually negative. Here the community can become richer and more effective. The group challenges the individual members to recognize their gifts they do not realize or acknowledge they possess. Gifts and talents are given to each one for everyone's benefit. This form of dialogue is undertaken only if each individual in the community is open to it. Otherwise it might wound and hurt, whereas it is meant to be healing and loving. We mostly only come to know ourselves through the eyes of others and only when the others have loving eyes and heart.

Appendix I

Twelve Steps for Christian Living

1. We admit our need for God's gift of salvation, that we are powerless over certain areas of our lives and that our lives are at times sinful and unmanageable.
2. We come to believe through the Holy Spirit that a power who came in the person of Jesus Christ and who is greater than ourselves can transform our weaknesses into strengths.
3. We make a decision to turn our will and our lives over to the care of Jesus Christ as we understand Him-hoping to understand Him more fully.
4. We make a searching and fearless moral inventory of ourselves-both our strengths and our weaknesses.
5. We admit to Christ, to ourselves, and to another human being the exact nature of our sins.
6. We become entirely ready to have Christ heal all of these defects of character that prevent us from having a more spiritual lifestyle.
7. We humbly ask Christ to transform all of our shortcomings.
8. We make a list of all persons we have harmed and become willing to make amends to them all.
9. We make direct amends to such persons whenever possible, except when to do so would injure them or others.
10. We continue to take personal inventory and when we are wrong, promptly admit it, and when we are right, thank God for the guidance.
11. We seek through prayer and meditation to improve our conscious contact with Jesus Christ, as we understand Him, praying for knowledge of God's will for us and the power to carry that out.
12. Having experienced a new sense of spirituality and realizing that this is a gift of God's grace, we are willing to share the message of Christ's love and forgiveness with others and to practice these principles in all our affairs.

Appendix II

An Approach to Life

"Go peacefully amid the noise and remember what peace there may be in silence. As far as possible, be on good terms with all persons. Speak your truth quickly and calmly, and listen to others, even the dull and ignorant, they too have their story. Avoid loud and aggressive persons, they are a vexation to the spirit, if you compare yourself with others, you may become bitter or vain, for always there will be greater and lesser persons than yourself. Enjoy your achievements as well as your plans. Keep interested in your own career however humble, it is a real possession in the changing fortunes of tide. Exercise caution in your business affairs, for the world is full of trickery. But let this not blind you to what virtue there is, for many persons strive for high ideals, and everywhere life is full of heroism. Be yourself. Especially do not feign affection, neither be cynical about love. Take kindly the counsel of the years, gracefully surrendering the things of youth. Nurture strength of spirit to shield you in sudden misfortune. But do not distress yourself with imaginings. Many fears are born of fatigue and loneliness. Beyond a wholesome discipline, be gentle with yourself. You are a child of the universe, no less than the trees and the stars. You have a right to be here. And whether or not it is clear to you, no doubt the universe is unfolding as it should. Therefore be at peace with God, whatever you conceive Him to be. And whatever your labors and aspirations, in the noisy confusion of life keep peace with your soul. With all its sham drudgery and broken dreams it is still a beautiful world. Be cheerful and strive to be happy.

Desiderata By Max Ehrmann

APPENDIX III

GENERAL GUIDANCE TO SOULS
by St. Alphonsus Liguori

1. Put all confidence in God and have a total mistrust in oneself. Have a strong resolution to conquer self. St. Teresa of Avila says, "If there is no neglect on our part, we should not doubt that God is ready to help us to become saints.
2. Beware of committing defects that are deliberate.
3. Do not become despondent: humble yourself. Do not disclose your temptations to imperfect souls, for, doing this will harm you and them.
4. Take care to detach yourselves from everything e.g. from relatives.
5. Rejoice within your spirit, when you see yourself made light-of, ridiculed etc.
6. Have a strong desire to love God. The Devil greatly fears resolute souls. The Lord demands no more from us than a worthy resolution in order for him to do the rest. (The Foundations St. Teresa p. 28.)
7. One must cultivate a great love for prayer, which is a furnace in which divine love burns. The saints, because they were lovers of God, have also become lovers of prayer.
8. Maintain a great uniformity with God's will, in all things contrary to our creaturely cravings. Progress does not consist in feeling more delight in God but in fulfilling his will.
9. Practice perfect obedience to the rules, to the superiors and to one's spiritual director. Obedience is the queen of all virtues, for all virtues obey obedience. St. Teresa taught, "From the soul resolved to love him, God demands nothing else but obedience."
10. Pay continued attention to God's presence, he who truly loves is ever mindful of one he loves. St. Teresa, "I do not fear that God will let one go without reward for raising his eyes mindful of him." (Camino de Perfectio 23.)

11. Make it your intention to please God in every act that you perform and say, "Lord I do this to please you." A good intention is called spiritual alchemy that turns into gold the most material actions.

Appendix IV

The Examination of Consciousness

"How do things stand between me and God? Where am I coming from, and where is my life in Christ growing?"

I can answer this satisfactorily only if I take leisure to reflect, for I am examining here a deep and dynamic personal relationship. Here is a way of doing that:

- First, I take time to thank God for the good things that came into my day. For instance, I thank God for sunshine or rain, for getting a chair fixed, for a phone call from a friend, for feeling good all day long, for having the energy to get a job done late in the evening. In this process, I may well come across some action that I did or some emotion or desire that I entertained for which I cannot thank God, since it was offensive or sinful.
- Second, having thanked God for all the day's gifts as much as I can, I beg that God will give me this further gift: to see clearly and in hope how I am growing more fully alive to God in them and through them, and also where they might be keeping me from growing.
- Third, I then examine carefully what my actions, omissions, thoughts, desires tell me about my relationship with God and with others and myself in God. Sometimes, a single event stands out dramatically; for instance: I lost my temper badly; I felt very great joy at a piece of news; I resisted making a decision someone asked me to make; I spent much too long a time on a simple task. Patiently, I ask myself what my action or my attitude meant. Did it embody love of God, or fear or distrust? Did it suggest that I have got over committed, and why would I get over committed?

All day long I felt anxious and worried; every time I saw a certain person, I wanted to have his or her attention; I got things done swiftly and easily: I erupted in anger over little things. Patiently, I ask myself what thus pattern means about my belief in God and my trust of and love for God.

- Fourth, then, I take what I have learned, to prayer, speaking to God and telling God whatever I need to say. I let God surprise me with insight and console me with faith and hope. I bring to God the larger needs that I feel right now: An old resentment that I seem unable to shake, an inveterate habit that I badly want to get rid of. A kind of living through the day without thanking and praising my Creator.
- Fifth, and finally, I determine to keep my spirit filled with gratitude, and to take steps to get rid of mind-sets that stand between my Creator and me. I set myself to change an attitude, shake off a fear, or grow in some special way. And I offer this larger movement in my life to God. I set my mind to accept any other change or shift in my person and myself that would come, were God to give me the larger gift I ask for. For God is the master of my life and myself; I place my trust there and not in myself.

Appendix V
Contemplation

If thou wouldst enter the Way of Contemplation,
Thou must take the path that leadeth thereto
The same is a conscience pure and undefiled,
A simple and well-regulated life,
A modest demeaning of thyself,
And the temperance in outward things.
Thou must remain the ungoverned desires of Nature,
Supply her wants with wisdom and discretion,
Ministering in the world without, to all who need, in love and mercy;
And, in the world within, emptying thyself of very vain imagining.
Gazing inward with an eye uplifted and open to the Eternal Truth;
Inwardly biding in simplicity, and stillness, and in utter peace.
So shalt thou bring with thee a burning earnestness of Love,
A fiery flame of devotion, leaping and ascending into the very Goodness of God Himself;
A loving longing of the soul to be with God in His eternity.
A turning from all things of self into the freedom of the Will of God,
With all the forces soul gathered into the unity of Spirit;
Thanking and glorifying God, and loving and serving Him, in everlasting reverence.
So lovingly following this life of virtue,
Thou mayest hope to come to the Life of Contemplation.
And, if thou abidest faithful to thy God and to thyself,
Then, in the hour when he shall manifest Himself,
Thou shalt behold His face.

Van Ruysbroeck, 1293-1381

Appendix VI

Sixteen Steps for Discovery and Empowerment

12. We affirm we have the power to take charge of our lives and we stop being dependent on substance or other people for our self-esteem and security.
13. We come to believe that God/Universe/Higher Power awakens the healing wisdom within us when we open ourselves to that power.
14. We make a decision to become our authentic selves and trust in the healing power of the truth.
15. We examine our beliefs, addictions, and dependent behavior in the context of living in a hierarchical patriarchal culture.
16. We share with another person and the Universe all those things inside of us for which we feel shame and guilt.
17. We affirm and enjoy out strengths, talents, and creativity, striving not to hide these qualities to protect others' egos.
18. We become willing to let go of shame, guilt, and any behavior that keeps us from loving our selves and others.
19. We make a list of people we have harmed and people who have harmed us, and take steps to clear our negative energy by making amends and sharing our grievances in a respectful way.
20. We express love and gratitude to others, and increasingly appreciate the wonder of life and the blessings we do have.
21. We continue to trust our reality and daily affirm that we see what we see, we know what we know, and we feel what we feel.
22. We promptly acknowledge our mistakes and make amends when appropriate, but we do not say we are sorry for things we have not done and we do not cover up, analyze, or take responsibility for the shortcomings of others.
23. We seek out situations, jobs, and people that affirm our intelligence, perceptions, and self worth and avoid situations or people who are hurtful, harmful or demeaning to us.
24. We take steps to heal our physical bodies, organize our lives reduce stress and have fun.

25. We seek to find our inward calling, and develop the will and wisdom to follow it.
26. We accept the ups and downs of life as natural events that can be used as lessons for our growth.
27. We grow in awareness that we are interrelated with all living things, and we contribute to restoring peace and balance on the planet.

Bibliography

Abhishiktananda. Saccidananda: *A Christian Approach to Advaitic Experience.* Delhi: ISPCK 1984.

Abraham J. Heschel, *The Prophets* (NY: Harper & Row, 1962)

Andrew Weil, *The Natural Mind* (Boston: Houghton Mifflin Co., 1972)

Argyle, M. *The Psychology of Happiness.* London: Methuen, 1987.

Ashley Montagu, *Touching* (NY:Perennial Library, 1972)

Asimov, I. And F. Walker.. *The March of the Millennia.* New York: Walker,1990.

Au, Wilkie, SJ. *By Way of the Heart: Toward a Holistic Christian Spirituality.* New York: Paulist Press, 1989.

Bellah, Robert N. et al. *The Good Society.* New York: Knopf, 1991.

Biallas, Leonard J. *World Religions*: A Story Approach. Mystic, Conn.: Twenty-Third Publications 1991.

Boff. Leonardo, and Clodovis Boff. *Introducing Liberation Theology.* Maryknoll, N.Y.: Orbit Books 1987.

Brown, H. Jackson. Chesterton, G.K. *Orthodoxy.* New York: Doubleday, 1973.

Burckhardt, Titus. *An Introduction to Sufi Doctrine.* Lahore, Sh. M. Ashraf, 1959.

Charland, William *A. Decide To Live.* USA, the Westminster Press, 1979.

Cohn, N. *The Pursuit of Millennium. London, 1957.*

Cone, James. *God of the Oppressed.* New York: Seabury Press 1975.

Conn, Joann Wolski, ed. Women's Spirituality: *Resources for Christian Development.* New York: Paulist Press, 1993.

De Mello, Anthony. *One Minute Wisdom.* New York: Doubleday, 1988.

De Mello. Wellsprings: *A Book of Spiritual Exercises.* Garden City: Doubleday, 1985.

Denett, D.C. 1991. *Consciousness Explained.* Boston: Little, Brown. DeVries, M. ed. 1992

Dietrich Bonhoeffer, *Letters and Papers from Prison* NY: Macmillan, 1967

Dillard, Annie. *Teaching a Stone to Talk*. New York: Harper and Row. Doherty, Catherine de 1988

Doohan, Leonard, *"The Spiritual Value of Leisure,"* Spirituality Today (June 1979): 164.

Dumm, Demetrius, OSB. *Flowers in the Desert*: A Spirituality of the Bible. New York: Paulist Press, 1987.

Dumoulin, Heinrich, SJ. *A History of Zen Buddhism*. Boston: Beacon Press 1963.

Dunne, John. *The Way of All the earth*. Notre Dame, Ind.: University of Norte Dame Press 1972.

Dupuis, Jacques. *Jesus Christ at the Encounter of World Religions*. Maryknoll, N.Y.: Orbit Books, 1991.

Schumacher E.F. *Small is Beautiful* NY: Perennial Library, 1975.

Edward Schillebeeckx, *Jesus: An Experiment in Christology* NY: Seabury, 1979, pp. 200-218.

Eliade, Mircea. 1957. *The Sacred and the Profane*. New York: Harper & Row.

Eno, R. *The Confucian Creation of Heaven*. Albany, N.Y: State University of New York Press, 1990.

Erikson, Erik. *Identity, Youth and Crisis*. New York: Norton, 1968.

Ernest Becker, *The Denial of Death* (NY: The free Press,1973)

Evans-Pritchard, E.E. [1956] *New Religion*. New York: Oxford University Press 1974.

Furlong, Monica, *"Connect and Collect,"* The Table 24 (March 1990): 380.

Gandhi, M. K.. *My Autobiography*. Boston: Beacon Press 1957.

Ginnis. M.C, Alan Loy. *Bringing Out The Best in People*. USA, Augsburg, 1980.

Greeley, Andrew. *The Friendship Game*. Garden City: Doubleday, 1970.

Griffiths, Bede. *Return to the Center*. Springfield: Templegate 1976.

Gutierrez, Gustavo. *A Theology of Liberation*. Maryknoll, N.Y.: Orbis Books1973.

Gutierrez, Gustavo. *We drink From Our Own Wells*: The Spiritual Journey of a People. Maryknoll, N.Y.: Orbis Books 1984.

Habermas, Jurgen. *The Theory of Communicative Action*, Vol. 1. Boston: Beacon Press 1984.

Habermas, Jurgen. *"God of Life, Idols of Death."* Monastic Studies 17:101-20, 1986.

Hammarskjold, Dag. *Markings.* New York: Knopf, 1965.

Harman and Ringgold. *Higher Creativity.* USA, Institute of Noetic sciences, 1984.

Heschel, Abraham Joshua. *I Asked for Wonder*: A Spiritual Anthology. New York: Crossroad, 1983.

Houston, Jean. *The Possible Human.* USA, J.P Teacher, 1982.

Howard, Vernon. *The Mystic's Path to Comic Power.* USA, Parker, 1973.

Hueck. *Soul of My Soul.* Notre Dame: Ave Maria Press, 1985.

Jose Miranda, *Marx and the Bible* (Maryknoll, NY: Orbis Books, 1974)

Julian of Norwich, *Showings* New York: Paulist, 1978

Karl Rahner, *Theological Dictionary* NY: Herder & Herder, 1965.

Kennedy, Eugene. *A Time for Being Human.* Chicago: Thomas More Press, 1977.

Koontz, Dean R. Strangers. New York: Putnam, 1986.

Kennedy, Eugene. *The Joy of Being Human.* Chicago: Thomas More Press, 1974.

Klausner, S.Z. *The Quest For Self-Control.* New York: The Free Press, 1965.

Koran, Al, *Bring Out The Magic In Your Mind.* USA, A. Thomas, 1980.

Kul, Kuthumi. *The Human Aura.* USA, Summit University, 1986.

Kushner, Harold S. *When Bad Things Happen to Good People.* New York: Schocken Books, 1981.

Lewis, C.S. *Beyond Personality.* New York: Macmillan, 1945.

Lewis, C.S. Surprised by Joy: *The Shape of My Early Life.* New York: Harcourt Brace Jovanovich, 1966.

Lewis, C.S. *The Four Loves.* San Diego: Harcourt Brace Jovanovich, 1960.

Live and Learn and Pass It On. Nashville: Routledge Hill Press, 1992.

Livingston, Patricia. *Lessons of the Heart*: Celebrating the Rhythms of Life. Notre Dame: Ave Maria Press, 1992.

Maslow, a. *Toward a Psychology of Being*. New York: Van Nostrand, 1980.

Matthew Fox, *Breakthrough: Meister Eckhart's Creation Spirituality in New Translation* (New York: Doubleday, 1980)

McFague, Sallie. *Models of God*: Theology for an Ecological, Nuclear Age. Philadelphia: Fortress Press 1987.

Merton, Thomas. *Zen and the Birds of Appetite*. New York: New Directions 1968.

Merton, Thomas. *The Sign of Jonas*. Garden City: Image Books, 1953.

Moore, Sebastian. *Let This Mind Be in You*: A Quest for Identity through Oedipus to Christ. New York: Harper and Row, 1985.

Moore, Thomas. *Care of the Soul*. New York: Harper Collins, 1992.

Murphy, Joseph. *The Power of Your Subconscious Mind*. USA, Bantam, 1985.

Myers, D. G. *The Pursuit of Happiness*. New York: William Morrow & Co 1992.

Nelson-Pallmeyer, Jack. *Brave New World Order*. Maryknoll, N.Y.: Orbis Books 1992.

Neville, Robert. Behind the Masks of God: *An Essay toward Comparative Theology*. Albany: State University of New York Press 1991.

Niebuhr, Reinhold. *The Irony of American History*. New York: Charles Scribner, 1952.

Nietzsche, F. *Also Sprach Zarathustra*. Leipzig; Kronen 1950.

Nouwen, Henri J.M. *Reaching Out*. Garden City: Doubleday, 1975.

Oates, Wayne. Confessions of a Workaholic: *The Facts about Work and Addiction*. Nashville: Abingdon, 1971.

Otto, Rudolf. 1923. *The Idea of the Holy. New York*. Oxford University Press.

Paul Tillich, *Systematic Theology, III* (Chicago: Harper& row, 1967)

Peck, M. Scott. *The Road Less Traveled*. New York: Simon and Schuster, 1978.

Peters, T. *The Cosmic Self*. San Francisco: HarperColins, 1991.

Pollard, Miriam, OCSO. *The Laughter of God*. Wilmington: Michael Glazier, 1986.

Prigogine, I., and I. Stingers. *Order out of Chaos.* New York: Bantam 1984.

Puls, Joan. Seek *Treasures in Small Fields*: Everyday Holiness. Mystic: Twenty-Third Publications, 1993.

Quoist, Michel. *With Open Heart.* New York: Crossroad Publishing, 1983.

Radakrishnan, S. *East and West.* New York 1956.

Ralston, Helen. *Christian Ashrams*: A New Religious Movement in Contemporary India 1987.

Rawls, John. *A Theory of Justice.* Cambridge, MA: Harvard University Press 1971.

Robert E. Ornstein, *The Psychology of Consciousness* (San Francisco: W.H. Freeman, 1972)

Rohr, Richard. *The Art of Living.* New York: Crossroad, 1991.

Roland E. Murphy, *"The Understanding of Revelation in Prophecy and Wisdom,"* Chicago Studies Spring, 1978

Rosemary Ruether, *Faith and Fratricide* NY: Seabury, 1974.

Rubenstein, Richard. *The Cunning of History.* New York: Harper & Row 1975.

Samra, Cal. The Joyful Jesus: *The Healing Power of Humor.* San Francisco: Harper, 1986.

Sartre, J. P. *Being and Nothingness.* New York: Philosophical Library. 1991.

Segundo, Juan Luis. *The Liberation of Theology.* Maryknoll, N.Y.: Orbis Books 1975.

Shea, John. *The Ch allenge of Jesus.* Chicago: Thomas More Press, 1975.

Shea, John. *The Spirit Master.* Chicago: Thomas More Press, 1987.

Sobrino, John. *Spirituality of Liberation*: Toward Political Holiness. Maryknoll, N.Y.: Orbis Books, 1987.

Stemberg, R, J. Wisdom: *Its Natural, Origins, and Development.* New York: Cambridge University Press, 1990.

Swimme, Brain. *"Science: A Partner in Creating the Vision."* 1988.

Thomas Merton, *No Man is an Island* Garden City, NY: Doubleday Image 1967.

Tracy, David. *Blessed Rage for Order:* The New Pluralism in Theology. New York: Seabury 1975.

Walsh, Roger. *Staying Alive*. U.S.A, New Science Library, 1984.

Walter Brueggemann, *The Prophetic Imagination* Philadelphia: Fortress, 1978

Wendell Berry, *The Unsettling of America: Culture &Agriculture* NY:Avon Books, 1977

Woods, ed., *Understanding Mysticism* Garden City, NY: Doubleday, 1980

Zaehner, R.C. (trans.) *Hindu Scriptures*. New York: Dutton & Dent, Everyman's Library 1938, 1966.

About the Author

The author serves as Professor of philosophy at the National Seminary of Lahore, Pakistan. His fields of interest are Spirituality, Educational Planning, English Literature, Comparative Religion and Future Studies. He has served as an educationist for the last nineteen years in Pakistan and fifteen years in Sri Lanka. He has published "An Introduction to Futuristic", "Self Actualization" and "A Word For Your Journey of Life" and "A companion to English language". He believes in humanism, peace power and people power.

Humans according to him, have to work on their inner selves, before they think of social change and global transformation. Private victories should precede public victories. The present need is a human being fully human, fully evolved and spiritually fit. Survival in the Third Millennium is reserved for the spirituality fit.